Intercultural Transitions in Higher Education

**Studies in Social Interaction**
**Series Editors: Steve Walsh, Paul Seedhouse and Christopher Jenks**

Presenting data from a range of social contexts including education, the media, the workplace and professional development, the *Studies in Social Interaction* series uncovers, among other things, the ways in which tasks are accomplished, identities formed and communities established. Each volume in the series places social interaction at the centre of discussion and presents a clear overview of the work that has been done in a particular context. Books in the series provide examples of how data can be approached and used to uncover social interaction themes and issues, and explore how research in social interaction can feed into a better understanding of professional practices and develop new research agendas. Through stimulating tasks and accompanying commentaries, readers are engaged and challenged to reflect on particular themes and relate the discussion to their own context.

**Series Editors**
**Steve Walsh** is Professor of Applied Linguistics at Newcastle University

**Paul Seedhouse** is Professor of Educational and Applied Linguistics at Newcastle University

**Christopher Jenks** is Assistant Professor of English and Intensive English/TESOL Coordinator at the University of South Dakota

**Titles available in the series:**

| | |
|---|---|
| *Social Interaction in Second Language Chat Rooms* | Christopher Jenks |
| *Social Interaction and L2 Classroom Discourse* | Olcay Sert |
| *Social Interaction and Teacher Cognition* | Li Li |
| *Social Interaction and English Language Teacher Identity* | John Gray and Tom Morton |
| *Intercultural Transitions in Higher Education* | Alina Schartner and Tony Johnstone Young |

Visit the Studies in Social Interaction website at www.edinburghuniversitypress.com/series/ssint

# Intercultural Transitions in Higher Education

## International Student Adjustment and Adaptation

Alina Schartner and Tony Johnstone Young

EDINBURGH
University Press

For Rupert, who is growing up to be a citizen of the world.

To Carolyn, Thomas and Anna, who are all the better for being 'international'. With love.

Edinburgh University Press is one of the leading university presses in the UK. We publish academic books and journals in our selected subject areas across the humanities and social sciences, combining cutting-edge scholarship with high editorial and production values to produce academic works of lasting importance. For more information visit our website: edinburghuniversitypress.com



Edinburgh University Press Ltd
The Tun – Holyrood Road, 12(2f) Jackson's Entry, Edinburgh EH8 8PJ

Typeset in Minion Pro by
Servis Filmsetting Ltd, Stockport, Cheshire and
printed and bound by CPI Group (UK) Ltd,
Croydon, CRO 4YY

A CIP record for this book is available from the British Library

ISBN 978 1 4744 3121 7 (hardback)
ISBN 978 1 4744 3122 4 (paperback)
ISBN 978 1 4744 3123 1 (webready PDF)
ISBN 978 1 4744 3124 8 (epub)

# CONTENTS


List of figures and tables vii
Acknowledgements ix

**Part I** **1**

1 Introduction 1
1.1 Aims, Structure and Scope 1
1.2 Context – The Scale and Patterns of International Student Mobility 3
1.3 Internationalisation of Higher Education 7
1.4 The 'International Student Experience' as an Intercultural Transition 9
1.5 Key Concepts and Glossary 14
1.6 Summary and Conclusions 17
References 17
2 The Current State of Knowledge About the 'International Student Experience' 22
2.1 Conceptual Approaches to Intercultural Transition 22
2.2 Adaptation and Adjustment of International Students 25
2.3 Contributory Factors to International Students' Adjustment 29
2.4 Conclusions 40
Note 40
References 41
3 Methodology 51
3.1 Research Setting 51
3.2 Research Design 51
3.3 Research Instruments 53
Note 60
References 60

**Part II** **63**

4 Academic Adjustment and Adaptation 63
4.1 Descriptive Statistics of Academic Adaptation 63
4.2 Academic Adjustment Over Time 65

4.3 Associations Between Contributory Factors and Academic Adaptation 71
4.4 Conclusion 79
References 80
5 Psychological Adjustment and Adaptation 83
5.1 Descriptive Statistics of Psychological Adaptation 83
5.2 Qualitative Findings 85
5.3 Associations Between Contributory Factors and Psychological Adaptation 106
5.4 Conclusion 112
References 112
6 Sociocultural Adjustment and Adaptation 115
6.1 Sociocultural Adjustment Over Time 116
6.2 Contributory Factors to Sociocultural Adaptation 127
References 136
7 Associations between Adjustment Domains 140
7.1 Sociocultural and Psychological Adjustment and Adaptation 141
7.2 Academic and Psychological Adjustment and Adaptation 144
7.3 Sociocultural and Academic Adjustment and Adaptation 146
7.4 Conclusion 148
Notes 149
References 149
8 Retrospectives on the 'International Student Experience' 150
8.1 Why 'Retrospective' Accounts? 152
8.2 Design, Participants and Analysis 152
8.3 Findings 154
8.4 Conclusions 164
References 165

**Part III** **167**

9 Conclusions 167
9.1 Revisiting the Research Questions 167
9.2 A Conceptual Model of International Student Adjustment and Adaptation 169
9.3 Agenda for Future Research 177
Note 177
References 178
10 Implications 180
10.1 HEIs 180
10.2 Research Implications 186
10.3 Policy Implications 187
10.4 Implications for Aspirant Students 189
References 189

Index 193

# FIGURES AND TABLES

## FIGURES

1.1 The 'triple transition' of international postgraduate students (Schartner 2014) 10
2.1 'W-curve' model of culture shock 23
2.2 An integrated framework of adjustment domains of salience to student sojourners 26
2.3 Student sojourners' adjustment domains 28
2.4 Model of international students' social ties (Source: Schartner 2015) 37
3.1 Qualitative data analysis procedure 59
4.1 Significant associations between contributory factors and academic adaptation 78
4.2 Academic adjustment trajectory of students in this study 80
5.1 Students' concerns in the initial sojourn stage 96
5.2 Psychological adjustment over time 106
5.3 Significant associations between contributory factors and psychological adaptation 111
6.1 Sociocultural adjustment amongst student sojourners over time 128
6.2 Significant associations between contributory factors and sociocultural adaptation 132
9.1 An integrated model of international student adjustment and adaptation 170
9.2 The broader theoretical background underpinning the model (Source: Schartner and Young 2016) 173

## TABLES

1.1 Countries offering tertiary programmes in English (Source: OECD 2012) 6
2.1 Example studies of sojourner adjustment using the Multicultural Personality Questionnaire 34
2.2 Bochner and colleagues' (1977) Functional Model of Friendship Networks 37
3.1 Demographics of survey respondents at Time 1 and Time 2 54

3.2 Interview analytical categories and example comments 59
4.1 Measures of central tendency for academic achievement 64
4.2 Interviewees' academic achievement scores 64
4.3 Bivariate correlations between the Relative Autonomy Index and academic achievement 73
4.4 Bivariate correlations between intercultural competence and academic achievement 74
4.5 Regression analysis of intercultural competence and academic achievement 74
4.6 Bivariate correlations between social contact and academic achievement 76
4.7 Regression analysis of social contact and academic achievement 76
4.8 Regression analysis of social support and academic achievement 77
5.1 Descriptive statistics for psychological wellbeing and satisfaction with life 84
5.2 Distribution of scores on the Satisfaction with Life Scale (SWLS) 84
5.3 Interviewees' psychological wellbeing and satisfaction with life scores over time 84
5.4 Regression analysis of English language ability at Time 2 and psychological adaptation 107
5.5 Regression analysis of the Relative Autonomy Index and psychological adaptation 107
5.6 Bivariate correlations between intercultural competence and psychological adaptation 108
5.7 Regression analysis of intercultural competence and psychological adaptation 109
5.8 Regression analysis of social contact and satisfaction with life 109
5.9 Bivariate correlations between social support and psychological adaptation 110
5.10 Regression analysis of social support and satisfaction with life 110
6.1 Sociocultural Adaptation Scale items rated as most difficult by respondents 115
6.2 Bivariate correlations between autonomy in the decision to study abroad and sociocultural adaptation 129
6.3 Bivariate correlations between intercultural competence and sociocultural adaptation 129
6.4 Regression analysis of intercultural competence and sociocultural adaptation 130
6.5 Regression analysis of social contact and sociocultural adaptation 130
6.6 Regression analysis of social support and sociocultural adaptation 131
8.1 Analytical categories and example comments in relation to sociocultural adjustment 154
9.1 Significant associations between contributory factors and adaptation measures in Young et al. (2013) and Schartner (2014), reported in Schartner and Young (2016) 175

# ACKNOWLEDGEMENTS

There are many people without whom this book would not have been possible. We would like to thank the series editors, Steve Walsh, Paul Seedhouse and Chris Jenks, for their support, encouragement and feedback. We also owe a great deal of gratitude to Mike Handford, Lou Harvey, Zhu Hua and Robert McKenzie, who acted as 'critical friends' and generously gave their time to read and comment on draft chapters. We are grateful to the anonymous reviewers, who offered invaluable advice and feedback on our book proposal and on its drafts. We owe our thanks to Edinburgh University Press for its support in publishing this book, in particular Laura Williamson, for her patience, advice and guidance. For research assistance on the 'retrospective' student accounts presented in Chapter 8, we would like to thank Kirsty Blewitt and Estelle Yong-Dessouroux. We are grateful to all those colleagues who share our interest in the 'international student experience' and with whom we have had the pleasure to work, both in the UK and further afield. Their work and camaraderie have inspired us and guided our thinking. They include Joana Almeida, Adam Brandt, John Edwards, Adrian Holliday, Hans Ladegaard, Yu Maemura, Rola Naeb, Maggie Pitts, Itesh Sachdev, Peter Sercombe, Navaporn Snodin, Sue Robson and Scott Windeatt. We have also had the pleasure of working with some excellent PhD students, who have developed and taken our work further; they include Fatimah Alsaadi, Yuwei Liang, Hanh Pho, Nattaya Srisakda and Xuan Zhao. A special word of gratitude is due to Carolyn Marr for meticulously checking references and helping us format our book. Last but not least, we need to thank the students, both 'home' and 'international', whose stories we unpack within this book. We are indebted to them for sharing their experiences with us, and feel humbled and privileged for having been allowed to be part of their journeys.

We thank all of these people for their contributions. Any omissions or errors are, of course, entirely our own.

In June 2016, the International Association of Language and Social Psychology (IALSP) awarded Alina Schartner the James J. Bradac early career prize for her work on the 'international student experience'. This recognition has inspired our book.

Research for this book was facilitated by a Newton Fund award to develop researcher links and support workshops as part of the *Internationalisation of Higher Education:*

*Developing Values-based Intercultural Research Approaches* project. It was also facilitated by a Newton Advanced Fellowship co-funded by the British Academy and the Thailand Research Fund, *Enhancing the Quality of the International Student and Staff Mobility Experience* (AF160059). We very gratefully acknowledge their support.

# PART I

## 1

# INTRODUCTION

### 1.1 AIMS, STRUCTURE AND SCOPE

This book addresses a global, international and intercultural phenomenon – the fact that more than five million people are studying for a higher education (HE) degree abroad (OECD 2018). These numbers have grown considerably in recent years, and despite attempts by some governments to slow or reduce them, are still on the rise (UIS 2013; OECD 2018). In this book, we specifically address the human side of this phenomenon. We explore what it is 'like' to be an international student (IS), and what makes it a positive and successful experience – or otherwise. We investigate how, within this phenomenon, people's experiences are researched, understood, supported and enhanced. The book is centred in ongoing research by the authors, conducted since 2011; some has been published elsewhere, some for the first time here. It also explores how others have investigated similar phenomena. We aim, essentially, to bring it all together in a conceptually new way and point to ways forward.

Specifically, we first present a survey and summary of our own and others' recent research, drawing together and analysing thought and findings from across the spectrum of relevant interest areas – social psychology, education, applied linguistics and intercultural communication studies. From this, we have developed a new heuristic integrated conceptual model of the IS experience that can gauge the adjustment and adaptation trajectories of this unique and important sojourner group. This integrates theory and recent empirical research exploring the academic, psychological and sociocultural aspects of, and influences on, the experience of study abroad. The model was developed through the deployment of a methodological toolkit that shows how different ontological perspectives on culture, interculturality and identity can be integrated into a mixed-methods research design. The toolkit will provide a guided practical application of the conceptual model by showcasing how qualitative process-oriented perspectives can be integrated with quantitative outcome-oriented approaches in the study of intercultural transition across different contexts. Through this toolkit, we will also show how the model can serve as a reference point for a research agenda. Another important contribution is a longitudinal perspective, which is very unusual in research in the area, where a phenomenon with effects that are likely to run through a lifetime is investigated. The data we present recognise that the 'international student experience' begins with factors that influence whether, when and where to study aboard, extends into the experience itself, and continues into the effects of the experience on the future life of former alumni.

The book is divided into three parts. Broadly, we first introduce, contextualise and discuss our approach. We then present, survey and discuss our research and that of others. Finally, we present applications, conclusions and implications arising from this research. More specifically, Part I consists of this introductory Chapter 1, which provides a general introduction; Chapter 2, which reviews relevant literature; and Chapter 3, which outlines our methodological approach. Chapter 1 introduces and discusses the idea of 'internationalisation', and outlines 'international' students' place in this increasingly important, complex and dynamic phenomenon. It also says something about the specific context of the work presented in this study –HE in the UK. Chapter 1 also details how approaches to 'intercultural' transitionary experiences undergone by ISs can be best captured with 'ecumenical' ontological and methodological approaches. These aim to take account of both the 'culture simple', positivist orientation manifest in much of the social psychological literature in the area, and the frequently competing 'culture complex' epistemological perspectives manifest in research that claims to approach intercultural interactions from a more critical, interpretivist, ontological standpoint. We argue that there is considerable value and originality, when addressing the nature and consequences for people of the 'international student experience', in drawing on both of these, usually antagonistic, perspectives. This chapter concludes by briefly unpacking some key concepts and terminology, such as adjustment, adaptation, sojourners, and 'international' and 'home' students. Chapter 2 then surveys, reviews and consolidates recent research into the 'international student experience'. It draws together research literature from the intersecting fields of intercultural communication, international education and applied linguistics, detailing research into ISs' experiences worldwide. Chapter 3 presents methodological applications of the ecumenical position outlined in Chapter 1. Here, we detail our mixed-methods approach and longitudinal research design, and present information on research participants, data collection instruments and analysis.

Part II presents empirical data informing a new model of IS adjustment and adaptation. Each chapter analyses and integrates interview and survey data from ISs, present or past, in mixed-methods research designs. The aim of Part II is to present the dynamics and patterns of IS adjustment over time, and the relationships between the intersecting domains of adjustment and adaptation, and their association with a range of contributory factors. The potential contributory factors integrated into the analysis are drawn from the literature detailed in Chapter 2 and include variables such as motivations to study abroad, prior knowledge about the host country, proficiency in the host language, previous academic achievement, and patterns of contact with and support from people such as hosts, co-nationals and ISs of other nationalities.

Chapter 4 introduces, integrates and discusses qualitative interview and quantitative survey-based data related to the academic adjustment and adaptation of ISs. This includes adjustments to the demands of academic life in the new environment, such as styles of learning and teaching at the host university, as well as explicit measures of academic achievement. The quantitative data demonstrate the positive effects that an explicit study of intercultural communication might have on academic adjustment and adaptation. Chapter 5 then turns the focus to students' psychological adjustment and adaptation. It details the dynamics and patterns of psychological adjustment over time and the relationships between a range of contributory factors and individual ISs' subjective sense of their psychological wellbeing and their general satisfaction with life in the new environment. Chapter 6's focus is on the third domain in the model – sociocultural adjustment and adaptation. Here, qualitative interview data provide a fine-grained and nuanced picture of participants' 'lived' sociocultural adjustment: this includes their experience of 'fitting into' the host environment, and their social contact with and support from 'home' students and others. The quantitative data demonstrate which factors contribute to sociocultural adaptation over time. Chapter 7 analyses and discusses the interrelationships between the three adjustment domains in the three previous chapters in Part II. Here we present data that demonstrate the links and conceptual overlaps between the domains, and discuss how these strong but complex interrelationships might influence future research and practice in 'internationalising' universities. Part II ends with Chapter 8, which deals with the presentation and analysis of data collected from international alumni – an analysis of survey and interview data relating to the retrospective experience of 'being international' in HE. Here we use the three domains of adjustment and adaptation in our model as frames of reference, and detail how these may relate to personal change, growth and perspectives in later life.

Part III details the many possible applications for our findings. Chapter 9 revisits our focus on the human side of 'internationalisation' detailed above, and offers some conclusions related to our empirical, methodological and theoretical contributions, which, we argue, are many and significant. It also details how the data presented in Part II have informed a guiding conceptual model of IS adjustment (over time) and adaptation ('outcomes'), which was developed by the authors, and presents the model itself. This model, we argue, can provide an important organising principle and point of reference for the burgeoning field of research into the IS experience. The chapter concludes with an agenda for further research and a call to arms. The final chapter (Chapter 10) discusses some of the implications from our research – for ISs and students-to-be, for host HEIs, for researchers and for policy makers.

## 1.2 CONTEXT – THE SCALE AND PATTERNS OF INTERNATIONAL STUDENT MOBILITY

There has been a huge global growth in the number of people studying abroad in HE over the last thirty years. Exact figures are hard to determine, but as we highlight above, the Organisation for Economic Cooperation and Development (OECD 2018) calculates that there are around five million students currently studying in higher education institutions (HEIs) outside their home countries worldwide. This is more than double the two million who were doing so in 1999 and more than triple the number only a decade before that. This growth has occurred in the context of what was, until very recently, an increasingly globalised world, in which economies are closely tied to others within their region and beyond. In the context of globalisation and an aggressively neoliberal political and socioeconomic world order, goods, capital and services have been flowing more freely across many borders and from many more sources than ever before. So, too, are people seeking employment, knowledge and skills. In terms of IS mobility, International Consultants for Education and Fairs (ICEF 2015: para 2) characterise things like this:

> Once accessible only to the world's elite, higher education is now open to the masses, particularly the burgeoning middle classes now found on every continent. And especially in countries lacking higher education capacity, students are looking for opportunities to study abroad.

The extent to which the burgeoning middle classes equate to 'the masses' is, of course, debatable. What is not debatable is that the phenomenon of IS mobility is huge and is having a considerable impact on people, institutions and countries.

About half of internationally mobile students move from Asia or Africa to predominantly English-speaking countries like the USA, UK, Canada or Australia. Another quarter move between countries in the European Higher Education Area, which comprises states across Europe and so includes everywhere from all the EU countries to the Holy See and the Russian Confederation (Marginson 2013). At the national level, IS enrolment varies greatly between countries, ranging from below 1 per cent for the vast majority of countries in the global South, to more than 10 per cent in some global Western contexts. ISs account for 10 per cent or more of the tertiary student population in New Zealand, the UK, Switzerland, Austria, Australia, the Netherlands, Belgium and Canada (OECD 2017). English-speaking countries are the most popular destination for ISs, with four countries hosting over half of globally mobile students (OECD 2018). In 2017, the USA hosted 30 per cent of the total number of ISs in the OECD area, followed by the UK (14 per cent) and Australia (10 per cent). However, France, Germany and the Russian Federation also hosted considerable numbers (OECD 2017). The largest group of ISs enrolled at HEIs in the OECD area are from Asia (55 per cent or 1.9 million), with China being the most dominant country of origin (some 860,000 students) (OECD 2018).

There are strong indications that general attitudes towards migration, particularly in the global North, are hardening, as evidenced by the 'Brexit' vote and the US presidential election outcomes in 2016, and the presidential elections in Brazil in 2018. We will return to this point in our Conclusion (Chapter 9, below). Nevertheless, all indications are that, on a global level, the phenomenon of IS mobility will continue to grow, although patterns of flows of students and distributions of 'market share' are likely to change.

Reasons for the increase in student mobility include changes in infrastructure and capacity of HEIs, as well as broader sociopolitical and socioeconomic factors. National governments frequently support and subsidise IS recruitment for reasons of soft power enhancement and increase in national global visibility, influence and prestige. So do supranational organisations like the European Union, which tend to see IS mobilities between national members as a means of creating greater cohesions across the Union, as well as an engine of individual personal growth and development (e.g. EACEA 2016).

For most universities around the world, the recruitment of ISs is now a central element in measures of institutional success as global research and teaching institutions. It is also, usually less overtly but no less crucially, of direct financial benefit and so is a means of continued viability or profitability for HEIs (Wright and Schartner 2013). In terms of world HE institutional rankings, among the multifarious evaluative ranking and rating surveys currently operating, numbers and ratios of international staff and of students are usually a key metric (e.g. QS 2018). The rapid expansion of the HE sector in many countries and the related intensification of financial pressure on education systems have made tuition fees an essential source of income for many universities (OECD 2010). ISs represent a particularly lucrative source of revenue, as their tuition fees are usually higher than those of domestic students. Fees are usually paid by the students themselves or by their families, or through bursaries or scholarships from either their own, or the receiving institutions', governments, or from a combination of these sources. Whatever the national or institutional motivations, recruitment of ISs provides a monetary benefit for HEIs in the receiving countries, while, at the same time, offering citizens of smaller or less developed countries and HE systems a relatively cost-effective alternative to national provision (Verbik and Lasanowski 2007).

As noted above, this benefit of IS recruitment has been particularly felt among host countries that are predominantly English first language-speaking, although they are now being challenged and patterns may be changing. Several factors have historically made predominantly English first language speaking-countries in the global North key players in the worldwide HE market (Verbik and Lasanowski 2007). Firstly, these countries have well-developed and relatively well-funded HE sectors. They have also consistently sourced students from a variety of countries, and so have created a diverse market and ensured relatively stable recruitment numbers, despite changes over time in areas of demand. Thirdly, they have traditionally recruited large numbers of students from India and China, which are still strong source countries (UKCISA 2018). Intrinsically linked to this successful establishment of target markets are aggressive, often highly professional and well-funded marketing strategies on behalf of the universities, established over a long period of time in most cases. Finally, these countries have the capacity to provide a service that is in high demand: the opportunity to study in English at internationally renowned facilities. Indeed, the perceived utility of the English language has also been identified as the main driving force behind the popularity of these countries as destinations for ISs (Forest and Altbach 2006).

While English-speaking countries remain popular, new destination countries for inward student mobility are emerging. In Europe, between 2013 and 2016, Estonia, Latvia, Poland and the Russian Federation each nearly doubled their incoming IS numbers. Other countries that saw a large increase include Turkey (an increase of 62 per cent), Mexico (58 per cent) and Chile (52 per cent) (OECD 2018).

As Coughlan (2011) sees it, the international HE market is becoming more like international air travel, with 'trade routes' of recruitment for the multibillion business of selling HE wrapping themselves around the globe. English-speaking universities

Table 1.1 Countries offering tertiary programmes in English (Source: OECD 2012)

| | |
|---|---|
| All or nearly all programmes offered in English | Australia, Canada, Ireland, New Zealand, UK, USA |
| Many programmes offered in English | Denmark, Finland, Netherlands, Sweden |
| Some programmes offered in English | Belgium (Flemish-speaking), Czech Republic, France, Germany, Hungary, Iceland, Japan, Korea, Norway, Poland, Portugal, Slovak Republic, Spain, Switzerland, Turkey |
| No or nearly no programmes offered in English | Austria, Belgium (French-speaking), Brazil, Chile, Greece, Israel, Italy, Luxembourg, Mexico, Russian Federation |

can therefore no longer rely on their central position in the global HE market, but are working very hard to maintain their dominant role in an increasingly challenging 'marketplace'.

As a reaction to the dominance of English-speaking countries, some European states have increased their marketing efforts in countries with which they share historical and linguistic relations (such as France with francophone Africa, Portugal with lusophone Africa and Latin America). Also, to overcome their perceived linguistic disadvantage, some countries previously using languages other than English have changed their medium of instruction for certain degree programmes to English (Forest and Altbach 2006), often very precipitately (Piller and Cho 2013). Change to English as a medium of instruction is especially seen in the Scandinavian and north-west European countries, where the use of English across curricula is increasingly widespread (see Table 1.1).

This book's main empirical focus is on the UK, which, for various reasons discussed below, is a particularly interesting and representative example of a 'mature' market for ISs. Expansion in IS numbers in the UK HE sector over the past four decades has been particularly marked. In 1973, there were 35,000 ISs sojourning in UK universities. By 1992, this number had increased to 95,000 (McNamara and Harris 2002). Currently, well over 700,000 non-UK students are enrolled at UK HEIs (HESA 2017). Overall, the increase in students undertaking full-time postgraduate degrees has been much bigger than the rise in full-time undergraduates, with around 37 per cent of master's students in the UK being 'international' (OECD 2017). Internationally, the picture is much the same, with postgraduate degrees attracting considerably more ISs than bachelor-level degrees. In the OECD area, some 19 per cent of students who graduated with a master's degree or equivalent in 2015 were ISs, compared to only 7 per cent of those who earned a bachelor's degree (OECD 2017). On average, there is more than one IS for every ten enrolled students at master's level, and the proportion of ISs at least doubles between bachelor's and master's levels in two-thirds of OECD countries. After Australia, the UK has the largest increase of ISs at master's level compared to bachelor's level (36 per cent versus 14 per cent) (OECD 2018).

The reasons why students come to the UK are similar to those for other predominantly anglophone countries. They include the perceived overall standard and quality of education in the UK, and the English language as a medium of instruction in a variety that is perceived as especially prestigious among many prospective students – 'British' English (e.g. Snodin and Young 2015). Also important is the generally good international reputation of UK education and the presence of well-known universities, often of long historical standing (McNamara and Harris 2002).

ISs make a significant contribution to the UK economy. Recent estimates suggest that, in 2014–15, on- and off-campus spending by ISs and their visitors generated £25.8 billion for the UK economy and supported more than 200,000 full-time jobs (Universities UK 2017). However, recent and apparently ongoing changes in immigration policy to counter perceived abuses of the student visa route place severe constraints on students from outside the European Economic Area (EEA, which includes all EU member states as well as Iceland, Liechtenstein, Norway and Switzerland). These policy-level changes have triggered a public debate about the effects of politics on UK HE. Uncertainties over the process and outcomes of UK 'Brexit' from the European Union mean that it is possible that such constraints will, in future, apply to all ISs, with potentially very serious effects on recruitment.

Despite these threats and uncertainties, the recruitment of ISs to UK universities remains large-scale; the substantial growth in absolute numbers observed above has, however, to some extent, slowed in the past few years. In 2004/5, around 4 per cent of ISs at UK universities came from other EU countries and 9 per cent came from outside the EU. In 2013/14, those numbers were 5.4 per cent and 13.5 per cent, respectively. However, this overall increase masks a fall in student numbers from the EU in 2012/13, with numbers 5.5 per cent lower in 2013/14 compared to 2011/12 (Universities UK 2015). Student enrolments from other EU countries decreased by 4 per cent between 2011/12 and 2015/16, with Ireland showing the largest percentage decrease (HESA 2017). However, non-UK students still constitute 19 per cent of the overall student body in the UK, with almost 70 per cent of students pursuing full-time taught postgraduate degrees. Although China, India, Malaysia and Nigeria were the top four sending countries of ISs to the UK in 2015–16 (HESA 2017), ISs as a whole come from a variety of different countries and thus represent a diverse and heterogeneous group. The participants in our studies, reported in Part II, reflected this multicultural heterogeneity.

In sum, the patterns of IS migration have shown considerable growth and a general flow from economically less developed locations to those in a more advanced state of economic development. Our focus, the UK, has been a major destination for and beneficiary of this flow.

## 1.3 INTERNATIONALISATION OF HIGHER EDUCATION

'Internationalisation' has been framed as the institutional response to this phenomenon of globalising HE (Young et al. 2017). Jane Knight's (2003: 2) definition of internationalisation has been one of the most frequently cited and, among researchers looking to frame 'internationalisation', perhaps the most influential. Knight defined it as 'the process of integrating an international, intercultural or global dimension into the purpose, functions or delivery of post-secondary education'. Within this broad definition, internationalisation encompasses a number of areas of activity, not solely associated with student mobility. These include:

- Recruitment of non-national staff
- The participation of HEIs, staff and students in international exchange programmes (like the Erasmus programme in Europe)
- Participation in internationally focused research
- The development of international 'branches' of HEIs
- The growth in the delivery of programmes in 'international' languages (predominantly English in recent years) or with an aim or focus of increasing international and/or intercultural understanding
- Attempts to 'internationalise at home': that is, to make the linguistic and intercultural benefits of international mobility available to the non-mobile majority of 'home' students and staff
- The recruitment of non-national students. (Young et al. 2017; Robson et al. 2017; Schartner and Young 2016).

The internationalisation of HE brings powerful practical and moral implications for universities who receive and host large numbers of ISs. There have been ever-increasing calls among those involved with the enhancement of the quality of the 'student experience' to value and promote diversity, and to approach international, multicultural student populations as resources and opportunities rather than as constraints, challenges or problems (e.g. Montgomery 2010). The surge in IS numbers has led to a burgeoning literature on their adjustment and adaptation, and the effects that their presence brings to campuses and classrooms around globe, including in the UK (see Chapter 2, below). An understanding of ISs' experiences and institutional commitment to students' needs is paramount if universities are to attract and retain ISs and aid them in their adjustment processes.

How actually to operationalise 'internationalisation' is one of the key contemporary debates in HE, both in the mature 'receiving' markets of the global North and in the increasingly important non-Northern hubs seeking to challenge their hegemony. Globally, it has become commonplace since 2000 for universities to proclaim their 'international' status. However, there has been little, if any, consensus about how this status can be justified, defined and operationalised institutionally (Robson et al. 2017). Internationalisation of HE has been associated with developments such as promoting change and improvement in the quality and relevance of HE programmes for diverse student bodies (Urban and Palmer 2014; Hénard et al. 2012; de Wit et al. 2015), and with enhanced strategic cooperation between HEIs transnationally (EACEA 2016). Such understandings of internationalisation accord with broader national and transnational goals, such as those of the EU strategy for internationalising European HE and the underlying strategic partnerships in the Erasmus+ scheme

(EACEA 2016), and with the Association of South East Asian Nations (ASEAN) Universities Network (AUN 2017). Internationalisation has thus been framed ubiquitously as an important, co-operative, positive and idealistic development, essential to prepare students for a globalised workplace, to strengthen research, and to foster development in an increasingly global knowledge economy (Altbach 2013).

However, in many HEIs, particularly among those in the West and in more long-standing Asian markets such as Japan (MEXT 2014), the strategic emphasis has increasingly shifted to competition, with internationalisation regarded as a means to generate revenue, to enhance national and institutional prestige and global ranking, and to increase the market share of ISs in an increasingly volatile HE landscape (IAU 2012; Seeber et al. 2016; Hazelkorn 2016: van der Wende 2001). A major challenge, which this book addresses directly and critically, will be for those working in international universities to foreground the positive benefits of internationalisation in such an increasingly competitive environment. This requires the political and economic rationales underpinning internationalisation strategies and processes to be approached with integrity (Inan et al. 2014), with greater emphasis placed on the social, cultural and academic goals of HE. Central to this must be prioritising the quality of the 'international student experience' in universities purporting to be internationalising entities.

## 1.4 THE 'INTERNATIONAL STUDENT EXPERIENCE' AS AN INTERCULTURAL TRANSITION

In examining the 'international student experience', this book draws on two key concepts for its main focus – notions of the intercultural (discussed below) and the idea of transition. The latter is relatively straightforward, the former much less so. To discuss our approach to transition first, we are guided by Meleis's (2010: 11) definition of a transition for a person as 'a passage from one fairly stable state to another fairly stable state […] triggered by critical events and changes in individuals or environments'. The move to a new national environment for the purpose of tertiary study is such a critical life event (Ward et al. 2001), which, to some extent, prompts the students' move from one state (that is, pre-sojourn state) to another (that is, post-arrival adaptation state) – this transition requires adjustments to the new environment by the individual – and, as we will see, also needs some kind of adjustive response from the host institution if this transition is likely to be a successful and positive experience (for examples of the forms this response might take, see Chapter 10).

International postgraduate students are the specific empirical focus for our research (see Part II, below). They present a particularly interesting case, as these students typically go through a 'triple transition' (Jindal-Snape and Ingram 2013, Figure 1.1). Firstly, they move to a new country, usually one with which they are less familiar than the one in which they received their primary education. Secondly, they move into an unfamiliar educational system, often one with a high degree of unfamiliarity across a range of academic and sociocultural domains. Thirdly, they move on to a new level of academic study (that is, the postgraduate level), which

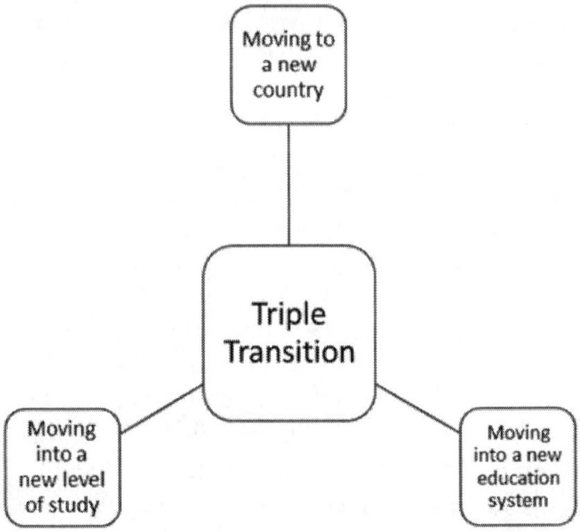


*Figure 1.1 The 'triple transition' of international postgraduate students (Schartner 2014)*

generally requires a greater deal of independence, self-reliance and, ultimately, academic achievement relative to undergraduate study. Research indicates that any of these student transitions can lead to adjustment problems such as anxiety, loss of self-esteem and low academic achievement for any student (Jindal-Snape 2010; see also Chapter 2 below), but ISs undertaking postgraduate degrees are confronted with all three transitional processes simultaneously and so are likely to be especially challenged. The very scale and intensity of the adjustments they go through therefore make them particularly worthy of study.

In this book we approach the transitions experienced by ISs as intercultural phenomena, and need to say something here about the nature of our perspectives on 'culture' and the intercultural. The need for perspectives in HE internationalisation that take account of intercultural factors is now being frequently raised, by ourselves and others:

> What is becoming increasingly clear is that the various manifestations of internationalisation currently operationalised are not in themselves panaceas for institutions seeking to engage positively with the globalizing education 'market', and that greater numbers of international students or a higher global institutional ranking do not necessarily reflect a higher degree of beneficial intercultural interaction or education. (Young et al. 2017: 189)

In order to deepen our understanding of the experiences of ISs 'in transition', we adopt an inclusive, epistemologically 'ecumenical' position in relation to notions of culture and cultural identity. Such an ecumenical position attempts to marry a relatively static, received, 'culture simple' stance to issues of intercultural transition with a more critical, interpretivist 'culture complex' approach (Schartner et al. 2019). We develop our ideas about this position below.

Often sitting alongside HEIs' claims to be 'international' entities is a related and equally prominent claim to be working toward the promotion of intercultural dialogue, learning or some variation of ideas of global citizenship, intercultural effectiveness or intercultural competence (Zhu et al. 2017). In calling for a recalibration of institutional aspirations fully aligned with these aspirations, particularly in the global North, Young (2016) calls for a move towards 'Internationalisation 2.0', which places intercultural perspectives and intercultural communication at the heart of universities' institutional goals and activities. He argues that this is not what they have hitherto tended to do, with financial motivations overriding interculturally focused mission statements and publicly declared institutional aims and aspirations. The exact conceptual nature of such intercultural perspectives, and how they are realised in how people communicate and interact across 'cultural boundaries', are central concerns of this book and one of its most significant contributions, and are therefore worthy of some focus in this introductory chapter.

Intercultural communication as a field of enquiry is concerned with how people from different backgrounds – backgrounds in some way 'cultural' – interact with each other. By 'cultural', we mean clusters of commonalities centred around everyday practices, understood with reference to normative attitudes and beliefs negotiated by groups whose interactions are conditioned by particular forms of social organisations (Corbett 2012). A central focus for scholars interested in intercultural communication is how cultural differences are perceived and made relevant through interactions. Also of interest is the impact that such interactions have on group and intergroup relations, and on people's sense of themselves, their attitudes and their behaviours in culturally unfamiliar situations, and where encountering and interacting with cultural 'others' (e.g. Zhu 2016; Young 2016). The recent boom in the study of inter- or cross-cultural communication, in universities and elsewhere, has occurred in tandem with the increased contact between, and perceived need to understand, cultural 'others' in the overall context of globalisation. Intercultural competences are increasingly promoted as desirable aspirations and target attributes in a range of academic and training contexts – for example, language education, human resource management, business, teacher education, social work, aid and development, engineering and medicine – and among religious organisations (Deardorff 2009; Zhu et al. 2017). There are also some indications that the study of intercultural communication might help sojourner adjustment and adaptation (Young and Schartner 2014; see below and Chapter 4).

Within the growing field of study that is 'intercultural communication', and indeed across the social sciences as a whole, it is possible to discern a continuum running between research influenced by broadly 'positivist' epistemologies at one end, and those with a more critical, interpretivist stance at the other. Positivist approaches are rooted in the natural sciences and an objectivist, natural science ontological position. These begin with assumptions that social phenomena and categories like 'culture', 'gender', 'ethnicity' and 'personality', which are used in everyday discourse, are isolatable, sufficiently stable to be approachable and researchable, and so 'real'.

Interpretivist approaches are rooted in constructivist ontologies. These hold that such phenomena and categories should be considered as social constructions formed from the perceptions and actions of social actors (Bryman 2016). At either end of this continuum sit, respectively, approaches to intercultural communication in cross-cultural psychology and the social psychology of language and communication at the positivist end, and epistemologies rooted in postcolonial and critical cultural theory at the interpretivist.

A criticism of an objectivist ontological stance is that individual and cultural identity can tend to be reified – made into an observable entity separate from and independent of social actors (Lukács 2000). They can also be essentialised: that is, approached as located 'inside' individuals, a product of cognition rooted in the processes of socialisation. From such a perspective, cultural identity can be approached as a characteristic of a person that tends to be absolute, relatively static and knowable (Benwell and Stokoe 2006). It can foster a tendency, in extreme cases, to equate nationality with cultural predispositions (e.g. Holliday et al. 2004) – with research rooted in assumptions that suggest, or overtly assume, that '(a) Culture = (a) Nation = (an) Independent Variable' (Young 2016). Figures such as Geert Hofstede operate from this stance (for a summary of the approach and associated publications, see Hofstede 2017). They see intercultural communication as influenced by core cultural values, indexical for different nationalities, or for people in countries in geographical proximity. Differences between these value systems can, to some extent, predict differences and associated difficulties between people from different national/cultural backgrounds. Such a stance has been very influential in theory informing practice in international business and human resource management, including, on some evidence, how universities themselves frame and approach 'international' students, as discussed below (Zhu et al. 2017).

The critical, interpretivist stance in intercultural studies tends to position itself as directly oppositional to the positivist stance identified above, characterising it as a dominant epistemology that needs to be challenged and, ideally, refuted, for its tendency to cultural simplification, reductionism and stereotyping (Young et al. 2017). It approaches cultural identities as emergent, dynamic, dialogically constructed and multiple. Such a position has been particularly influential in applied linguistics over recent years, and is illustrated in much of the work of scholars such as Claire Kramsch (e.g. 1998) and Adrian Holliday (e.g. 2013), among many others. Holliday (2017: 207) summarises this position in this way:

> It is no longer possible to talk simplistically about cultural differences or what it is like to travel to 'another culture' as though it is a solid and boundaried place [...] This opening up results from a postmodern realisation that the concept of culture is socially and ideologically constructed, and a critical cosmopolitan view that culture is open to travel and creative innovation across boundaries.

An interpretivist approach arguably accounts for the observed realities of real-life, real-time intercultural interaction more accurately. It may even be more ethically focused in its explicit rejection of stereotyping and 'othering', and so better aligned with idealistic calls for truly 'intercultural' goals for internationalising universities. However, the practical, applied benefits of such an approach are perhaps harder to discern at organisational and institutional levels. This may explain the ongoing influence outside the interpretivist research community of more objectivist perspectives on the intercultural in organisational policy and practice (Young et al. 2017; Zhu et al. 2017).

Our stance in this book, and in much of our recent work, attempts a 'middle-ground', 'ecumenical' (Atkinson 1999) approach to considerations of the intercultural, which marries the benefits of a positivist approach with those of an interpretivist approach. In doing so, we pick up ideas evident in the work of Michael Byram (1997) and Dwight Atkinson (1999) during the 'cultural turn' in applied linguistics in the 1990s. Addressing changing perspectives and priorities in foreign language education, these scholars called for approaches to the intercultural that attempted to take account of both positivist and interpretivist perspectives, getting the best out of both world-views, while acknowledging the strengths and the limitations in both. As Atkinson (1999: 649) puts it, when proposing ways forward for the study of culture in language learning:

> I am trying to present a way of looking at the vexed notion of culture ecumenically – of taking into account a wide range of cultural understandings and critiques, and trying to show that they do not necessarily need to be viewed as oppositional or mutually exclusive. To put it more positively, I believe that I am trying to show how concepts that have often been seen as working against each other can work together, and in so doing provide us with more expansive and useful vantage points.

This contention segues with our own position vis-à-vis culture. We see culture as a powerful and pervasive but messy and imprecise concept. It is rooted in people in terms of some kind of individual and social identity, permeable and dynamic but bounded sufficiently for some kind of useful analysis and understandings in relation to external circumstances and social organisations to be carried out. Within these parameters, notions like personality, adjustment and adaptation can be studied both as definable and measurable concepts and processes, and as the contingent, almost infinitely variable natures and experience of individuals. In order to capture a 'thick', generalisable picture of the intercultural transitions of 'international' students, and one sufficiently fine-grained and individualised to be true to the individual experience in all its myriad richness, we need to try to bring the two perspectives – the positivist and the interpretive – together.

This approach is detailed when we discuss our methodology in detail in Chapter 3, below. For now, it is sufficient to state that to operationalise our 'ecumenical' position, we employ a mixed-methods (or 'multi-strategy' – Bryman 2001) approach in the studies reported in this book. This combines both quantitative and qualitative research methodologies. The former are usually rooted in positivist epistemologies, the latter in interpretivism. Bringing the two together allows us to augment the strengths of each of these methods, while mitigating the weaknesses. For example, then, we are able to refer to quantified data on the academic, psychological and sociocultural adaptation of ISs, and the interrelationships between these different domains, beyond the specific context of study and beyond the particular groups of students who were our participants. We are also able to draw on qualitative interview data that are highly individual-, person- and context-specific with which to deepen our understandings of what particular people are going through more or less while they are going through it, in terms of how they are perceiving and responding to the changed, transitional, circumstances in which they are finding themselves. One dataset converges with, talks to and enriches the other, enabling a multilevel analysis of the complex phenomena we are exploring (Dörnyei 2007). This convergence and corroboration, we contend, can only serve to improve the validity of our research outcomes. It can also help us, we hope, reach a wider audience than a study cleaving closely to one particular paradigmatic stance.

## 1.5 KEY CONCEPTS AND GLOSSARY

An issue bedevilling studies of 'internationalisation' in global HE, and of the 'international student experience' – and, indeed, of intercultural 'transitions' in general – is a lack of agreement and clarity around the meaning(s) of key concepts and terminology (Matsumoto and Hwang 2013). To end this introductory chapter, we therefore explore, unpack and – where necessary – define concepts and terminology that are important in the presentation of our own and others' research in these areas.

### 1.5.1 ADAPTATION AND ADJUSTMENT

Ambiguity surrounds key terms and concepts used to describe the affective, cognitive and behavioural changes experienced by intercultural sojourners (Kim 2001). The determining variable for a successful sojourn abroad is typically conceived in the literature in terms of 'adjustment' or 'adaptation' to the new environment (Ward et al. 2001), and these notions are employed as the two main conceptual frames of reference in this book. However, there is little consistency in the literature in defining and conceptualising adjustment and adaptation: indeed, many researchers and theoretical frameworks make no clear distinction between the two – often, the terms are used interchangeably (Stanton et al. 2007). For clarity and consistency, we use 'adjustment' to refer to the dynamic, interactive processes involved in functioning in the host environment (Anderson 1994), while we use 'adaptation' to refer to discernible outcomes of these adjustive processes (Pitts 2005). In this conceptualisation, adjustment is best approached longitudinally as a process that can be explored over time, while adaptation can be viewed as measurable outcomes of the sojourn in areas of high salience to the student sojourner, including academic, psychological and sociocultural aspects.

While much of the literature reported below (Chapter 2) does not make this distinction explicit, it is crucial for this book and the work it reports that we make such a differentiation. We aim to monitor academic, psychological and sociocultural adjustment processes and experiences in and among students over time, but also measure and attempt to predict outcomes of these (that is, adaptation). In addition, and in accordance with Ward and colleagues (2001), we distinguish 'psychological' and 'sociocultural' domains of adjustment and adaptation. Moreover, as the students in this study sojourn for the purpose of obtaining a degree, 'academic' adjustment and adaptation are also included as a conceptual focal point. The three adjustment domains are further discussed in Chapter 2.

### 1.5.2 SOJOURNERS

Similar ambiguity surrounds the term 'sojourner', which has been used to refer to a range of groups such as refugees, missionaries, diplomats, military and humanitarian aid personnel, and expatriates on overseas assignments, as well as ISs (Ward et al. 2001). For the purpose of our research, we approach the students at the heart of our investigations as voluntary sojourners. They are not, primarily, individuals who might live or seek to live in a new society more or less permanently (as immigrants), but are more like those who undergo intercultural transition as a more temporary state. While some transition experiences might be shared by all sojourners, regardless of the length of their stay abroad, some might be more specific to either long-term or short-term timeframes. It is also the case that some individuals relocate out of necessity (as, for example, refugees or displaced persons), whereas others 'volunteer' to relocate for a set amount of time, after which they intend to return to their country of origin or relocate to another country yet again (Ady 1995; Ward et al. 2001; Pitts 2005). The latter assumption is of course not always hard and fast. For example, many ISs remain in their country of choice after completion of their studies to look for work (Ward et al. 2001).

In our research, the term 'sojourner' refers to a person who has temporarily relocated to a territory outside of her or his country of origin for an extended period of time and for a specific purpose, such as obtaining a university degree (Ward et al. 2001; Pitts 2005). It is important to note that what distinguishes sojourners from tourists or travellers is that the length and nature of their stay abroad usually demand a certain degree of immersion and adjustment beyond that that might be needed by a visitor (Martin and Harrell 1996; Ward et al. 2001). For example, ISs need to adjust to differences in the education system in order to be successful academically (Zhou and Todman 2009). As we detail in our Conclusion, the HEIs operating within these education systems also need to adjust if they are to help ISs through this complex process.

### 1.5.3 INTERNATIONAL AND HOME STUDENTS

Although it is important to acknowledge that ISs represent a diverse and heterogeneous set of people, they do nevertheless share some common characteristics and circumstances that allow them to be identified as a group (Misra and Castillo 2004; see Chapter 2 below). Various terms have been used to refer to this sojourner group, including 'international students', 'foreign students' and 'overseas students'. All these terms commonly describe individuals who leave their countries of origin to undertake tertiary study abroad. However, it is important to distinguish between those students who relocate to obtain a degree and those who travel abroad as exchange students for a more limited period and who, without obtaining a degree from the 'foreign' university, instead return to their universities of origin to complete their degrees (Pitts 2005). The experiences of these two groups might differ quite substantially, particularly in terms of academic demands. In this book, the term 'international students' refers to individuals who have left their country of origin for the purpose of study and are now pursuing tertiary education in a different country: that is, they are enrolled in HE programmes outside of the country where they have received their prior education (OECD 2012). Our specific research focus, as noted above, is on postgraduate students who are undertaking a full programme of study abroad.

Who exactly is considered an 'international' student may vary from country to country for legal or tuition fee purposes (Gürüz 2008). ISs have previously been defined as non-citizens of the country in which they study; however, this definition is now widely regarded as inappropriate, as it includes permanent residents as a result of immigration and can therefore lead to an overestimation of IS numbers (OECD 2010). In the UK, at the time of writing, students from EU member states are counted as 'international' in the national statistics (cf. UKCISA 2018), while they are classed as 'home' students for tuition fee purposes and therefore pay the same rate as UK students. Students from EEA member states, such as Iceland, Liechtenstein, Switzerland and Norway, are in an intermediate position, as they currently pay the higher 'international' fees but do not need to obtain a visa to live or study in the UK. These terminologies and designations are likely to change as a result of the negotiations currently under way to secure the UK's exit from the EU.

For simplicity, in our research, the terms 'non-UK students' and 'ISs' are used interchangeably throughout to refer to all students who have relocated to the UK to study. We also specifically refer to 'international postgraduate students', as those that have relocated abroad for one year or more to complete a master's or doctoral degree, to distinguish this group from undergraduate students.

These groups contrast with 'home' students. A range of terms are commonly used to refer to students who are attending university in the country where they have previously been educated (Carroll and Ryan 2005). This includes 'home students', 'domestic students', 'host (country) students' and 'local students'. In this study, these terms will be used synonymously to refer to students who have spent their formative years in the country of their citizenship and are now enrolled at a university in that country, with the intention of securing a degree there. The distinction between 'international' and 'home' students is, in many ways, blurred, with some home students exhibiting traits that might be considered more characteristic of ISs (for example, using English as a second language) and vice versa (Harrison and Peacock 2008). Nevertheless, as we shall see, there are characteristics of ISs that make their experiences sufficiently distinctive to be able to approach them as a distinct category, while acknowledging that there is no single, unitary 'international student experience'.

## 1.6 SUMMARY AND CONCLUSIONS

In this chapter we have outlined the aims, structure and conceptual, empirical and methodological scope of this book. We have also explored the context for our research focus – IS mobility and its effects on those undertaking it. We have critically examined the nature of 'internationalisation' in HE, and how it is framed and approached by governments and institutions as a response to student mobility. We have explained how the 'international student experience' can be conceptualised and studied as an intercultural transition and, in doing so, unpacked notions of 'culture' and 'the intercultural' in relation to our work and more broadly. A major contribution of our work, we have argued, is how an 'ecumenical' position on culture and the intercultural can be framed and operationalised in examining the phenomena of internationally mobile students' adjustment and adaptation: that is, the process and outcomes of their individual intercultural transitions. Relatedly, we have defined, critically examined and unpacked key concepts such as adjustment, adaptation, sojourning and sojourners in order to frame our approach and to understand better the effects of mobility on individuals undertaking study abroad.

In the following chapter we critically review and consolidate recent research on the 'international student experience' in the fields of intercultural communication, education and applied linguistics. We discuss and integrate findings from both quantitative and qualitative studies on IS adjustment and adaptation, detailing contributory factors identified in the literature.

## REFERENCES

Ady, J. (1995), 'Toward a differential demand model of sojourner adjustment', in R. Wiseman (ed.), *Intercultural Communication Theory*, Thousand Oaks, CA: Sage, pp. 92–114.

Altbach, P. G. (2013), 'Advancing the national and global knowledge economy: the role of research universities in developing countries', *Studies in Higher Education*, 38(3), 316–30.

Anderson, L. E. (1994), 'A new look at an old construct: cross-cultural adaptation', *International Journal of Intercultural Relations*, 18, 293–328.

Atkinson, D. (1999), 'TESOL and culture', *TESOL Quarterly*, 33, 625–54.

AUN (2017), 'Association of South East Asian Nations (ASEAN) Universities Network'. Available at: <http://www.aunsec.org/> (last accessed 1 April 2017).

Benwell, B., and E. Stokoe (2006), *Discourse and Identity*, Edinburgh: Edinburgh University Press.

Bryman, A. (2001), *Social Research Methods*, Oxford: Oxford University Press.

Bryman, A. (2016), *Social Research Methods*, 5th edn, Oxford: Oxford University Press.

Byram, M. (1997), *Teaching and Assessing Intercultural Communicative Competence*, Clevedon: Multilingual Matters.

Carroll, J., and J. Ryan (2005), *Teaching International Students: Improving Learning for All*, London: Routledge.

Corbett, J. (2012), *Discourse and Intercultural Language Education*, British Association for Applied Linguistics SIG in Intercultural Communication Annual Seminar, Nottingham Trent University, May.

Coughlan, S. (2011), 'Record numbers of international students', *BBC News*, 10 March. Available at: <http://www.bbc.co.uk/news/business-12671198> (last accessed 13 December 2018).

Deardorff, D. (2009), 'Preface', in D. K. Deardorff (ed.), *The SAGE Handbook of Intercultural Competence*, Thousand Oaks, CA: Sage, pp. xi–xiv.

de Wit, H., F. Hunter, L. Howard and E. Egron-Polak (2015), *The Internationalisation of Higher Education*, Brussels: European Parliament, Committee on Culture and Education.

Dörnyei, Z. (2007), *Research Methods in Applied Linguistics*, Oxford: Oxford University Press.

EACEA (Education, Audiovisual and Culture Executive Agency of the European Commission) (2016), 'http://eacea.ec.europa.eu/home/erasmus-plus/actions/key-action-2-cooperation-for-innovation-and-exchange-good-practices/capacity-0_en> (last accessed 13 December 2018).

Forest, J. J. F., and P. G. Altbach (2006), *International Handbook of Higher Education*, vol. 1, Dordrecht: Springer.

Gürüz, K. (2008), *Higher Education and International Student Mobility in the Global Knowledge Economy*, Albany, NY: State University of New York Press.

Harrison, N., and N. Peacock (2008), 'Mindful or mindless: do UK student drinking cultures and stereotypes undermine intercultural contact?', in Higher Education Academy (ed.), *University Life Uncovered: Making Sense of the Student Experience*, pp. 44–56. Available at: <https://www.heacademy.ac.uk/system/files/university-life-uncovered_0.pdf> (last accessed 10 December 2016).

Hazelkorn, E. (2016), *Global Rankings and the Geopolitics of Higher Education*, London: Routledge.

Hénard, F., L. Diamond and D. Roseveare (2012), *Approaches to Internationalisation and Their Implications for Strategic Management and Institutional Practice: A Guide for Higher Education Institutions*, Institutional Management in Higher Education, OECD. Available at: <https://www.oecd.org/education/imhe/Approaches%20to%20internationalisation%20-%20final%20-%20web.pdf> (last accessed 31 July 2019).

HESA (Higher Education Statistics Agency) (2017), *Higher Education Student Enrolments and Qualifications Obtained at Higher Education Providers in the United Kingdom 2015/16*. Available at: <https://www.hesa.ac.uk/news/12-01-2017/sfr242-student-enrolments-and-qualifications> (last accessed 10 December 2018).

Hofstede, G. (2017), *Geert Hofstede*. Available at: <https://geert-hofstede.com/> (last accessed 13 December 2018).

Holliday, A. (2013), *Understanding Intercultural Communication: Negotiating a Grammar of Culture*, Abingdon: Routledge.

Holliday, A. (2017), 'PhD students, interculturality, reflexivity, community and internationalisation', *Journal of Multilingual and Multicultural Development*, 38(3), 206–18.

IAU (International Association of Universities) (2012), 'Affirming academic values in internationalization of higher education: a call for action', *Global Higher Education*. <https://www.iau-aiu.net/IMG/pdf/affirming_academic_values_in_internationalization_of_higher_education.pdf> (last accessed 13 December 2018).

ICEF Monitor (2015), *The State of International Student Mobility in 2015*. Available at: <http://monitor.icef.com/2015/11/the-state-of-international-student-mobility-in-2015> (last accessed 10 December 2018).

Inan, A., D. Wick, H. G. van Liempd and M. Fastner (2014), *Internationalisation with Integrity: Modelling a New Approach. European Association for International Education*, 25 July. Available at: <http://www.eaie.org/blog/internationalisation-with-integrity/> (last accessed 13 December 2018).

Jindal-Snape, D. (2010), 'Setting the scene: educational transitions and moving stories', in D. Jindal-Snape (ed.), *Educational Transitions: Moving Stories from Around the World*, New York: Routledge, pp. 1–10.

Jindal-Snape, D., and R. Ingram (2013), 'Understanding and supporting triple transitions of international doctoral students: ELT and SuReCom Models', *Journal of Perspectives in Applied Academic Practice*, 1(1), 17–24.

Kim, Y. Y. (2001), *Becoming Intercultural: An Integrative Theory of Communication and Cross-cultural Adaptation*, Thousand Oaks, CA: Sage.

Knight, J. (2003), 'Updated internationalization definition', *International Higher Education*, 33, 2–3.

Kramsch, C. (1998), *Language and Culture*, Oxford: Oxford University Press.

Lukács, G. (2000), *History and Class Consciousness: Studies in Marxist Dialectics*, Cambridge, MA: MIT Press.

McNamara, D., and R. Harris (2002), 'Introduction', in D. McNamara and R. Harris (eds), *Overseas Students in Higher Education: Issues in Teaching and Learning*, London: Taylor & Francis, pp. 1–11.

Marginson, S. (2013), 'Equals or others? Mobile students in a nationally-bordered world', in S. Sovic and M. Blythman (eds), *International Students Negotiating Higher Education*, Abingdon: Routledge, pp. 9–27.

Martin, J. N., and T. Harrell (1996), 'Re-entry training for intercultural sojourners', in D. Landis and R. S. Bhagat (eds), *Handbook of Intercultural Training*, 2nd edn, Thousand Oaks, CA: Sage, pp. 307–26.

Matsumoto, D., and H. C. Hwang (2013), 'Assessing cross-cultural competence: a review of available tests', *Journal of Cross-Cultural Psychology*, 44(6), 849–73.

Meleis, A. I. (2010), 'Transitions as a nursing theory', in A. I. Meleis (ed.), *Transitions Theory: Middle-range and Situation-specific Theories in Nursing Research and Practice*, New York: Springer, pp. 11–13.

MEXT (Ministry of Education, Culture, Sports, Science and Technology – Japan) (2014), *Selection of the FY 2014 Top Global University Project*. Available at: <http://www.mext.go.jp/b_menu/houdou/26/09/__icsFiles/afieldfile/2014/10/07/1352218_02.pdf> (last accessed 13 December 2018).

Misra, R., and L. G. Castillo (2004), 'Academic stress among college students: comparison of American and international students', *International Journal of Stress Management*, 11(2), 132–48.

Montgomery, C. (2010), *Understanding the International Student Experience*, Basingstoke: Palgrave Macmillan.

OECD (Organisation for Economic Co-Operation and Development) (2010), *Education at a Glance 2010: OECD Indicators*, OECD. Available at: <http://www.oecd.org/dataoecd/45/39/45926093.pdf> (last accessed 10 December 2018).

OECD (2012), *Education at a Glance 2012: OECD Indicators*, OECD. Available at: <https://www.oecd-ilibrary.org/education/education-at-a-glance-2012_eag-2012-en> (last accessed 10 December 2018).

OECD (2017), *Education at a Glance 2017: OECD Indicators*, OECD. Available at: <https://www.oecd-ilibrary.org/education/education-at-a-glance-2017_eag-2017-en> (last accessed 10 December 2018).

OECD (2018), *Education at a Glance 2018: OECD Indicators*, OECD. Available at: <http://www.oecd.org/education/education-at-a-glance/> (last accessed 10 December 2018).

Piller, I., and J. Cho (2013), 'Neoliberalism as language policy', *Language in Society*, 42(1), 23–44.

Pitts, M. J. (2005), *The Role of Communication in Cross-national Adjustment and Identity Transitions Among Student Sojourners*, Unpublished doctoral thesis, Pennsylvania State University, USA.

QS (2018), *World University Rankings Methodology*. Available at: <https://www.topuniversities.com/qs-world-university-rankings/methodology> (last accessed 10 December 2018).

Robson, S., J. Almeida, J. and A. Schartner (2017), 'Internationalization at home: time for review and development?', *European Journal of Higher Education*, 8(1), 19–35.

Schartner, A. (2014), *Cross-cultural Transition in Higher Education: The Academic, Psychological and Sociocultural Adjustment and Adaptation of International Postgraduate Students at a British University*, Unpublished doctoral thesis, Newcastle University, UK.

Schartner, A., and T. J. Young (2016), 'Towards an integrated conceptual model of international student adjustment and adaptation', *European Journal of Higher Education*, 6(4), 372–86.

Schartner, A., T. J. Young, A. Brandt, M. Handford and Y. Maemura (2019), 'Intercultural communication as a graduate attribute: a needs analysis among engineering students and university staff in the UK and Japan', Manuscript submitted to *The European Journal of Engineering Education*.

Seeber, M., M. Cattaneo, J. Huisman and S. Paleari (2016), Why do higher education institutions internationalize? An investigation of the multilevel determinants of internationalization rationales', *Higher Education*, 72(5), 685–702.

Snodin, N., and. J. Young (2015), '"Native-speaker" varieties of English: Thai perceptions and attitudes', *Asian Englishes*, 17(3), 248–60.

Stanton, A., T. A. Revenson and H. Tennen (2007), 'Health psychology: psychological adjustment to chronic disease', *Annual Review of Psychology*, 58, 565–92.

UIS (UNESCO Institute for Statistics) (2013), *Global Flow of Tertiary-level Students*. Available at: <http://uis.unesco.org/en/topic/higher-education> (last accessed 13 December 2018).

UKCISA (2018), *International Student Statistics: UK Higher Education*. Available at: <https://www.ukcisa.org.uk/Research--Policy/Statistics/International-student-statistics-UK-higher-education> (last accessed 13 December 2018).

Universities UK International (2017), *International Facts and Figures*. Available at: <https://www.universitiesuk.ac.uk/policy-and-analysis/reports/Documents/International/International_Facts_and_Figures_2017.pdf> (last accessed 21 July 2018).

Universities UK (2015), *Patterns and Trends in UK Higher Education*. Available at: <https://www.universitiesuk.ac.uk/policy-and-analysis/reports/Documents/2015/patterns-and-trends-2015.pdf > (last accessed 10 December 2018).

Urban, S. L., and L. B. Palmer (2014), 'International students as a resource for internationalization of higher education', *Journal of Studies in International Education*, 18(4), 305–24.

van der Wende, M. (2001), 'Studies in Internationalization', *Journal of Studies in International Education*, 5(2), 165–9.

Verbik, L., and V. Lasanowski (2007), *International Student Mobility: Patterns and Trends*. Available at: <http://heer.qaa.ac.uk/SearchForSummaries/Summaries/Pages/SCEE232.aspx> (last accessed 10 December 2018).

Ward, C., S. Bochner and A. Furnham (2001), *The Psychology of Culture Shock*, 2nd edn, Hove: Routledge.

Wright, C., and A. Schartner (2013), '"I can't … I won't?" International students at the threshold of social interaction', *Journal of Research in International Education*, 12(2), 113–28.

Young, T. J. (2016). 'Intercultural Research and Internationalisation in Higher Education', Keynote to *Newton Fund Researcher Links Workshop: Internationalisation of Higher*

*Education: Developing Values-based Intercultural Research Approaches*, Dusit Thani Hotel, Bangkok, Thailand.

Young, T. J., M. Handford and A. Schartner (2017), 'Introduction: the internationalising university: an intercultural endeavour?', *Journal of Multilingual and Multicultural Development* (Special Issue), 38(3), 189–91.

Young T. J., and A. Schartner (2014), 'The effects of cross-cultural communication education on international students' adjustment and adaptation', *Journal of Multilingual and Multicultural Development*, 35(6), 547–62.

Zhou, Y., and J. Todman (2009), 'Patterns of adaptation of Chinese postgraduate students in the United Kingdom', *Journal of Studies in International Education*, 13(4), 467–86.

Zhu, H. (2016), 'Identifying research paradigms', in Zhu Hua (ed.), *Research Methods in Intercultural Communication*, Chichester: John Wiley, pp. 3–22.

Zhu, H., M. Handford and T. J. Young (2017), 'Framing interculturality: a corpus-based analysis of online promotional discourse of higher education intercultural communication courses', *Journal of Multilingual and Multicultural Development*, 38(3), 283–300.

2

# THE CURRENT STATE OF KNOWLEDGE ABOUT THE 'INTERNATIONAL STUDENT EXPERIENCE'

In this chapter, we review and consolidate recent research on intercultural transitions in HE, with a specific focus on the 'international student experience', in the fields of intercultural communication, education and applied linguistics. We attempt to synthesise a body of research that remains, as we shall see, both fragmented and under-theorised. In particular, we discuss and integrate findings from across quantitative and qualitative studies on IS adjustment and adaptation, detailing contributory factors commonly identified in the literature. The review below, alongside the data presented in Part II of this book, serves as the empirical underpinning for our conceptual model (detailed in Chapter 9).

This chapter is organised as follows: firstly, we review common theoretical approaches to the study of intercultural transition (2.1). Secondly, we discuss specific areas of salience to student sojourners' intercultural transition, including academic, psychological and sociocultural adjustment and adaption (2.2). Thirdly, we present contributory factors to ISs' adjustment and adaptation commonly identified in the literature (2.3). Finally, we sum up where current research is at, and the questions that we feel arise from the state of current knowledge (2.4).

## 2.1 CONCEPTUAL APPROACHES TO INTERCULTURAL TRANSITION

For the purpose of this book, we view a study sojourn abroad as a major life event that requires a transition on an emotional, behavioural and cognitive level (see 'ABC model' below). The 'international student experience' invariably brings the individual into contact with new cultural environments and this requires a degree of intercultural transition. We understand the latter as 'alterations that occur in individuals and in their environments as a consequence of culture-contact situation' (Laosa 1998: 3). These changes involve a range of complex psychological and social processes (Ward et al. 2001), and a variety of theoretical approaches have been proposed in an attempt to capture these dynamics. However, conceptualisations of intercultural transition are far from consistent across the literature, as Kim (2001: 11) highlights: 'The complex nature of the phenomenon manifests itself in the variety of existing conceptions, making it difficult for individual investigators to gain a clear picture of the body of knowledge accumulated over the decades.'

One of the most popular and frequently cited theories of intercultural transition is the 'U curve' model (Lysgaard 1955). This recuperation model encompasses four stages: an initial 'honeymoon' phase of excitement and euphoria, which is followed by a phase of disenchantment or 'culture shock', a stage of recovery and, eventually, full adaptation. Together, these four stages resemble a U-curve shape. Oberg (1960: 24) describes culture shock as 'anxiety that results from losing all our familiar signs and symbols of social intercourse', which can be manifested in, for example, longing for home, feelings of helplessness, anger and hostility, and concerns about daily activities. Gullahorn and Gullahorn (1963) extended the U-curve to a 'W-curve' model, suggesting that, upon re-entry into the country of origin, sojourners experience the four stages of intercultural transition yet again (see Figure 2.1).

Despite its popular appeal – in particular, in the intercultural management and training literature (see, for example, UKCISA 2018), there is actually little empirical evidence for a U-curve pattern in intercultural transition (Church 1982; Furnham and Bochner 1986). Recent studies of ISs do not support the notion of early 'honeymoon' euphoria, but instead depict the early stages of transition as a time of anxiety and nervousness (Ward and Kennedy 1996a, 1996b; Brown 2008a, 2008b; Brown and Holloway 2008; Schartner 2014). Additionally, the linear pattern of recuperation depicted in the U-curve model may not accurately reflect different domains of transition. There is some evidence, for example, that psychological adjustment tends to remain variable over time rather than necessarily following an ascending pattern (Ward et al. 1998; Schartner 2014).

In response to some of the perceived limitations of the U-curve model, researchers began to develop approaches that depicted the sojourner as a more proactive individual. Rather than counselling and therapy for the 'culturally shocked' sojourner, the role of coping mechanisms, preparation, orientation, and the acquisition of

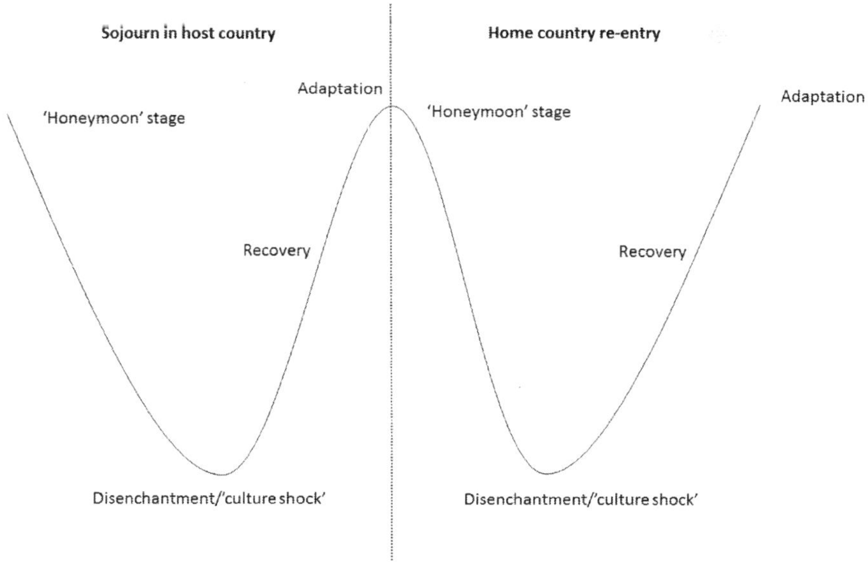


*Figure 2.1 'W-curve' model of culture shock*

culturally relevant knowledge and social skills were increasingly emphasised (e.g. Bochner 1982, 1986; Furnham and Bochner 1982). Major influences here included scholarly work in stress and coping (e.g. Lazarus and Folkman 1984), social learning theory (e.g. Argyle 1980), and social cognition and intergroup perceptions (e.g. Kosmitzki 1996; Kunda 1999). As a result, three theoretical approaches to the study of intercultural transition, termed by Ward and colleagues (2001) the 'ABC model', have become fairly well established since the 1990s:

1. Stress and coping approaches, representing the affective (A) component of intercultural transition
2. Culture-learning and social skills perspectives, reflecting behavioural (B) elements
3. Social identification theories, reflecting cognitive (C) processes.

The first, stress and coping approaches (e.g. Berry 1997) highlight the significance of life changes for those undergoing intercultural transition and subsequent 'acculturative stress' (Berry 1970). Coping strategies are required to deal with this acculturative stress (Ward et al. 2001). The extent to which one is able to cope with acculturative stress may depend on both individual and situational variables, including personality (e.g. Ward and Kennedy 1992; Ward and Chang 1997), social support (e.g. Adelman 1988; Hayes and Lin 1994), cultural distance (Berry 1997), and degree and quality of social relationships (Furnham and Alibhai 1985; Young et al. 2013).

The second approach, culture learning and social skills perspectives, focuses on behavioural elements. This approach suggests that, upon arrival in the host country, sojourners experience difficulties in managing everyday social encounters. The learning of the salient characteristics of the new environment will eventually help the sojourner to function effectively and confidently (Furnham and Bochner 1982, 1986). This may include the acquisition of culturally relevant verbal and non-verbal communication skills (Gardner 1952; Ruben and Kealey 1979), as well as the learning of social behaviours (Triandis 1977, 1980). Intercultural transition is conceptualised here as a growth-facilitating experience, where initial adjustment difficulties are followed by relatively steady improvement, resembling an ascending learning curve.

The third major conceptual approach is social identification theories. Drawing on the study of social cognition (e.g. Kunda 1999) and social identity theory (Tajfel 1978), social identification theories are concerned with the way in which people view themselves in the social world, and how they perceive in-group and out-group members (Ward et al. 2001). This approach therefore investigates the cognitive elements of intercultural transition, such as pre-sojourn expectations (e.g. Pitts 2009), stereotypes and intergroup attitudes (e.g. Gudykunst 1983), cultural identity (e.g. Kim 2001), or value changes as a result of intercultural transition (e.g. Arends- Tóth and van de Vijver 2006).

Both our empirical work (reported in Part II) and our conceptual model (presented in Chapter 9) are informed by these three theoretical approaches. We feel that the 'international student experience' encompasses affective (A), behavioural (B) and cognitive (C) processes. For example, on an affective (A) level, in order to function effectively in the new academic environment (that is, meet the demands of their degree programme), student sojourners must employ coping strategies to deal with acculturative stress triggered by the transition from academic home to host 'culture'. They must also learn new behaviours (B), related to academic conventions and practices at the host university, in order to negotiate the new academic environment successfully. Finally, the students' norms and values may be challenged as they encounter new ways of doing things, leading to cognitive (C) changes. In the case of one-year taught postgraduate students, the group under study in this book, these processes are most likely to happen swiftly as students are expected to manage a 'condensed', heavy and demanding workload within a relatively short timeframe (Scudamore 2013).

## 2.2 ADAPTATION AND ADJUSTMENT OF INTERNATIONAL STUDENTS

The 'international student experience' involves processes of adjustment in several domains. In this book, and particularly in our conceptual model (Chapter 9), we focus on (1) academic adjustment, (2) psychological adjustment and (3) sociocultural adjustment. In Chapters 4 to 7 we present empirical data, on both adjustment processes and adjustment outcomes, regarding these three domains. In the following section, we discuss how student sojourners' adjustment and adaptation is conceptualised in the literature, and we review relevant empirical research.

Intercultural transition is a multifaceted phenomenon (Berry 2006). In order to be able to study adjustment and adaptation of ISs (see Chapters 4 to 7) we had to define key criteria for a 'successful' IS sojourn clearly. The international business sojourner literature was helpful here. Kealey and Ruben (1983) discern three domains in which sojourners on work assignments abroad should be successful:

1. Professional competence, defined as skills and knowledge needed to carry out the daily tasks and responsibilities in the work environment
2. Psychological adjustment, defined as the ability to feel happy and satisfied in the new environment
3. Intercultural interaction, defined as being interested in and being able to interact with people of other cultures.

In a similar conceptualisation, Black and Stephens (1989), whose studies focus on intercultural adjustment in the management field, discern the following spheres of sojourner adjustment:

1. General adjustment (managing daily life)
2. Work adjustment (accomplishing work-related objectives)
3. Interaction adjustment (interacting effectively with host nationals).

Another frequently cited conceptualisation of sojourner adjustment is Ward and colleagues' (2001) distinction between psychological and sociocultural adjustment. The former refers to affective responses to the new environment, including

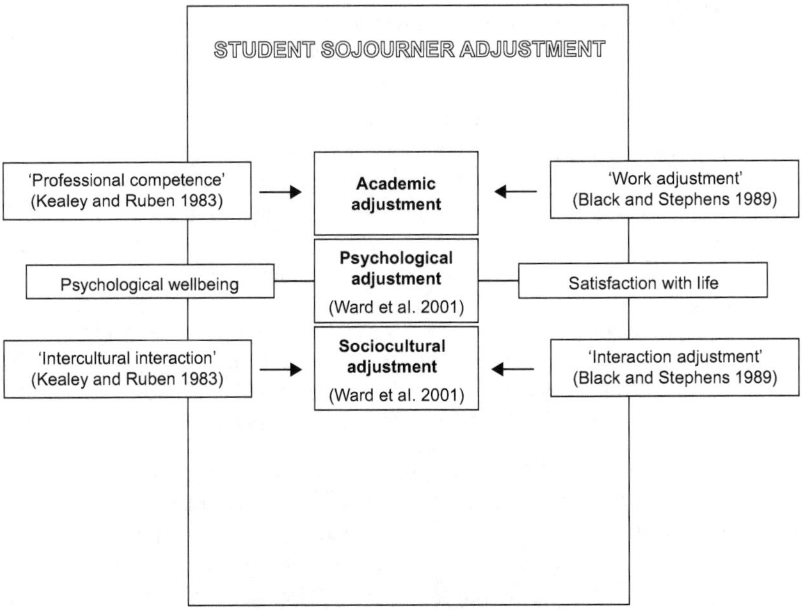


*Figure 2.2 An integrated framework of adjustment domains of salience to student sojourners*

psychological wellbeing and satisfaction with life in that new environment, while the latter refers to cognitive and behavioural factors associated with effective performance in the host country, such as the ability to 'fit in' socially and interact successfully with others in the new environment.

Ward and colleagues' (2001) notion of sociocultural adjustment corresponds closely to Kealey and Ruben's (1983) notion of intercultural interaction and Black and Stephens's (1989) concept of interaction adjustment, although ISs' social contact is not limited to host nationals but involves contact with co-nationals and other non-co-nationals as well (Bochner et al. 1977; Schartner 2015). If we replace professional competence or work adjustment with academic achievement, the criteria above provide a suitable framework for understanding adjustment domains that are central to a 'successful' IS sojourn (Figure 2.2).

### 2.2.1 ACADEMIC ADJUSTMENT

Academic adjustment is defined here as adjustment to the specific demands of academic study, including styles of teaching and learning at the host university. As such, it includes the way classes are conducted, relationships between students and staff, and assessment procedures (Ballard 1987; Ryan 2005). Academic achievement, defined here as evidence of learning measured by successful completion of course requirements and grade point averages (GPAs), is at the centre of the IS sojourn, as it is, in general, of primary importance to the student sojourners themselves (Young et al. 2013). A number of terms have been used in the literature to refer to the process that ISs undergo when transitioning into an unfamiliar academic environment. The literature suggests that ISs may experience 'academic shock' (Ryan 2005), 'learning shock' (Griffiths et al. 2005) or 'education shock' (Yamazaki 2005) due to unfamiliar learning and teaching approaches encountered at the host university, including what counts as 'knowledge' (Scudamore 2013). Gilbert (2000: 14) claims that 'academic culture shock' is caused by 'incongruent schemata about higher education in the students' home country and in the host country'. Learning and teaching approaches can differ between countries, as can priorities in terms of their educational policies (Groom and Maunonen-Eskelinen 2006). What is more, each university has its own practices and conventions. Thus, even ISs with previous academic experience, such as those studying abroad for a postgraduate degree, might be novices in the 'academic culture' of their host university due to a lack of familiarity with local learning and teaching practices (Garson 2005; Luxon and Peelo 2009).

Overall, and in very general terms, research suggests that most ISs are generally satisfied with their academic experiences in the host country (Lee and Wesche 2000; Schutz and Richards 2003). However, they have also been found to experience some academic anxiety and difficulties as part of their intercultural transition (Lewthwaite 1997). In fact, academic adjustment has been described in some literature as more difficult than other domains such as sociocultural adjustment, and researchers have pointed to the long-lasting nature of 'academic shock' (e.g. Ryan 2005; Gu et al. 2010). None the less, Carroll (2005) claims that the early days of learning in the new academic culture are among the most stressful for student sojourners. Although ISs share some of their academic adjustment challenges with local peers who enter academia for the first time or who may be moving to a new level of academic study (Andrade 2006), there are some adjustment matters that are more salient to the former, including, for many, learning while developing host language ability (Arkoudis 2006). It is also believed that ISs are often under greater pressure from their families to succeed academically (Robertson et al. 2000).

### 2.2.2 PSYCHOLOGICAL ADJUSTMENT

Psychological adjustment refers to affective responses to the new environment, including psychological wellbeing and satisfaction with life (Ward et al. 2001). Ward and colleagues argue that psychological adjustment is best understood within a stress and coping framework, with the greatest psychological difficulties expected to be encountered in the initial sojourn stage, when the sojourner is faced with the most immediate life changes and when coping resources and social support in the new environment are limited. Research suggests that psychological adjustment is likely to be influenced by personality variables, social support and life change events (Berry 2005). Although a drop in psychological adjustment difficulties is generally expected over time, longitudinal patterns are difficult to predict as they are likely to be influenced by a variety of environmental and transitional factors. For example, hectic assignment and examination periods might impact on ISs' wellbeing throughout the sojourn (Schartner 2014).

### 2.2.3 SOCIOCULTURAL ADJUSTMENT

Sociocultural adjustment refers to cognitive and behavioural factors associated with effective performance in the host country, such as the ability to 'fit in' and interact successfully with others in the new environment (Ward et al. 2001). 'Successful' sociocultural adjustment is thought to be determined by a variety of factors, including previous intercultural experience, host language proficiency, social ties and cultural distance (Li and Gasser 2005; Swami 2009; Swami et al. 2010), with research suggesting that a larger perceived distance between the sojourners' 'home culture' and 'host culture' may result in greater adjustment difficulties (Ward and Kennedy 1993; Galchenko and van de Vijver 2007). Sociocultural adjustment difficulties are expected to peak in the initial sojourn stages, when the sojourner has the least familiarity with and knowledge of the host society and when meaningful relationships in the new environment are still limited (Ward et al. 1998). Situated within a culture-learning and social skills framework, sociocultural adjustment is typically described as a learning curve that ascends fairly rapidly during the first few months of the sojourn and subsequently levels off over time as students become increasingly familiar with the host society's norms and rules (Ward et al. 2001). However, recent research has shown that sociocultural adjustment patterns are far from uniform (Coles and Swami 2012), and that few sojourners experience what has hitherto been seen as 'typical patterns of adjustment'. For example, Wright and Schartner (2013) found evidence for a more dynamic sociocultural adjustment pattern than is commonly

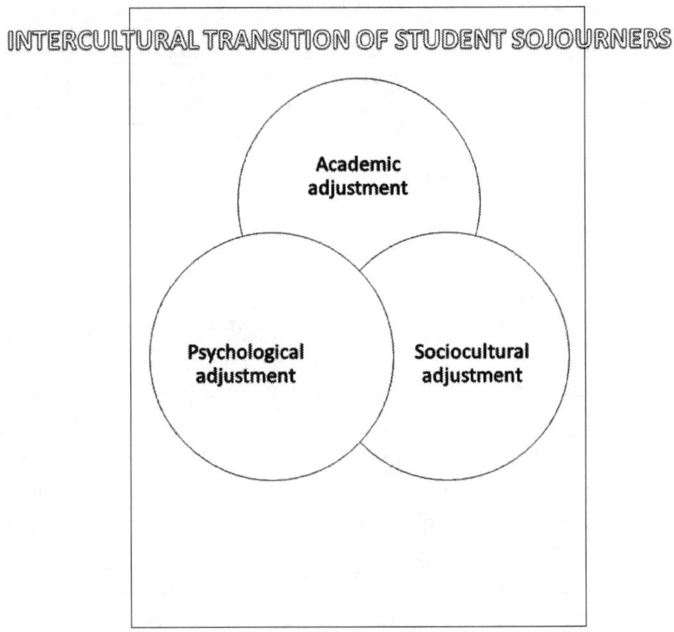


*Figure 2.3 Student sojourners' adjustment domains*

suggested. Their mixed-methods study tracked social interaction and sociocultural adjustment among twenty international postgraduates over a one-year UK-based master's programme. Findings showed that participants remained conflicted on a threshold of interaction throughout, reporting little engagement but also reluctance to take up available opportunities for social interaction. The authors challenge linear models of sociocultural adjustment and suggest that there may be greater individual variation along the sociocultural adjustment path than is commonly recognised.

Recent research suggests that the three domains discussed above interact with and influence one another over the course of the sojourn (see Chapter 7). In this book, and in our model (Chapter 9), we therefore conceptualise the intercultural adjustment of student sojourners as a multidimensional phenomenon and portray academic, psychological and sociocultural adjustment as three overlapping and interconnected spheres (Figure 2.3).

## 2.3 CONTRIBUTORY FACTORS TO INTERNATIONAL STUDENTS' ADJUSTMENT

As researchers have investigated sojourner adjustment and have searched for generalisable patterns, they have found that there is considerable variation between individuals (Kim 2001; Masgoret and Ward 2006). The next section therefore considers contributory factors to IS adjustment, as identified in the literature. Berry (2006) distinguishes between contributory factors that exist prior to the sojourn (henceforth 'pre-sojourn' factors) and those that arise during the process of intercultural transition (henceforth 'in-sojourn' factors). We apply this distinction throughout this book and in our conceptual model (Chapter 9). Ward and colleagues (2001) further distinguish between micro-level factors (that is, characteristics of the individual sojourner, such as age, personality and language ability) and macro-level factors (that is, characteristics of the situation, such as cultural distance between 'home' and 'host' country). An understanding of macro-level factors is important to establish the context in which intercultural transition takes place (Arends-Tóth and van de Vijver 2006). In the case of ISs' macro-level factors, such as the national discourse on immigration in the host country, can influence how the study sojourn abroad is experienced by the individual and can ultimately impact on their adjustment.

Kim (2001: 147) states:

> Strangers' communication and adaptation in a new cultural environment cannot be fully understood without taking into account the conditions of the environment [...] different conditions of the environment evoke different responses in strangers by serving as the cultural, social, and political forces in accordance to which they must strive to increase their chances for meeting personal and social goals.

Research on ISs in various contexts suggests that feelings and experiences of discrimination, for example, can be linked to poor psychological wellbeing and depression (Atri et al. 2006; Wei at al. 2007), increased levels of homesickness (Poyrazli and Lopez 2007) and fewer contacts with members of the host society (Mori 2000). Perceived discrimination has also been found to be a predictor of adjustment difficulties (Duru and Poyrazli 2011) and to affect ISs' acculturation strategies, reflected in increased endorsement of one's own cultural background and avoidance of members of the host society (Ramos et al. 2016).

It is important to note that, while we acknowledge that intercultural adjustment and adaptation are always products of interactions between the individual sojourner and the wider conditions in the host society, this book takes mainly a micro-level approach, with the focus being on the individual, as is typically the case in socio-psychological studies on sojourner adjustment (Ward et al. 2001). Relative to the macro-level, the role of micro-level factors in intercultural transition has attracted considerable research attention. We discuss below individual-level contributory factors commonly identified in the literature.

### 2.3.1 HOST LANGUAGE PROFICIENCY

Proficiency in the local language, or lack thereof, is often conceived as the most crucial factor in ISs' intercultural transition (Sovic 2008) and consequently has received considerable research attention over the years (see Andrade 2006 for a review). Studies have consistently shown that proficiency in the local language, or in a lingua franca such as English if this is the main language of instruction and assessment, is absolutely crucial to academic success (e.g. Ramsay et al. 2007; Gu et al. 2010). Language difficulties can have a negative impact upon aspects such as essay writing, understanding lectures, oral and written examinations, and the ability to contribute to classroom discussions (Smith and Khawaja 2011). In our earlier work (Young et al. 2013) we reported a positive relationship between self-perceived English language ability of students sojourning in the UK and their subsequent academic achievement.

There are also some indications in the literature that language proficiency, self-perceived or otherwise, can influence student sojourners' adjustment beyond the purely academic (Poyrazli et al. 2004; Duru and Poyrazli 2011; Yang et al. 2006; Sumer et al. 2008; Young et al. 2013; Schartner 2014). For example, Poyrazli and colleagues have found that lower levels of language proficiency may contribute to acculturative stress or even depression (Poyrazli et al. 2004; Sumer et al. 2008). Poor language skills may also impede ISs' sociocultural adjustment (e.g. Schutz and Richards 2003; Yang et al. 2006), in particular their interactions with members of the local community (e.g. Poyrazli et al. 2002), although the role of motivation beyond language proficiency has also been acknowledged (Yu and Downing 2012).

### 2.3.2 KNOWLEDGE ABOUT THE HOST COUNTRY

'Preparedness' for the host environment is said to be an important predisposition for internationally mobile individuals. This includes the acquisition of cultural knowledge (and of the host language) prior to relocation (Kim 2017). However, relatively little is known regarding ISs in this respect, as most studies on the effect of pre-arrival preparation to date remain limited to international business sojourners

(Littrell et al. 2006). None the less, the importance of pre-arrival knowledge has been repeatedly noted in the theoretical literature (e.g. Kim 2001; Ward et al. 2001), and there is some, albeit limited, empirical evidence for a positive relationship between knowledge about the host environment and subsequent adjustment in IS samples. For example, Chapman and colleagues (1988) found that prior knowledge of the programme of study was a significant predictor of the academic achievement of an international postgraduate student sample in the USA. In a more recent study, Tsang (2001) found a significant positive relationship between pre-departure knowledge and the general and interaction adjustment of students sojourning in Singapore. Research also suggests that student sojourners tend to prepare for their sojourn in largely superficial, organisational terms (e.g. Pitts 2005) and that, on the whole, preparation rarely goes beyond the purely linguistic (Copland and Garton 2011).

### 2.3.3 PRIOR OVERSEAS EXPERIENCE

Prior overseas experience is generally conceived as having a positive impact on ISs' intercultural transition (Gudykunst and Nishida 2001), although the exact nature of this relationship has yet to be comprehensively determined. Studies of business expatriates suggest that the first-hand practical experience of intercultural transition, and the skills previously acquired abroad, might subsequently be applied to new settings and can therefore ease adjustment to a new environment (Masgoret and Ward 2006; Lee and Sukoco 2010).

### 2.3.4 MOTIVATION FOR STUDY ABROAD

The reasons why people embark on a sojourn abroad have mostly been studied within the concept of 'push/pull motivations' (Berry 2006). 'Push' factors refer to conditions in the home country that initiate the decision to embark on a sojourn abroad, including economic, social and political forces. 'Pull' factors are those that attract the sojourner to another country (Mazzarol and Soutar 2002). Much of the motivation research to date has focused on long-term immigrants, and the motivation of student sojourners remains an under-studied area (Li and Bray 2007). Nevertheless, some studies have identified factors that influence the choice to study abroad in general or the selection of a particular destination country in particular, including perceived prestige and quality of education and tuition and living costs (Mazzarol and Soutar 2002), immigration prospects after graduation (e.g. Baas 2006), degree programmes not offered in the home country (e.g. Nyaupane et al. 2010), established social ties in the destination country (e.g. Nyaupane et al. 2011), environmental considerations such as climate and lifestyle (Bodycott 2009), geographical proximity (Kemp et al. 1998), and the influence of parents, relatives and peers (e.g. Lim et al. 2011; Pimpa 2003). The high utility of a foreign-earned degree in their home country and the emotional, financial and social costs of quitting have been found to motivate ISs to persevere with their degree, even if they do experience difficulties (Zhou 2015).

The role of motivation in ISs' intercultural transition is still relatively underexplored (Smith and Khawaja 2011), but research by Chirkov and colleagues has recently identified self-determined motivation for study abroad as a powerful predictor of adjustment (Chirkov et al. 2007; Chirkov et al. 2008). Chirkov and colleagues' work is grounded in self-determination theory (SDT; Deci and Ryan 2012) which assesses an individual's level of self-determined motivation by considering the degree to which her or his behaviour is autonomous or controlled by others.

According to this theory, four types of behaviour regulation can be distinguished on a self-determination continuum (see Chirkov et al. 2007):

1. *Intrinsic motivation* occurs when people engage in an activity for its own sake because it meets their genuine interests and needs (for example, students move abroad because they find this move challenging and exciting).
2. *Identified regulation* occurs when people internalise external outcomes (for example, students study abroad because the move appears important to their career goals).
3. *Introjected regulation* occurs when people engage in an activity to gain social approval or avoid feeling guilty (for example, students do not receive direct pressure but they feel they 'ought' to study abroad).
4. *External regulation* occurs when people perform an activity to avoid punishment or to obtain rewards (for example, parents insist on them studying abroad or promise a reward).

On this continuum, intrinsic motivation represents full autonomy in the decision to study abroad, whereas external regulation reflects a complete lack of self-determination. Chirkov and colleagues' (2007, 2008) findings suggest that when ISs' decision to study abroad is self-determined, the chances of succeeding in the new environment are higher compared to when the decision is influenced or controlled by others. In a sample of Chinese ISs in Belgium and Canada, a high degree of autonomy in the decision to study abroad was linked to self-determination in academic activities, willingness to learn more about the host culture and overall psychological wellbeing (Chirkov et al. 2007). In a follow-up study of ISs in Canada, Chirkov and colleagues (2008) found that the degree of autonomy in the decision to study abroad was a predictor of overall wellbeing and social difficulties during the sojourn.

### 2.3.5 INTERCULTURAL COMPETENCE

The concept of intercultural competence (IC) is increasingly conceived as a form of individual disposition that is vital for the intercultural transition of ISs (Leong 2007). There has been considerable scholarly debate about IC (Salisbury 2011), and a range of similar concepts exist in the literature, including intercultural communicative competence, cross-cultural awareness, intercultural sensitivity, multicultural effectiveness and global competencies (for a review see Fantini and Tirmizi 2006). In a meta-analysis, Spitzberg and Changnon (2009) discovered over 300 different conceptual approaches to IC. In this book, we use the team 'intercultural competence', as it is thought to be the most widely used in the literature (Van Bakel et al. 2014).

We define IC as 'a complex set of abilities needed to perform effectively and appropriately when interacting with others who are linguistically and culturally different from oneself' (Fantini and Tirmizi 2006: 12).

Reflecting conceptual ambiguity, there is a range of instruments that attempt to measure IC: more than forty-four, according to a review by Fantini (2009). These instruments conceptualise IC in various ways, including affective, behavioural and personality aspects, indicating that there is little consensus as to the dimensions that constitute IC (Spitzberg and Changnon 2009).

In this book, we report on research that used the Multicultural Personality Questionnaire (MPQ), designed to assess 'the effectiveness of individuals in dealing with groups or individuals that differ culturally from themselves' (van Oudenhoven et al. 2007). The MPQ has been identified as one of the most 'promising' psychometric instruments for measuring IC (Matsumoto and Hwang 2013: 867). The MPQ was specifically designed to assess effectiveness in intercultural encounters, and has been found to be more predictive of effectiveness in intercultural settings than more general personality scales such as the 'Big Five' (van der Zee and van Oudenhoven 2000): 'The MPQ questions refer to behaviour in multicultural situations [...] even the MPQ-scales that closely correspond with Big Five-scales are designed to cover more specifically those aspects that are of relevance to multicultural success' (van Oudenhoven and van der Zee 2002: 680).

The most recent ninety-item[1] English version of the MPQ includes five distinct dimensions of IC:

1. *Cultural empathy* (CE) reflects the ability to 'empathise with the feelings, thoughts and behaviours of members from different cultural groups' (van Oudenhoven and van der Zee 2002: 680). This dimension is also often more broadly referred to as 'sensitivity' in the literature (e.g. Hawes and Kealey 1981) and has been identified repeatedly as a dimension of IC by a range of scholars (e.g. Arthur and Bennett 1995; Deardorff 2006).
2. *Open-mindedness* (OM) refers to an open and unprejudiced attitude towards others, and includes aspects such as 'interest in the local people' (Harris 1973) and 'freedom from prejudice' (Ronen 1989).
3. *Social initiative* (SI) refers to the ability to take the initiative and approach social situations actively. With regard to cross-cultural transition, researchers have pointed to the importance of the ability to instigate and maintain contacts and to take the initiative (e.g. Hawes and Kealey 1981; Spreitzer et al. 1997).
4. *Emotional stability* (ES) reflects a tendency to remain calm in stressful situations. A sojourn abroad has been characterised as a stressful life event by various scholars (e.g. Berry 2006); thus the ability to cope with psychological stress has repeatedly been identified as a key factor of IC (Church 1982).
5. *Flexibility* (FL) refers to the ability to learn from experiences and adjust behaviour accordingly. As sojourners enter the host environment, familiar ways of handling things might no longer work (van Oudenhoven and van der Zee 2002). Thus, flexibility is crucial in order to become effective in the new environment (Arthur and Bennet 1995; Spreitzer et al. 1997).

There has been some debate in the literature as to whether IC is 'trainable' and malleable through intercultural experiences, or whether it is, in fact, a collection of more stable personality traits (see Schartner 2016). Some authors distinguish more dynamic aspects of IC from those that are thought to be relatively stable (e.g. Leiba-O'Sullivan 1999; Bird et al. 2010). CE, OM and SI are thought to be more dynamic over time (Herfst et al. 2008), whereas ES is more often seen as a relatively stable personality trait (Ones and Viswesvaran 1997). However, recent studies of ISs in the UK (Schartner 2016) and in China (An and Chiang 2015) found evidence for the malleability of IC dimensions over time, including ES. Thus, although there is some debate over the flexibility of constructs such as the 'multicultural personality', recent research employing the MPQ has shown that it is indeed possible to approach IC in this way – to see it as a malleable set of characteristics that are nevertheless stable enough to capture in research.

The MPQ has been used repeatedly in research on sojourner adjustment and has demonstrated predictive validity for a range of adjustment outcomes in a number of studies on business sojourners (e.g. van Oudenhoven et al. 2003; Peltokorpi 2008) and IS samples (e.g. van Oudenhoven and van der Zee 2002; Leong 2007; Young et al. 2013). It is a reliable instrument and internal consistencies for the five subscales among diverse IS samples are generally high, with Cronbach's alpha ranging from 0.74 to 0.87 in Yakunina and colleagues (2012) and from 0.71 to 0.82 in Young and colleagues (2013). Table 2.1 presents an overview of empirical studies of sojourner adjustment that have employed the MPQ. What is striking is that most studies to date, including those of ISs, have employed a cross-sectional/concurrent research design (that is, the MPQ dimensions and adjustment outcomes were measured once and at the same time). Longitudinal research designs remain comparatively scarce, with some exceptions (Mol et al. 2001; van Oudenhoven and van der Zee 2002; Leong 2007; Schartner 2014).

In studies of ISs, the MPQ dimensions emerged as significant predictors for a range of adjustment outcomes, including indicators of academic, psychological and sociocultural adaptation (Table 2.1).

Table 2.1 Example studies of sojourner adjustment using the Multicultural Personality Questionnaire

| | Authors | Sample | Research design | Variables predicted |
|---|---|---|---|---|
| 1 | Basow and Gaugler (2017) | US exchange students in Costa Rica (N = 120) | Longitudinal | Psychological adjustment (ES, SI, CE) |
| 2 | Peltokorpi and Froese (2014) | Expatriates in Brazil and Japan (N = 199) | Cross-sectional/ concurrent | Job satisfaction (CE, ES) |
| 3 | Lee and Ciftci (2013) | International students in the USA (N = 330) | Cross-sectional/ concurrent | Social support; academic self-efficacy; sociocultural adaptation |

Table 2.1 Continued

| | Authors | Sample | Research design | Variables predicted |
|---|---|---|---|---|
| 4 | Young et al. (2013) | International students undertaking taught MA programmes in the UK (N = 102) | Cross-sectional/ concurrent | Academic achievement (CE, OM, SI); psychological wellbeing (ES, OM); satisfaction with life (ES) |
| 5 | Yakunina et al. (2012) | International students in the USA (N = 341) | Cross-sectional/ concurrent | Psychological adjustment (ES, SI) |
| 6 | Peltokorpi and Froese (2012) | Expatriates in Japan (N = 181) | Cross-sectional/ concurrent | Interaction adjustment (OM); general adjustment (CE, ES); work adjustment (SI) |
| 7 | Peltokorpi (2008) | Expatriates in Japan (N = 110) | Cross-sectional/ concurrent | Interaction adjustment (CE); general adjustment (CE) ES); job satisfaction (ES) |
| 8 | Leong (2007) | Singaporean undergraduates students on a study abroad programme (N = 166) | Longitudinal | Psychological and sociocultural adaptation (SI) |
| 9 | Ali et al. (2003) | Expatriate spouses in 29 countries (N = 247) | Cross-sectional/ concurrent | Satisfaction with life (OM, ES); intercultural interaction (OM); sociocultural adjustment (OM) |
| 10 | van Oudenhoven et al. (2003) | Expatriates in Taiwan (N = 102) | Cross-sectional/ concurrent | Physical health (ES); psychological wellbeing (ES, SI); life satisfaction (CE, ES); job satisfaction (FL); social support (CE, ES, FL) |
| 11 | van Oudenhoven and van der Zee (2002) | International business students in the Netherlands (N = 171, 47%) | Longitudinal | Mental health (29% explained variance); subjective wellbeing (19%); social support (30%); academic achievement (7%) |
| 12 | Mol et al. (2001) | International high-school students in Taiwan (N = 205) | Longitudinal | Life satisfaction (OM, ES); physical health (ES); psychological wellbeing (ES); social support (OM, SI); participation in extracurricular activities (OM, ES) |

Note: CE = cultural empathy; ES = emotional stability; FL = flexibility; OM = open-mindedness; SI = social initiative.

### 2.3.6 SOCIAL CONTACT

A sojourn abroad entails leaving one's comfort zone and involves the temporary loss of social ties and familiar social support systems (Hayes and Lin 1994). This may result in a lack of social connectedness for the individual student sojourner (Ward et al. 2001), as 'international university students arrive in the host country generally denuded of social capital' (Neri and Ville 2008: 1515). Consequently, the formation of new social ties becomes a paramount objective for ISs (Ong and Ward 2005). Research has confirmed the importance of social connectedness for ISs' adjustment, suggesting that those with a strong social network report lower levels of stress and more positive effects from study abroad in general (Russell et al. 2010). In comparison to their domestic peers, ISs need to make extra efforts to achieve social integration in the new environment, as their familiar social networks are usually not within easy reach (Rienties et al. 2012), although the spread of social networking sites and online communication tools such as Skype are changing this somewhat (for a review see Sleeman et al. 2016). Recent research indicates that social media play an important support function for ISs and that they may use them more than their domestic counterparts (Gray et al. 2010). Social media use can fulfil two primary functions for student sojourners: firstly, it can help provide a sense of connectedness to the home country, reducing acculturative stress (see Sandel's 2014 study of ISs in the US), and secondly, it can provide a window into the host culture (see, for example, Li and Chen's 2014 study of Chinese ISs' use of Facebook).

A considerable body of research has highlighted the importance of social connectedness for student sojourners' subjective wellbeing and their academic and sociocultural adjustment (see Ward et al. 2001 for a review), and studies have recently used degree of social contact as a predictor for academic and psychosocial adaptation (Young et al. 2013). However, few systematic attempts have been made to monitor the trajectories of ISs' social ties over time using qualitative methods of inquiry (exceptions include Montgomery and McDowell 2009, and Schartner 2015). Most studies to date have employed a cross-sectional quantitative design and have typically counted the number of friends students had in the host country (e.g. Bochner et al. 1986; Furnham and Alibhai 1985; Neri and Ville 2008; Hendrickson et al. 2011).

In this book, we aim to explore social contact not only as a contributory variable for adjustment, but also in relation to the trajectories of students' social ties over time and the functions of different social groups, including co-nationals, host nationals and non-co-national ISs. These three groups emerged as significant in Bochner and colleagues' (1977) Functional Model of Friendship Networks, based on a study of thirty ISs sojourning in Hawaii. The researchers asked participants to identify their five 'best friends' and the five people with whom they spent most of their time. Findings suggested that students develop three distinct friendship networks, each with a different function (Table 2.2).

Furnham and Alibhai (1985) replicated Bochner and colleagues' study with a larger and more diverse sample of 140 student sojourners in the UK. Findings corresponded largely with Bochner and colleagues' 1977 model. However, a more recent study by Hendrickson and colleagues (2011) found that student sojourners in Hawaii

Table 2.2 Bochner and colleagues' (1977) Functional Model of Friendship Networks

| Network | Members | Typical function |
|---|---|---|
| Co-national (primary) | Has contact with other sojourning compatriots | Close friendships; expression and rehearsal of the culture of origin |
| Host national (secondary) | Bonds with significant host nationals (e.g. academics, officials) | Instrumental; support with language and academic difficulties |
| Non-co-national (tertiary) | Has contact with non-co-nationals, including fellow international students | Companionship for recreational activities |

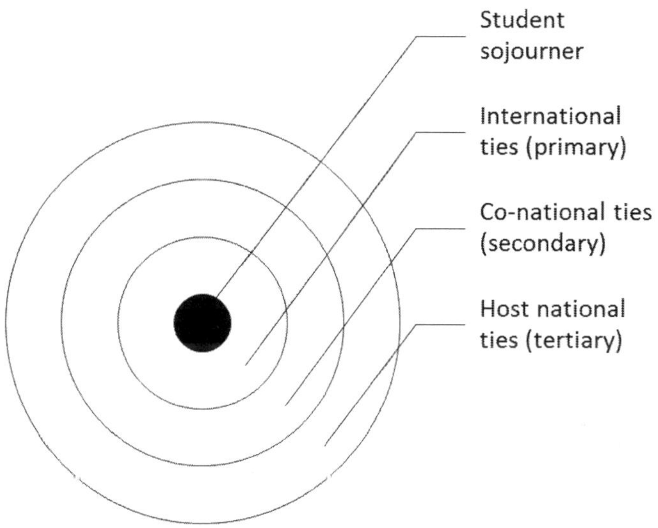


*Figure 2.4 Model of international students' social ties (Source: Schartner 2015)*

reported higher ratios of host nationals in their social network than co-nationals, possibly due to the study design, which asked students to provide an exhaustive list of their friends, as opposed to a specific number of 'best' friends. In a recent longitudinal study of international postgraduate students in the UK, Schartner (2015) found evidence for strong 'international ties' (that is, friendships with non-co-nationals), which emerged as the most important social network for ISs (Figure 2.4).

Overall, three key trends with regard to social contact patterns can be discerned in the wider IS literature. Firstly, and in line with Bochner and colleagues' 1977 model, a number of studies have identified ties with co-nationals as the primary social network of student sojourners (e.g. Furnham and Alibhai 1985; Maundeni 2001; Neri and Ville 2008). Co-national ties are thought to fulfil an important support function among individuals undergoing intercultural transition by buffering acculturative stress (Kim 2001; Woolf 2007). It is also believed that co-national friendships have the potential to increase student sojourners' self-esteem (Al-Sharideh and Goe 1998).

However, researchers also caution against the reliance on co-national friendships and point to the potentially adverse effects of co-national contact on language development and adjustment to the host environment (Maundeni 2001). Kim (2001) postulates that although co-national contact offers short-term support, it may be detrimental to long-term adaptation. It is also believed that strong co-national ties may negatively affect overall student satisfaction and feelings of social connectedness (Hendrickson et al. 2011). Indeed, Kashima and Loh (2006) found psychological adjustment of student sojourners in Australia to be explained by both host and international ties, but not by co-national ties. It has also been suggested that high degrees of co-national contact may inhibit ISs from forming meaningful bonds with members of the host society (Church 1982).

Although many aspects of the IS sojourn require interactions with members of the host society, both on and off campus (Al-Sharideh and Goe 1998), a recurrent trend across the literature is a lack of integration with the host society. Research across locations has shown fairly conclusively that while ISs desire and often expect to form relationships with host nationals, they find it difficult to instigate and sustain meaningful contact (Brown 2008a; Wright and Schartner 2013; Schartner 2015). In a large-scale survey by the UK Council for International Student Affairs, 70 per cent of taught postgraduate students surveyed in the UK stated that they had no British friends at all (Merrick 2004). Despite this paucity of host ties, the literature points to the benefits of host national contact, including its ability to evoke 'host communicative competence' (Kim 2001) in the student sojourner. Although there is some evidence that contact with host nationals can be intimidating and distressing in some circumstances (Greenland and Brown 2005), research has found that, on the whole, host national contact relates positively to ISs' adjustment and adaptation, including overall sojourn satisfaction and aspects of academic achievement (e.g. Ward and Masgoret 2004; Young et al. 2013), and host language proficiency (e.g. Furnham and Erdmann 1995; Gareis et al. 2011). Researchers have also suggested that contact with members of the host society allows ISs to learn about local traditions and practices, and thereby acquire the social and behavioural skills necessary to 'fit in' and function effectively in the host society (Li and Gasser 2005; Bochner 2006). However, host contact seems to be, by and large, instrumental and formulaic rather than emotionally supportive (Wright and Schartner 2013; Schartner 2015).

Several authors have pointed to factors that might inhibit interactions with domestic students and the local community more broadly, including indifference on the part of the hosts (Montgomery 2010) and skewed student intake (Merrick 2004; Schartner 2015). In their UK-based study, Harrison and Peacock (2008) found that local students avoided working with ISs because of the perceived weak English language ability of the latter. They also found that UK students had more individualised conceptions of students from European, anglophone and Latin American countries, compared to those from 'the rest of the world'. Students in the latter group were, for example, categorised by wider geography (such as African) or religion (such as Muslim). Similarly, in a recent US study (Birnbaum et al. 2012), student sojourners from Central America perceived a lack of interest among host students in interacting with newcomers. A UK-based study by Brown and Richards (2012), however, yielded mixed results. They found some negative reactions among British postgraduate students who were asked to reflect on the high number of ISs on their degree programmes, while others appreciated this cultural diversity.

The role of contact between student sojourners of different nationalities – what Sovic (2009) terms 'cosmopolitan friendships' – is comparatively under-explored (Marginson et al. 2010) but has recently attracted growing research attention. For example, in a study of social contact patterns among a sample of 100 ISs in Australia, Kashima and Loh (2006) found that respondents generally had more co-national and international ties than host national ties. Results also suggested that the more international ties students had, the better adjusted they were psychologically and the more they also identified with their Australian host university. Similarly, Montgomery and McDowell's (2009) and Schartner's (2015) longitudinal UK-based studies found evidence for a closely-knit and highly supportive 'international community of practice', and Young and colleagues (2013) found that more international ties led to higher academic achievement.

There is also some evidence that the dynamics of social ties might vary by country of origin. For example, in a US-based, Glass and colleagues (2014) found that non-European students reported more friendships with co-national peers and fewer contacts with host nationals.

### 2.3.7 SOCIAL SUPPORT

The quality of social ties has also received considerable research attention, and is often measured through the variable of social support (SS), a key coping resource in intercultural transition. ISs are generally thought to have a greater need for support than their domestic peers (Andrade 2006), as they face unique challenges salient to their status as temporary visitors, including homesickness and, for some, language and communication difficulties (Ong and Ward 2005). Intercultural transition involves the loss, at least temporarily, of readily available familiar support structures:

> Sojourning individuals necessarily experience a disruption or loss of social support systems and the familiar means by which support is socially communicated [...] they are also forced to evolve new ways of obtaining some of the required support, which includes maintaining regular long-distance communication with important sources of support at home and developing new support systems in the host country. (Ong and Ward 2005: 638)

Ong and Ward (2005) distinguish between socio-emotional support and instrumental support. The former includes, firstly, emotional support, including display of love, concern and sympathy; and, secondly, social companionship, including feelings of belonging to a social group. The latter includes, firstly, tangible assistance – for example, in the form of financial aid or material resources; and, secondly, informational support, including advice and feedback.

A USA-based study by Chavajay (2013) showed that ISs perceived greater socio-emotional and instrumental support from international peers relative to local people.

Studies have also shown a mitigating effect of SS on acculturative stress (Misra et al. 2003; Yeh and Inose 2003; Lee, Koeske and Sales 2004; Smith and Khawaja 2011), and a negative association between SS and psychological distress (see Zhang and Goodson 2011 for a review). SS was positively related to cultural adjustment of ISs in Thailand (Rujiprak 2016), and in our own study of postgraduate students sojourning in the UK (Young et al. 2013) we found a significant positive relationship between SS and students' psychological wellbeing, but no significant association between SS and academic achievement and satisfaction with life. Conversely, a study of ISs in Turkey found that SS was a significant predictor of academic adjustment (Cura and Isik 2015). Higher perceived SS was related to better mental health in a sample of mainland Chinese university students in Hong Kong (Chui and Chan 2017). The important role of online social support in intercultural adjustment is also being increasingly acknowledged (Chen and Yang 2015). In this book, we explore the relationship between SS and a range of adjustment outcomes.

## 2.4 CONCLUSIONS

While research on the 'international student experience' is burgeoning, lines of enquiry often remain fragmented, with few studies taking a holistic approach that comprises a focus on academic and psychological, as well as sociocultural, adjustment and adaptation. Moreover, the area remains under-theorised (Schartner and Young 2016) and the experiences of ISs are strikingly absent from most of the prevailing theoretical models. One aim of this book is therefore to introduce a guiding conceptual model that captures a range of contributory factors and adjustment outcomes.

In response to the literature review above, we formulated the following set of research questions, which guided our empirical enquiry (see Part II of this book):

- How do commonly identified contributory factors (host language ability, knowledge about the host country, prior overseas experience, autonomy in the decision to study abroad, intercultural competence, social contact and social support) relate to different aspects of academic adaptation measured over the whole programme?
- How do these contributory factors relate to psychological adaptation?
- How do they relate to sociocultural adaptation?
- What are the patterns and dynamics of student sojourners' academic, psychological and sociocultural adjustment over the course of the programme?
- What are the interrelationships of academic, psychological and sociocultural adjustment and adaptation?

In the following chapter (Chapter 3), we detail the methodological approach adopted for this book.

## NOTE

1. A new forty-item short form of the MPQ was published in 2013 by van der Zee and colleagues but was not available at the time of data collection for this book.

## REFERENCES

Adelman, M. B. (1988), 'Cross-cultural adjustment: a theoretical perspective on social support', *International Journal of Intercultural Relations*, 12(3), 183–204.

Al-Sharideh, K. A., and. R. Goe (1998), 'Ethnic communities within the university: an examination of factors influencing the personal adjustment of international students', *Research in Higher Education*, 39(6), 699–725.

Ali, A., K. I. van der Zee and G. Sanders (2003), 'Determinants of intercultural adjustment among expatriate spouses', *International Journal of Intercultural Relations*, 27, 563–80.

An, R., and S.-Y. Chiang (2015), 'International students' culture learning and cultural adaptation in China', *Journal of Multilingual and Multicultural Development*, 36(7), 661–76.

Andrade, M. S. (2006), 'International students in English-speaking universities: adjustment factors', *Journal of Research in International Education*, 5(2), 131–54.

Arends-Tóth, J., and. J. R. van de Vijver (2006), 'Assessment of psychological acculturation', in D. L. Sam and J. W. Berry (eds), *The Cambridge Handbook of Acculturation Psychology*, Cambridge: Cambridge University Press, pp. 142–60.

Argyle, M. (1980), 'Interactions skills and social competence', in P. Feldman and J. Orford (eds), *Psychological Problems: The Social Context*, Chichester: John Wiley.

Arkoudis, S. (2006), *Teaching International Students: Strategies to Enhance Learning*, University of Melbourne. Available at: <https://melbourne-cshe.unimelb.edu.au/__data/assets/pdf_file/0004/2299045/international.pdf> (last accessed 10 December 2018).

Arthur, W., and W. Bennett (1995), 'The international assignee: the relative importance of factors perceived to contribute to success', *Personnel Psychology*, 48(1), 99–115.

Atri, A., M. Sharma and R. Cottrell (2006), 'Role of social support, hardiness and acculturation as predictors of mental health among international students of Asian Indian origin', *International Quarterly of Community Health Education*, 27(1), 59–73.

Baas, M. (2006), 'Students of migration: Indian overseas students and the question of permanent residency', *People and Place*, 14(1), 8–16.

Ballard, B. (1987), 'Academic adjustment: the other side of the export dollar', *Higher Education Research and Development*, 6(2), 109–19.

Basow, S. A., and T. Gaugler (2017), 'Predicting adjustment of US college students studying abroad: beyond the multicultural personality', *International Journal of Intercultural Relations*, 56, 39–51.

Berry, J. W. (1970), 'Marginality, stress and ethnic identification in an acculturated aboriginal community', *Journal of Cross-Cultural Psychology*, 1, 239–52.

Berry, J. W. (1997), 'Immigration, acculturation, and adaptation', *Applied Psychology*, 46(1), 5–34.

Berry, J. W. (2005), 'Acculturation: living successfully in two cultures', *International Journal of Intercultural Relations*, 29, 697–712.

Berry, J. W. (2006), 'Acculturative stress', in P. T. P. Wong and L. C. S. Wong (eds), *Handbook of Multicultural Perspectives on Stress and Coping*, New York: Springer, pp. 287–98.

Bird, A., M. Mendenhall, M. J. Stevens and G. Oddou (2010), 'Defining the content domain of intercultural competence for global leaders', *Journal of Managerial Psychology*, 25(8), 810–28.

Birnbaum, B., B. Cardona, M. Milian and M. Gonzales (2012), 'Strangers in a strange land: how non-traditional international adult students see a United States university', *Journal of International Education and Leadership*, 2(2). Available at: <http://www.jielusa.org/

wp-content/uploads/2012/01/Strangers-in-a-Strange-Land_Birnbaum.pdf> (last accessed 25 February 2019).

Black, J. S., and G. K. Stephens (1989), 'The influence of the spouse on American expatriate adjustment in Pacific Rim overseas assignments', *Journal of Management*, 15, 529–44.

Bochner, S. (1982), 'The social psychology of cross-cultural relations', in S. Bochner (ed.), *Cultures in Contact: Studies in Cross-cultural Interaction*, Oxford: Pergamon, pp. 5–44.

Bochner, S. (1986), 'Coping with unfamiliar cultures: adjustment or culture learning?', *Australian Journal of Psychology*, 38(3), 347–58.

Bochner, S. (2006), 'Sojourners', in D. L. Sam and J. W. Berry (eds), *The Cambridge Handbook of Acculturation Psychology*, Cambridge: Cambridge University Press, pp. 181–97.

Bochner, S., N. Hutnik and A. Furnham (1986), 'The friendship patterns of overseas and host students in an Oxford student residence', *Journal of Social Psychology*, 125, 689–94.

Bochner, S., B. M. McLeod and A. Lin (1977), 'Friendship patterns of overseas students: a functional model', *International Journal of Psychology*, 12(4), 277–94.

Bodycott, P. (2009), 'Choosing a higher education study abroad destination: what mainland Chinese parents and students rate as important', *Journal of Research in International Education*, 8(3), 349–73.

Brown, L. (2008a), *The Adjustment Journey of International Postgraduate Students at a University in England*, Unpublished doctoral thesis, Bournemouth University, UK.

Brown, L. (2008b), 'The incidence of study-related stress in international students in the initial stage of the international sojourn', *Journal of Studies in International Education*, 12(1), 5–28.

Brown, L., and I. Holloway (2008), 'The initial stage of the international sojourn: excitement or culture shock?', *British Journal of Guidance and Counselling*, 36(1), 33–49.

Brown, L., and S. Richards (2012), 'The British host: just how welcoming are we?, *Journal of Further and Higher Education*, 36(1), 57–79.

Carroll, J. (2005), 'Strategies for becoming more explicit', in J. Carroll and J. Ryan (eds), *Teaching International Students: Improving Learning for All*, London: Routledge, pp. 26–35.

Chapman, D., T. Y. Wan and M. Xu (1988), 'Academic adjustment of international students in American universities', *Education and Research*, 6(2), 96–10.

Chavajay, J. (2013), 'Perceived social support among international students at a U.S. university', *Psychological Reports*, 112(2), 667–77.

Chen, L., and X. Yang (2015), 'Nature and effectiveness of online social support for intercultural adaptation of mainland Chinese international students', *International Journal of Communication*, 9, 2161–81.

Chirkov, V. I., S. Safdar, J. de Guzman and K. Playford (2008), 'Further examining the role motivation to study abroad plays in the adaptation of international students in Canada', *International Journal of Intercultural Relations*, 32(5), 427–40.

Chirkov, V. I., M. Vansteenkiste, R. Tao and M. Lynch (2007), 'The role of motivation to study abroad in the adaptation of international students: a self-determination theory approach', *International Journal of Intercultural Relations*, 31(2), 199–222.

Chui, R. C.-F., and C.-K. Chan (2017), 'School adjustment, social support, and mental health of mainland Chinese college students in Hong Kong', *Journal of College Student Development*, 58(1), 88–100.

Church, A. T. (1982), 'Sojourner adjustment', *Psychological Bulletin*, 91(3), 540–72.

Coles, R., and V. Swami (2012), 'The sociocultural adjustment trajectory of international university students and the role of university structures: a qualitative investigation', *Journal of Research in International Education*, 11(1), 87–100.

Copland, F., and S. Garton (2011), 'I felt that I do live in the UK now: international students' self-reports of their English language speaking experiences on a pre-sessional programme', *Language and Education*, 25(3), 241–55.

Cura, U., and A. N. Isik (2015), 'Impact of acculturative stress and social support on academic adjustment of international students', *Egitim ve Bilim - Education and Science*, 41(1840), 333–47.

Deardorff, D. (2006), 'Identification and assessment of intercultural competence as a student outcome of internationalisation', in M. Byram and A. Feng (eds), *Living and Studying Abroad: Research and Practice*, Clevedon: Multilingual Matters, pp. 232–56.

Deci, E., and R. Ryan (2012), 'Self-determination theory', in P. A. van Lange, A. Kruglanski and E. Higgins (eds), *Handbook of Theories of Social Psychology*, vol. 1, Thousand Oaks, CA: Sage, pp. 416–37.

Duru, E., and S. Poyrazli (2011), 'The role of demographics, English language competency, perceived discrimination and social connectedness in predicting level of adjustment difficulties among Turkish international students in the U.S.', *The International Journal of Psychology*, 46, 446–54.

Fantini, A. E. (2009), 'Assessing intercultural competence: issues and tools', in D. K. Deardorff (ed.), *The Sage Handbook of Intercultural Competence*, London: Sage, pp. 456–76.

Fantini, A. E., and A. Tirmizi (2006), *Exploring and Assessing Intercultural Competence*, World Learning Publications. Available at: <http://digitalcollections.sit.edu/worldlearning_publications/1> (last accessed 10 December 2018).

Furnham, A., and N. Alibhai (1985), 'The friendship networks of foreign students: a replication and extension of the functional model', *International Journal of Psychology*, 20(3–4), 709–22.

Furnham, A., and S. Bochner (1982), 'Social difficulty in a foreign culture: an empirical analysis of culture shock', in S. Bochner (ed.), *Cultures in Contact: Studies in Cross-cultural Interaction*, Oxford: Pergamon, pp. 161–98.

Furnham, A., and S. Bochner (1986), *Culture Shock: Psychological Reactions to Unfamiliar Environments*, London: Methuen.

Furnham, A., and S. Erdmann (1995), 'Psychological and sociocultural variables as predictors of adjustment in cross-cultural transitions', *Psychologia*, 38(4), 238–51.

Galchenko, I., and F. J. R. van de Vijver (2007), 'The role of perceived cultural distance in acculturation among exchange students in Russia', *International Journal of Intercultural Relationships*, 31, 187–97.

Gardner, J. W. (1952), 'The foreign student in America', *Foreign Affairs*, 30(4), 637–50.

Gareis, E., R. Merkin and J. Goldman (2011), 'Intercultural friendship: linking communication variables and friendship success', *Journal of Intercultural Communication Research*, 40, 155–73.

Garson, B. (2005), 'Teaching abroad: a cross-cultural journey', *Journal for Education and Business*, 80(6), 322–6.

Gilbert, S. (2000), *Japanese Students in American Higher Education: A Cross-cultural Analysis of Academic Culture*, Unpublished MA thesis, Stanford University, USA.

Glass, C. R., E. Gomez and A. Urzua (2014), 'Recreation, intercultural friendship, and international students' adaptation to college by region of origin', *International Journal of Intercultural Relations*, 42, 104–17.

Gray, K., S. Chang and G. Kennedy (2010), 'Use of social web technologies by international and domestic undergraduate students: implications for internationalising learning and teaching in Australian universities', *Technology, Pedagogy and Education*, 19(1), 31–46.

Greenland, K., and R. Brown (2005), 'Acculturation and acculturative stress among Japanese students in the United Kingdom', *Journal of Social Psychology*, 145(4), 373–89.

Griffiths, D., D. Winstanley and Y. Gabriel (2005), 'Learning shock: the trauma of return to formal learning', *Management Learning*, 36, 275–97.

Groom, B., and I. Maunonen-Eskelinen (2006), 'The use of portfolios to develop reflective practice in teacher training: a comparative and collaborative approach between two teacher training providers in the UK and Finland', *Teaching in Higher Education*, 11(3), 291–300.

Gu, Q., M. Schweisfurth and C. Day (2010), 'Learning and growing in a "foreign" context: intercultural experiences of international students', *Compare*, 40(1), 7–23.

Gudykunst, W. B. (1983), 'Toward a typology of stranger–host relationships', *International Journal of Intercultural Relations*, 7(4), 401–13.

Gudykunst, W., and T. Nishida (2001), 'Anxiety, uncertainty, and perceived effectiveness of communication across relationships and cultures', *International Journal of Intercultural Relations*, 25, 55–71.

Gullahorn, J. E., and J. T. Gullahorn (1966), 'American students abroad: professional versus personal development', *The Annals*, 368, 43–59.

Harris, J. G. (1973), 'A science of the South Pacific: an analysis of the character structure of the Peace Corps volunteer', *American Psychologist*, 28, 232–47.

Harrison, N., and N. Peacock (2008), 'Mindful or mindless: do UK student drinking cultures and stereotypes undermine intercultural contact?', in Higher Education Academy (ed.), *University Life Uncovered: Making Sense of the Student Experience*, pp. 44–56. Available at: <https://www.heacademy.ac.uk/system/files/university-life-uncovered_0.pdf> (last accessed 10 December 2016).

Hawes, F., and D. J. Kealey (1981), 'An empirical study of Canadian technical assistance', *International Journal of Intercultural Relations*, 5, 239–58.

Hayes, R. L., and H.-R. Lin (1994), 'Coming to America: developing social support systems for international students', *Journal of Multicultural Counseling and Development*, 22(1), 7–16.

Hendrickson, B., D. Rosen and K. Aune (2011), 'An analysis of friendship networks, social connectedness, homesickness, and satisfaction levels of international students', *International Journal of Intercultural Relations*, 35(3), 281–95.

Herfst, S. L., J. P. van Oudenhoven and M. E. Timmerman (2008), 'Intercultural effectiveness training in three Western immigrant countries: a cross-cultural evaluation of critical incidents', *International Journal of Intercultural Relations*, 32, 67–80.

Kashima, E. S., and E. Loh (2006), 'International students' acculturation: effects of international, conational, and local ties and need for closure', *International Journal of Intercultural Relations*, 30, 471–85.

Kealey, D. J., and B. D. Ruben (1983), 'Cross-cultural personnel selection: criteria, issues and methods', in D. Landis and R. Brislin (eds), *Handbook for Intercultural Training. Volume 1: Issues in Theory and Design*, New York: Pergamon, pp. 155–75.

Kemp, S., G. Madden and M. Simpson (1998), 'Emerging Australian education markets: a discrete choice model of Taiwanese and Indonesian student intended study destination', *Education Economics*, 6(2), 159–69.

Kim, Y. Y. (2001), *Becoming Intercultural: An Integrative Theory of Communication and Cross-cultural Adaptation*, Thousand Oaks, CA: Sage.

Kim, Y. Y. (2017), 'Cross-cultural adaptation', *Oxford Research Encyclopedias. Communication*, DOI: 10.1093/acrefore/9780190228613.013.21.

Kosmitzki, C. (1996), 'The reaffirmation of cultural identity in cross-cultural encounters', *Personality and Social Psychology Bulletin*, 22, 238–48.

Kunda, Z. (1999), *Social Cognition: Making Sense of People*, Cambridge, MA: MIT Press.

Laosa, L. M. (1998), *Intercultural Transitions in Human Development and Education*, Educational Testing Service, New Jersey. Available at: <https://onlinelibrary.wiley.com/doi/pdf/10.1002/j.2333-8504.1998.tb01770.x> (last accessed 10 December 2018).

Lazarus, R. S., and S. Folkman (1984), *Stress, Appraisal, and Coping*, New York: Springer.

Lee, J.-S., G. F. Koeske and E. Sales (2004), 'Social support buffering of acculturative stress: a study of mental health symptoms among Korean international students', *International Journal of Intercultural Relations*, 28, 399–414.

Lee, J.-Y., and A. Ciftci (2013), 'Asian international students' socio-cultural adaptation: influence of multicultural personality, assertiveness, academic self-efficacy, and social support', *International Journal of Intercultural Relations*, 38, 97–105.

Lee, K., and M. Wesche (2000), 'Korean students' adaption to post-secondary studies in Canada: a case study', *Canadian Modern Language Review*, 56(4), 637–85.

Lee, L.-Y., and B. M. Sukoco (2010), 'The effects of cultural intelligence on expatriate performance: the moderating effects of international experience', *The International Journal of Human Resource Management*, 21(7), 963–81.

Leiba-O'Sullivan, S. (1999), 'The distinction between stable and dynamic cross-cultural competencies: implications for expatriate trainability', *Journal of International Business Studies*, 30(4), 709–25.

Leong, C.-H. (2007), 'Predictive validity of the Multicultural Personality Questionnaire: a longitudinal study on the socio-psychological adaptation of Asian undergraduates who took part in a study-abroad program', *International Journal of Intercultural Relations*, 31(5), 545–59.

Lewthwaite, M. (1996), 'A study of international students' perspectives on cross-cultural adaptation', *International Journal for the Advancement of Counselling*, 19(2), 167–85.

Li, A., and M. B. Gasser (2005), 'Predicting Asian international students' sociocultural adjustment: a test of two mediation models', *International Journal of Intercultural Relations*, 29(5), 561–76.

Li, M., and M. Bray (2007), 'Cross-border flows of students for higher education: push–pull factors and motivations of mainland Chinese students in Hong Kong and Macau', *Higher Education*, 53, 791–818.

Li, X., and W. Chen (2014), 'Facebook or Renren? A comparative study of social networking site use and social capital among Chinese international students in the United States', *Computers in Human Behavior*, 35, 116–123.

Lim, Y. M., C. S. Yap and T. H. Lee (2011), 'Destination choice, service quality, satisfaction, and consumerism: international students in Malaysian institutions of higher education', *African Journal of Business Management*, 5(5), 1691–702.

Littrell, L. N., E. Salas, K. P. Hess, M. Paley and S. Riedel (2006), 'Expatriate preparation: a critical analysis of 25 years of cross-cultural training research', *Human Resource Development Review*, 5(3), 355–88.

Luxon, T., and M. Peelo (2009), 'Academic sojourners, teaching and internationalisation: the experience of non-UK staff in a British university', *Teaching in Higher Education*, 14(6), 649–59.

Lysgaard, S. (1955), 'Adjustment in a foreign society: Norwegian Fulbright grantees visiting the United States', *International Social Science Bulletin*, 7, 45–51.

Marginson, S., C. Nyland, E. Sawir and H. Forbes-Mewett (2010), *International Student Security*, Port Melbourne: Cambridge University Press.

Masgoret, A.-M., and C. Ward (2006), 'Culture learning approach to acculturation', in D. L. Sam and J. W. Berry (eds), *The Cambridge Handbook of Acculturation Psychology*, Cambridge: Cambridge University Press, pp. 58–77.

Matsumoto, D., and H. C. Hwang (2013), 'Assessing cross-cultural competence: a review of available tests', *Journal of Cross-Cultural Psychology*, 44(6), 849–73.

Maundeni, T. (2001), 'The role of social networks in the adjustment of African students to British society: students' perceptions', *Race, Ethnicity and Education*, 4(3), 253–76.

Mazzarol, T., and G. N. Soutar (2002), '"Push-pull" factors influencing international student destination choice', *International Journal of Educational Management*, 16, 82–90.

Merrick, B. (2004), *Broadening our Horizons: International Students in UK Universities and Colleges*, UK Council for Overseas Student Affairs (UKCOSA). *Report of the UKCOSA Survey*. Available at: <http://www.ukcosa.org.uk/files/pdf/BOHreport.pdf> (last accessed 10 December 2018).

Misra, R., M. Crist and C. J. Burant (2003), 'Relationships among life stress, social support, academic stressors, and reactions to stressors of international students in the United States', *International Journal of Stress Management*, 10(2), 137–57.

Mol, S., J. P. van Oudenhoven and K. I. van der Zee (2001), 'Validation of the MPQ amongst an internationally oriented student population in Taiwan', in F. Salili and R. Hoosain (eds), *Research in Multicultural Education and International Perspectives*, Greenwich, CT: Information Age, pp. 167–86.

Montgomery, C. (2010), *Understanding the International Student Experience*, Basingstoke: Palgrave Macmillan.

Montgomery, C., and L. McDowell (2009), 'Social networks and the international student experience: a community of practice?', *Journal of Studies in International Education*, 13(4), 455–66.

Mori, S. (2000), 'Addressing mental health concerns of international students', *Journal of Counseling & Development*, 78, 137–44.

Neri, F., and S. Ville (2008), 'Social capital renewal and the academic performance of international students in Australia', *The Journal of Socio-Economics*, 37, 1515–538.

Nyaupane, G. P., C. M. Paris and V. Teye (2010), 'Why do students study abroad? Exploring motivations beyond earning academic credits', *Tourism Analysis*, 15(2), 263–8.

Nyaupane, G. P., C. M. Paris and V. Teye (2011), 'Study abroad motivations, destination selection and pre-trip attitude formation', *International Journal of Tourism Research*, 13, 205–17.

Oberg, K. (1960), 'Cultural shock: adjustment to new cultural environments', *Practical Anthropology*, 7, 177–82.

Ones, D. S., and C. Viswesvaran (1997), 'Personality determinants in the prediction of aspects of expatriate job success', in D. M. Saunders and Z. Aycan (eds), *New Approaches to Employee Management: Vol. 4. Expatriate Management: Theory and Research*, Stamford, CT: JAI Press, pp. 63–92.

Ong, A. S. J., and C. Ward (2005), 'The construction and validation of a social support measure for sojourners: the Index of Sojourner Social Support (ISSS) Scale', *Journal of Cross-Cultural Psychology*, 36(6), 637–61.

Peltokorpi, V. (2008), 'Cross-cultural adjustment of expatriates in Japan', *The International Journal of Human Resource Management*, 19(9), 1588–606.

Peltokorpi, V., and F. J. Froese (2012), 'The impact of expatriate personality traits on cross-cultural adjustment: a study with expatriates in Japan', *International Business Review*, 21(4), 734–46.

Pimpa, N. (2003), 'The influence of peers and student recruitment agencies on Thai students' choices of international education', *Journal of Studies in International Education*, 7(2), 178–92.

Pitts, M. J. (2005), *The role of Communication in Cross-national Adjustment and Identity Transitions Among Student Sojourners*, Unpublished doctoral thesis, Pennsylvania State University, USA.

Pitts, M. J. (2009), 'Identity and the role of expectations, stress, and talk in short-term student sojourner adjustment: an application of the integrative theory of communication and cross-cultural adaptation', *International Journal of Intercultural Relations*, 33(6), 450–62.

Poyrazli, S., C. Arbona, A. Nora, R. McPherson and S. Pisecco (2002), 'Relation between assertiveness, academic self-efficacy, and psychosocial adjustment among international graduate students', *Journal of College Student Development*, 43(5), 632–42.

Poyrazli, S., P. R. Kavanaugh, A. Baker and N. Al-Timimi (2004), 'Social support and demographic correlates of acculturative stress in international students', *Journal of College Counseling*, 7, 73–82.

Poyrazli, S., and M. D. Lopez (2007), 'An exploratory study on perceived discrimination and homesickness: a comparison of international students to the U.S. students', *The Journal of Psychology*, 141, 263–80.

Ramos, M. R., C. Cassidy, S. Reichler and S. A. Haslam (2016), 'A longitudinal study of the effects of discrimination on the acculturation strategies of international students', *Journal of Cross-cultural Psychology*, 47(3), 401–20.

Ramsay, S., E. Jones and M. Barker (2007), 'Relationship between adjustment and support types: young and mature-aged local and international first year university students', *Higher Education*, 54(2), 247–65.

Rienties, B., S. Beausaert, T. Grohnert, S. Niemantsverdriet and P. Kommers (2012), 'Understanding academic performance of international students: the role of ethnicity, academic and social integration', *Higher Education*, 63(6), 685–700.

Robertson, M., M. Line, S. Jones and S. Thomas (2000), 'International students, learning environments and perceptions: a case study using the Delphi technique', *Higher Education Research & Development*, 19(1), 89–101.

Ronen, S. (1989), 'Training the international assignee', in I. L. Goldstein (ed.), *Training and Development in Organizations*, San Francisco: Jossey-Bass, pp. 417–53.

Ruben, B. D., and D. J. Kealey (1979), 'Behavioral assessment of communication competency and the prediction of cross-cultural adaptation', *International Journal of Intercultural Relations*, 3(1), 15–47.

Rujiprak, V. (2016), 'Cultural and psychological adjustment of international students in Thailand', *International Journal of Behavioral Science*, 11(2), 127–42.

Russell, J., D. Rosenthal and G. Thomson (2010), 'The international student experience: three styles of adaptation', *Higher Education*, 60(2), 235–49.

Ryan, J. (2005), 'Improving teaching and learning practices for international students: implications for curriculum, pedagogy and assessment', in J. Carroll and J. Ryan (eds), *Teaching International Students: Improving Learning for All*, Abingdon: Routledge, pp. 92–101.

Salisbury, M. H. (2011), *The Effect of Study Abroad on Intercultural Competence among Undergraduate College Students*, Unpublished doctoral thesis, University of Iowa, USA.

Sandel, T. L. (2014), '"Oh, I'm here!" Social media's impact on the cross-cultural adaptation of students studying abroad', *Journal of Intercultural Communication Research*, 43(1), 1–29.

Schartner, A. (2014), *Cross-cultural Transition in Higher Education: The Academic, Psychological and Sociocultural Adjustment and Adaptation of International Postgraduate Students at a British University*, Unpublished doctoral thesis, Newcastle University, UK.

Schartner, A. (2015), '"You cannot talk with all of the strangers in a pub": a longitudinal case study of international postgraduate students' social ties at a British university', *Higher Education*, 69(2), 225–41.

Schartner A. (2016), 'The effect of study abroad on intercultural competence: a longitudinal case study of international postgraduate students at a British university', *Journal of Multilingual and Multicultural Development*, 37(4), 402–18.

Schartner, A., and T. J. Young (2016), 'Towards an integrated conceptual model of international student adjustment and adaptation', *European Journal of Higher Education*, 6(4), 372–86.

Schutz, A., and M. Richards (2003), 'International students' experience of graduate study in Canada', *Journal of the International Society for Teacher Education*, 7(1), 10–26.

Scudamore, R. (2013), *Engaging Home and International Students: A Guide for New Lecturers*. Available at: <https://www.heacademy.ac.uk/system/files/rachelscudamorereportfeb2013.pdf> (last accessed 10 December 2018).

Sleeman, J., C. Lang and N. Lemon (2016), 'Social media challenges and affordances for international students: bridges, boundaries, and hybrid spaces', *Journal of Studies in International Education*, 20(5), 1–25.

Smith, R. A., and N. G. Khawaja (2011), 'A review of the acculturation experiences of international students', *International Journal of Intercultural Relations*, 35(6), 699–71.

Sovic, S. (2008), 'Coping with stress: the perspective of international students', *Art, Design & Communication in Higher Education*, 6(3), 145–58.

Sovic, S. (2009), 'Hi-bye friends and the herd instinct: international and home students in the creative arts', *Higher Education*, 58(6), 747–61.

Spitzberg, B. H., and G. Changnon (2009), 'Conceptualizing intercultural competence', in D. K. Deardorff (ed.), *The Sage Handbook of Intercultural Competence*, Thousand Oaks, CA: Sage, pp. 2–52.

Spreitzer, G. M., M. W. McCall, Jr, and J. D. Mahoney (1997), 'Early identification of international executive potential', *Journal of Applied Psychology*, 82(1), 6–29.

Sumer, S., S. Poyrazli and K. Grahame (2008), 'Predictors of depression and anxiety among international students', *Journal of Counseling and Development*, 86, 429–37.

Swami, V. (2009), 'Predictors of sociocultural adjustment among sojourning Malaysian students in Britain', *International Journal of Psychology*, 44(4), 266–73.

Swami, V., A. Arteche, T. Chamorro-Premuzic and A. Furnham (2010), 'Sociocultural adjustment among sojourning Malaysian students in Britain: a replication and path analytic extension', *Social Psychiatry & Psychiatric Epidemiology*, 45(1), 57–65.

Tajfel, H. (ed.) (1978), *Differentiation Between Social Groups: Studies in the Social Psychology of Intergroup Relations*, London: Academic Press.

Triandis, H.C. (1977), *Interpersonal Behavior*, Monterey, CA: Brook/Cole.

Triandis, H.C. (1980), 'Values, attitudes, and interpersonal behavior', in H. Howe and M. Page (eds), *Nebraska Symposium on Motivation, 1979*, vol. 27, Lincoln: University of Nebraska Press, pp. 195–295.

Tsang, E. W. K. (2001), 'Adjustment of mainland Chinese academics and students to Singapore', *International Journal of Intercultural Relations*, 25(4), 347–72.

UKCISA (UK Council for International Student Affairs) (2018), *Facing Culture Shock*. Available at: <https://www.ukcisa.org.uk/Information--Advice/Preparation-and-Arrival/Facing-culture-shock> (last accessed 19 December 2018).

van Bakel, M., M. Gerritsen and J. P. van Oudenhoven (2014), 'Impact of a local host on the intercultural competence of expatriates', *The International Journal of Human Resource Management*, 25(14), 2050–67.

van der Zee, K. I., and J. P. van Oudenhoven (2000), 'The Multicultural Personality Questionnaire: a multidimensional instrument of multicultural effectiveness', *European Journal of Personality*, 14(4), 291–309.

van Oudenhoven, J. P., S. Mol and K. I. van der Zee (2003), 'Study of the adjustment of Western expatriates in Taiwan ROC with the Multicultural Personality Questionnaire', *Asian Journal of Social Psychology*, 6(2), 159–70.

van Oudenhoven, J. P., M. E. Timmerman and K. I. van der Zee (2007), 'Cross-cultural equivalence and validity of the Multicultural Personality Questionnaire in an intercultural context', *Journal of Intercultural Communication*, 13, 51–65.

van Oudenhoven, J. P., and K. I. van der Zee (2002), 'Predicting multicultural effectiveness of international students: the Multicultural Personality Questionnaire', *International Journal of Intercultural Relations*, 26(6), 679–94.

Ward, C., S. Bochner and A. Furnham (2001), *The Psychology of Culture Shock*, 2nd edn, Hove: Routledge.

Ward, C., and W. C. Chang (1997), '"Cultural fit": a new perspective on personality and sojourner adjustment', *International Journal of Intercultural Relations*, 21(4), 525–33.

Ward, C., and A. Kennedy (1992), 'Locus of control, mood disturbance and social difficulty during cross-cultural transitions', *International Journal of Intercultural Relations*, 16(2), 175–94.

Ward, C., and A. Kennedy (1993), 'Where's the culture in cross-cultural transition? Comparative studies of sojourner adjustment', *Journal of Cross-cultural Psychology*, 24, 221–49.

Ward, C., and A. Kennedy (1996a), 'Before and after cross-cultural transition: a study of New Zealand volunteers on field assignments', in H. Grad, A. Blanco and J. Georgas (eds), *Key Issues in Cross-cultural Psychology*, Lisse: Swets & Zeitlinger, pp. 138–54.

Ward, C., and A. Kennedy (1996b), 'Crossing cultures: the relationship between psychological and sociocultural dimensions of cross-cultural adjustment', in J. Pandey, D. Sinha and D. P. S. Bhawuk (eds), *Asian Contributions to Cross-cultural Psychology*, New Delhi: Sage, pp. 289–306.

Ward, C., and A.-M. Masgoret (2004), *The Experiences of International Students in New Zealand: Report on the Results of the National Survey*, Centre for Applied Cross-cultural Research and School of Psychology, Victoria University of Wellington. Available at: <https://www.educationcounts.govt.nz/publications/international/14700> (last accessed 10 December 2018).

Ward, C., Y. Okura, A. Kennedy and T. Kojima (1998), 'The U-curve on trial: a longitudinal study of psychological and sociocultural adjustment during cross-cultural transition', *International Journal of Intercultural Relations*, 22(3), 277–91.

Wei, M., P. P. Heppner, M. Mallen, T. Y. Ku, K. Y.-H. Liao and T.-F. Wu (2007), 'Acculturative stress, perfectionism, years in the United States, and depression among Chinese international students', *Journal of Counseling Psychology*, 54(4), 385–94.

Woolf, M. (2007), 'Impossible things before breakfast: myths in education abroad', *Journal of Studies in International Education*, 11, 496–509.

Wright, C., and A. Schartner (2013), '"I can't … I won't?" International students at the threshold of social interaction', *Journal of Research in International Education*, 12(2), 113–28.

Yakunina, E. S., I. K. Weigold, A. Weigold, S. Hercegovac and N. Elsayed (2012), 'The multicultural personality: does it predict international students' openness to diversity and adjustment?', *International Journal of Intercultural Relations*, 36(4), 533–40.

Yamazaki, Y. (2005), 'Learning styles and typologies of cultural differences: a theoretical and empirical comparison', *International Journal of Intercultural Relations*, 29(5), 521–48.

Yang, R. P.-J., K. A. Noels and K. D. Saumure (2006), 'Multiple routes to cross-cultural adaptation for international students: mapping the paths between self-construals, English language confidence, and adjustment', *International Journal of Intercultural Relations*, 30(4), 487–506.

Yeh, C. J., and M. Inose (2003), 'International students' reported English fluency, social support satisfaction, and social connectedness as predictors of acculturative stress', *Counselling Psychology Quarterly*, 16(1), 15–28.

Young, T. J., P. G. Sercombe, I. Sachdev, R. Naeb and A. Schartner (2013), 'Success factors for international postgraduate students' adjustment: exploring the roles of intercultural competence, language proficiency, social contact and social support', *European Journal of Higher Education*, 3, 151–71.

Yu, B., and K. Downing (2012), 'Determinants of international students' adaptation: examining effects of integrative motivation, instrumental motivation and second language proficiency', *Educational Studies*, 38(4), 457–71.

Zhang, J., and P. Goodson (2011), 'Predictors of international students' psychosocial adjustment to life in the United States: a systematic review', *International Journal of Intercultural Relations*, 35(2), 139–62.

Zhou, J. (2015), 'International students' motivation to pursue and complete a Ph.D. in the US', *Higher Education*, 69(5), 719–33.

# 3
# METHODOLOGY

In this chapter, we detail the methodological approach for the empirical findings presented in Part II of this book (Chapters 4 to 7). Below, we outline first the research setting (3.1), followed by the research design (3.2). We then detail the research instruments (3.3), including the quantitative self-report surveys (3.3.1), the interviews (3.3.2) and the qualitative alumni survey.

## 3.1 RESEARCH SETTING

The setting for our research was a British university (student population approximately 20,000), and participants were current and former non-UK students undertaking one-year taught master's (MA) programmes in the humanities and social sciences, specifically MA degrees in Cross-Cultural Communication, and in Applied Linguistics and Teaching English as a Second Language (TESOL). The two programmes were very similar in terms of structure and student cohort composition. Both were highly 'international' (with around 90 per cent of students being non-UK) and heterogeneous in terms of nationalities represented (typically twenty or more). As such, they were not untypical of UK postgraduate taught degrees where the IS enrolment figure currently stands at 70 per cent (UKCISA 2018). In order to maximise homogeneity, it seemed reasonable to keep participation limited to these two programmes. Our roles as teachers on the programmes allowed us to access the students relatively easily and enabled us to capture the full temporal range of their experiences. The first author's role as an 'international' postgraduate researcher at the time of data collection also helped to build rapport, which was crucial in light of our longitudinal research design. A limitation of our approach is that our research remained limited to a very specific group of people, from one particular disciplinary area, and we are conscious that any conclusions must be drawn cautiously. Nevertheless, we felt that the students on these two programmes would provide a rich 'microcosm', as we expected them to be likely to be engaged in thinking about their own transitions and open to taking part in reflection on their own experiences.

## 3.2 RESEARCH DESIGN

We were interested in 'tracking' the same group of student sojourners over a period of time. Therefore, we adopted a 'within-subjects' (Goodwin 2010: 224) longitudinal research design. Our research was mixed-methods in nature, comprising semi-structured interviews and self-report surveys. An ecumenical epistemological approach allowed us to draw on both qualitative and quantitative paradigms, in an attempt to monitor students' lived experiences, as well as measuring outcomes. We were guided by the notion that complex research phenomena call for multifaceted research approaches.

> The complexity of our research problems calls for answers beyond simple numbers in a quantitative sense or words in a qualitative sense. A combination of both forms of data can provide the most complete analysis of problems. Researchers can situate numbers in the contexts and words of participants, and they can frame the words of participants with numbers, trends and statistical results. Both forms of data are necessary today. (Pashaeizad 2010: 14)

A longitudinal mixed-methods design was most suitable for the purpose of our research, as we aimed both to monitor adjustment over time and to measure a range of adjustment outcomes, including academic, psychological and sociocultural adaptation. Longitudinal research designs of this kind are still relatively rare in the literature on ISs' adjustment and adaptation (Zhou and Todman 2009). The predictive element of the study (quantitative self-report surveys) aimed to explore which contributory factors predicted ISs' adaptation to life and study in the UK, while the monitoring element (qualitative interviews) aimed to capture the patterns of students' academic, psychological and sociocultural adjustment over time. To capture retrospective accounts of students' experiences (see Chapter 8), we also included an additional reflective element (qualitative self-report survey).

Data were collected from a total of 295 participants across four stages:

- Stage 1: Participants (N = 223) completed a self-report survey (Time 1, October of the year of study).
- Stage 2: Three waves of semi-structured individual interviews were conducted with a subsample of student volunteers (N = 20), in October, February and June of the year of study.
- Stage 3: Participants (N = 143) completed a second self-report survey (Time 2, June, nine months into the programme).
- Stage 4: Qualitative online questionnaires were completed by a sample of alumni of the two programmes (N = 70).

The survey administered at Time 1 (Stage 1 of data collection) allowed us to measure contributory factors to ISs' adjustment, while the survey at Time 2 (Stage 3) measured adjustment outcomes in the form of adaptation indices using well-established, reliable, close-ended measures and statistical procedures (Creswell and Plano 2007; Rauscher and Greenfield 2009). The use of regular interviews *in situ* (Stage 2) allowed us to capture the 'lived' experiences of the students, exploring nuances and focusing on the individual sojourner and his/her construction of reality (Denzin and Lincoln 1998). Finally, the questionnaires with graduates (Stage 4) enabled us to capture retrospective accounts of the experience.

Data integration occurred at a number of points, as is recommended for mixed-methods research (Rauscher and Greenfield 2009). To a small extent, it occurred during the data-collection stage, as the self-report surveys included both quantitative and qualitative response options. Integration also occurred in the data-analysis stage, when the interview transcripts were analysed for both frequency (quantitative) and intensity of comments (qualitative). The final, and perhaps most substantial, stage of integration occurred in the discussion of findings.

## 3.3 RESEARCH INSTRUMENTS

We detail below the research instruments, starting with the quantitative questionnaires (Stages 1 and 3 of data collection), followed by the interviews (Stage 2) and finally qualitative alumni survey (Stage 4).

### 3.3.1 THE QUANTITATIVE SELF-REPORT SURVEYS

A total of 239 students undertaking MA programmes in Cross-Cultural Communication (MA CCC) and in Applied Linguistics and TESOL (MA ALT) completed the quantitative questionnaire at Time 1 (October). After an initial analysis of respondents' demographic data, sixteen participants had to be excluded from further analysis, as they had previously obtained degrees from UK universities. Of the 223 students who had completed the Time 1 survey, 143 also completed the Time 2 survey (64 per cent response rate).

Table 3.1 details the demographics of the respondents. The sample as a whole was relatively young, with a mean age of around 24 years at both times, and ranging in age from 20 to 42 years. The vast majority of respondents were female, mirroring the gender bias in this group and previous cohorts (see above). Most respondents came from the People's Republic of China, the main sending country of ISs to the UK (UKCISA 2018). The remainder came from a variety of countries or territories.[1] Seventeen students were first-language speakers (L1) of English, mainly from Canada and the USA. All students who were second-language (L2) English speakers had obtained the minimum English language entrance requirement for their programmes of study of International English Language Testing System (IELTS) 6.5 or equivalent.

Measures for the surveys, detailed below, were mostly taken directly or with slight modifications from existing scales, although some were specifically developed for this study. Scales and survey items were selected based on the information needed to address the research questions (cf. Rosenthal et al. 2006). With the exception of demographic items and a final open-ended question, all questions were answered on five-point Likert scales. All participants received an English version of the surveys, and informed consent was obtained from all participants prior to collecting data.

Table 3.1 Demographics of survey respondents at Time 1 and Time 2

| | Time 1 (N = 223) | Time 2 (N = 143) |
|---|---|---|
| **Gender** | | |
| Female | 200 (90%) | 127 (89%) |
| Male | 23 (10%) | 16 (11%) |
| **Age** | M = 24.04<br>20–24: 155 students<br>25–29: 46 students<br>30–35: 9 students<br>35+: 2 students | M = 24.22<br>20–24: 97 students<br>25–29: 32 students<br>30–35: 8 students<br>35+: 2 students |
| **Place of origin** | | |
| People's Republic of China | 121 (55%) | 63 (44%) |
| Europe | 37 | 35 |
| Americas/Caribbean | 20 | 13 |
| East Asia | 30 | 24 |
| Middle East | 10 | 6 |
| Africa | 2 | 2 |
| **Subject area** | | |
| MA CCC | 129 (58%) | 109 (76%) |
| MA ALT | 94 (42%) | 34 (24%) |
| **Cohort** | | |
| 2011/12 | 99 (44%) | 67 (47%) |
| 2012/13 | 124 (56%) | 76 (53%) |
| **Overseas experience ≥ 5 months** | 91 (41%) | 67 (45%) |

Note: MA ALT = MA programme in Applied Linguistics and Teaching English as a Second Language; MA CCC = MA programme in Cross-Cultural Communication.

The surveys at Time 1 and Time 2 comprised some identical measurements, including scales on intercultural competence (IC), English language ability (ELA), satisfaction with life (SWL), psychological wellbeing (PWB) and knowledge about the UK (KNW). In the Time 1 survey (124 items), respondents were also asked to provide the following demographic background information: date of arrival in the UK, place of origin, age, gender, first language, previous overseas experience, and type of residence in the UK (for example, private, university accommodation, home stay). One scale measured students' degree of autonomy in the decision to study abroad.

The Time 2 survey (178 items) comprised scales measuring academic and socio-cultural adaptation, and the degree of social contact and social support in the host environment. At both times, the questionnaire was administered at the end of a lecture and it took respondents between 15 and 20 minutes to complete the survey. In order to be able to track their responses, participants were asked to provide their student identity numbers in both surveys. A detailed discussion of the scales used to measure contributory factors and adjustment outcomes follows below, starting with the contributory factors.

**English language ability (ELA)**

A self-report measure was included in both surveys to assess students' own perceived competence in the English language. Initial analysis of students' pre-programme IELTS and Test of English as a Foreign Language (TOEFL) scores had shown very little variation, with the vast majority of students fulfilling the English language entrance requirement of IELTS 6.5 or equivalent. Thus, a self-report measure, relating ability to self-concept, seemed reasonable (cf. Young et al. 2013). A self-report measure could provide insights into students' self-confidence in their own abilities, which is not usually captured in standardised tests but has been found in some studies to be a more important predictor of adjustment outcomes than actual linguistic competence (e.g. MacIntyre et al. 1997; MacIntyre et al. 1998). A four-item scale asked, 'At this point, how satisfied are you with your ability to communicate in the English language?' Following Ying and Liese (1991), respondents were asked to self-rate their abilities in four skill areas – reading, writing, listening and speaking – on a five-point Likert scale ranging from 1 [not at all satisfied] to 5 [very satisfied], with high mean scores representing high perceived competence in English.

**Knowledge about the UK (KNW)**

One single item in the Time 1 survey asked, 'How much, would you say, did you know about the UK before coming here?' The Time 2 survey asked, 'At this point, how much do you feel you know about the UK?' Students rated their answer on a five-point scale, ranging from 1 [no knowledge at all] to 5 [a lot of knowledge]. This single-item measure aimed to gauge, broadly, students' own perception of their pre- and post-sojourn KNW.

**Autonomy in the decision to study abroad**

To assess the degree of students' autonomy in the decision to study abroad, the Self-regulation Questionnaire-Study Abroad (SRQ-SA; Chirkov et al. 2008) was used. This ten-item scale measures the degree of self-determination in the decision to study abroad and differentiates between four types of motivation on a self-determination continuum: intrinsic motivation (INTRI, two items), identified regulation (IDENT, two items), introjected regulation (INTRO, four items) and external regulation (EXTER, two items). The items were rated on a five-point Likert scale, ranging from 1 [totally not applicable] to 5 [completely applicable]. From these items, a Relative Autonomy Index (RAI; cf. Chirkov et al. 2007) was computed by weighting the four subscales, based on their intercorrelations [+2 = INTRI, +1 = IDENT, –1 = INTRO, –2 = EXTER]. A positive score symbolised the prevalence of autonomous motivation over controlled motivation, and a negative score represented the prevalence of controlled motivation over self-determined motivation.

**Intercultural competence (IC)**

In order to assess participants' intercultural competence, the ninety-one-item English version of the MPQ (van Oudenhoven and van der Zee 2002) was used. This instrument has been widely used in sojourner research, including with IS samples, and its statistical reliability has repeatedly been tested and confirmed in a number of studies (see 2.3 above). The MPQ included ninety-one items, each relating to one of five dimensions of IC: cultural empathy (CE, eighteen items), open-mindedness (OM, eighteen items), social initiative (SI, seventeen items), emotional stability (ES, twenty items) and flexibility (FL, eighteen items). Respondents could give their answers on a five-point Likert scale, ranging from 1 [totally not applicable] to 5 [completely applicable].

#### Social contact

Four single items in the Time 2 survey measured the degree of overall social contact that students had with British students, co-nationals, non-co-national ISs and other British people in the local community. Participants were asked to rate the degree of contact with these four groups on a five-point Likert scale ranging from 1 [almost never] to 5 [very often].

#### Social support

In order to measure the degree of social support (SS) students received while sojourning in England, Ong and Ward's (2005) Index of Sojourner Social Support (ISSS) was included in the Time 2 survey. This seventeen-item scale was specifically developed to assess SS in an intercultural context and allowed for separate scores to be computed for socio-emotional SS and instrumental SS. Students were presented with a range of statements about people's behaviour towards them, and were asked to rate on a five-point scale how often people displayed these behaviours during their stay in the UK. Answers could range from 1 [almost never] to 5 [very often]. Example items included 'Listen and talk to you whenever you feel down' (socio-emotional SS) and 'Accompany you somewhere' (instrumental SS).

#### Academic adaptation

Academic adaptation was assessed in terms of academic achievement on the degree programme. Academic achievement here refers to evidence of learning, measured in the form of GPAs (Andrade 2006). Students' grades were obtained from the host university with their permission. We used an unusually fine-grained measure of academic achievement, reflecting the assessment structure of the degree programmes: an overall degree GPA (for the taught and research elements of the degree combined) and separate GPAs (for the taught element and for the research element of the degree, respectively). Separating the research and taught grades allowed for a more detailed analysis of aspects of academic achievement, with the measure of achievement on the taught element representing the more structured and guided element, and the measure of achievement on the research element reflecting achievement in more independent study (cf. Young et al. 2013).

#### Psychological adaptation

Two indicators of psychological adaptation were included in the Time 2 survey, measuring both student satisfaction and emotional responses to the host environment (cf. Rosenthal et al. 2006): psychological wellbeing (PWB) and satisfaction with life (SWL). A common distinction when measuring psychological responses to the host environment (Ward et al. 2001), SWL reflected a more cognitive dimension of subjective wellbeing (Chirkov et al. 2007) and PWB reflected a more affective dimension (Sam 2000). Both constructs were found to correlate significantly with each other in prior research but researchers have argued that each construct needs, none the less, to be studied in its own right (Diener et al. 1999).

To assess PWB, scales were obtained from the RAND Mental Health Inventory. Eleven items asked students how they had been feeling over the past four weeks. Example items include: 'I have felt full of energy' (+) and 'I have been a very nervous person' (–). Answers could vary from 1 [none of the time] to 5 [all the time]. As a measure of SWL, Diener and colleagues' (1985) five-item Satisfaction with Life Scale (SWLS) was used. Example items include: 'The conditions of my life are excellent' and 'If I could live my life over, I would change almost nothing'. Answers could vary from 1 [totally not applicable] to 5 [completely applicable].

**Sociocultural adaptation**

To assess students' sociocultural adaptation, a thirty-seven-item scale was constructed, based on Ward and Kennedy's (1999) Sociocultural Adaptation Scale (SCAS) and Furnham and Bochner's (1982) Social Situations Questionnaire (SSQ). Ward and Kennedy's SCAS was originally based on the SSQ but included some additional adaptive skills, such as 'dealing with the climate' and 'getting used to local food' (cf. Ward et al. 2001). Students were asked to indicate how much difficulty they experienced in various social situations in the host country. Response options ranged from 1 [no difficulty] to 5 [extreme difficulty]. Scores were then mirrored so that a higher score on the SCAS would reflect better sociocultural adaptation. Example items included 'Finding food that you enjoy' and 'Understanding jokes and humour'.

Survey data were analysed using the Statistical Package for Social Sciences (SPSS). Pearson product–moment correlation analyses were performed to investigate relationships between the contributory factors and outcome variables. Linear simple and multiple regression analyses using the enter method were conducted to assess the predictive validity of the contributory factors for the adaptation indices. Independent-sample t-tests were performed to compare mean differences between groups, and paired-sample t-tests were performed to investigate changes in mean scores over time. An alpha-level of .05 was used for statistical tests unless otherwise indicated, as is recommended in the social sciences (Capraro 2007). Before any analysis was conducted, the data were carefully screened to identify incomplete surveys and outliers, and determine whether they met the underlying assumptions of parametric tests (Tabachnick and Fidell 2007). Normality of variables is generally assessed using statistical and/or graphical methods (Leimeister 2009). The shape of each distribution was therefore scrutinised visually using histograms, by superimposing a normal curve over the top and by producing Q–Q plots for each variable. Apparent outliers in the data were identified, assessed and, in some cases, omitted from the dataset, as is recommended for inferential statistics (Field 2005). After omitting outliers, these visual screens showed normal distributions for all variables.

### 3.3.2 THE INTERVIEWS

Individual interviews were chosen as the best method for accessing students' 'lived experiences', as it was felt that focus group situations might have inhibited participants with lower English language ability and less confidence in public speaking (Brown 2008).

Student volunteers for the interviews were sought in lectures. The only inclusion criteria for selecting interviewees were that they should not hold any degrees from UK universities and that they should vary in nationality as a group. Motivation to participate in the interviews was high and sixty students volunteered in total. All sixty volunteers were contacted via e-mail to confirm their initial expression of interest. Of those who replied, the first twenty were selected as participants on the basis of availability. This resulted in a fairly representative sample of twenty interviewees (six males and fourteen females), between the ages of twenty-two and twenty-eight, and representing thirteen different countries.

The interviews were conducted in a location on campus, usually in an empty classroom or a quiet seating area in a university building. They varied in length, lasting between twenty minutes and one hour. The same interviewer, who was also an 'international' student, conducted all interviews. This allowed for rapport to be built, helped to maintain commitment from participants, and allowed for consistency of interview style and approach. While an interview guide was used as 'scaffolding' for all interviews, flexibility and spontaneity were preserved by using probing questions emerging from the students' accounts (Mason 2002). The aim of the interviews was to explore how the students themselves felt they were adjusting and how they experienced the various aspects of life and study in the UK. The interviewees were asked broadly about the areas covered in the survey: namely, to talk about their experiences in daily life, their academic studies, their sense of wellbeing and their social interaction with others. Initial interview questions were open-ended (for example, 'How are things going for you at the moment?'). This technique allowed for themes to emerge from the students' own accounts. All interviews were recorded, transcribed for analysis and then anonymised.

Interview data were analysed using thematic analysis (Braun and Clarke 2006). This involved careful scrutiny of each transcript and repeated listening to the audio recordings until recurring patterns or themes began to emerge, as agreed by both authors (Holloway and Wheeler 2002). A 'theme' is understood here as "a pattern in the information that at minimum describes and organises the possible observations and at maximum interprets aspects of the phenomenon' (Boyatzis 1998: 161). Using the NVivo software, students' comments were initially sorted into four broad analytical categories: 'positive', 'negative', 'neutral' and 'problematising' comments. A comment was classified as 'problematising' if the student identified an aspect of their sojourn as problematic while not overtly exhibiting a negative orientation or describing a negative experience (Table 3.2).

In a second analytical step, every statement in the four broad categories was further analysed for content and placed under an appropriate heading or thematic 'node', along with any others that were sufficiently similar (Hannan 2007). Here, the interest was in the general adjustment trajectory, as well as individual nuances. It is important

Table 3.2 Interview analytical categories and example comments

| Analytical category | Example comments |
|---|---|
| Positive – *Positive orientation/experience* | 'I like it [the programme] because it's very international' (Romanian student, T2)<br>'It was nice working with other people as opposed to just yourself going to the library'(US student, T1) |
| Negative – *Negative orientation/experience* | 'I am not happy with the dissertation part because there are too many students' (Turkish student, T2)<br>'Sometimes I felt I had to teach my course mates and that I didn't expect. I came here to learn'(Finnish student, T2) |
| Problematising – *Highlighting the problematic/complex nature of an issue* | 'It is a little bit more challenging to work in a group with more Chinese students' (Latvian student, T2)<br>'It takes lots of time to analyse literature, to read it, because, you know, I'm, like, translating at the same time while reading' (Lithuanian student, T2) |
| Neutral – *An impartial statement without making a judgement* | 'I'm kind of surprised because there aren't that many British students taking the master's degree' (Romanian student, T1)<br>'The classroom environment here is very different from Malaysia' (Malaysian student, T1) |

Note: T1 = Time 1; T2 = Time 2.

to note that the importance of a theme might not necessarily be reflected merely by its frequency (Hesse-Biber 2010); thus analysis focused on frequency, as well as intensity, of comments. In practice, this meant that responses were coded by frequency, specificity and emotionality in order to discern the importance of a theme across the dataset and for each participant (Figure 3.1; see also Young and Schartner 2014).

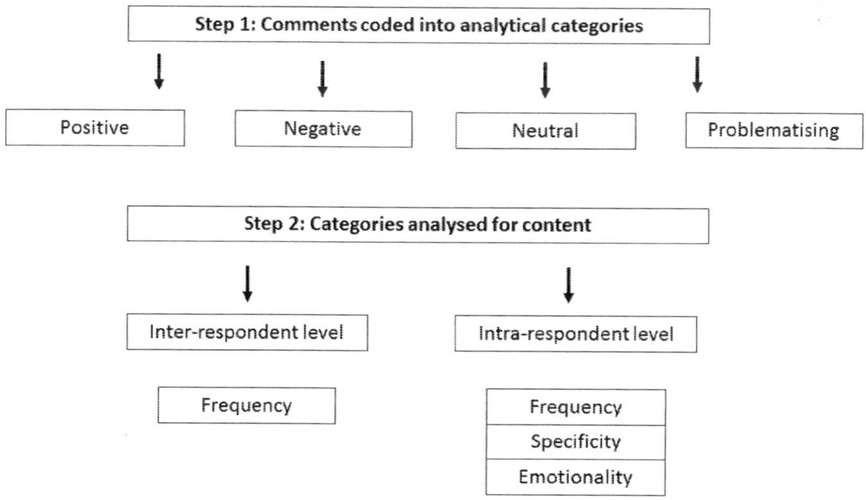


*Figure 3.1 Qualitative data analysis procedure*

### 3.3.3 THE QUALITATIVE ALUMNI SURVEY

The qualitative questionnaire reflected Stage 4 of the data collection and was aimed at collecting retrospective accounts of the student experience from graduates. It was distributed via e-mail and included the following three open questions:

- What are your main memories of doing the degree?
- How has the degree influenced your professional life?
- How has the degree influenced your personal life?

Responses were sorted thematically into the following categories: 'academic', 'psychological', 'sociocultural', 'outcomes' and 'other'. Mapping on to the analytical procedure for the interviews, each comment was then sorted into four further categories ('positive', 'negative', 'neutral', 'problematising'), which were further analysed for emerging themes. Of the respondents who completed the questionnaire (N = 70), thirty had graduated from an MA CCC and forty from an MA ALT between the years of 1991 and 2013. We hoped that alumni's retrospective impressions of a highly internationalised MA programme would add a new temporal perspective to the study of student adjustment and adaptation. Data from this element of our research are presented in Chapter 8.

The methodological approach detailed above served the purpose of our research well. It allowed us to integrate qualitative process-oriented perspectives with quantitative outcome-oriented approaches in a single study. The longitudinal design adopted in our research is very unusual in studies of student sojourner adjustment and adaptation, and the data we present in Part II of this book recognise that the IS experience begins with factors that influence whether, when and where to study aboard, extends into the experience itself, and continues into the effects of the experience on the future life of former international alumni.

In the following section of the book (Part II), we demonstrate how our mixed-methods longitudinal approach was applied, and present and consolidate empirical findings from our research.

## NOTE

1. In some cases, students identified territories that are not officially recognised as nation states as their places of origin (e.g. Palestine, Kurdistan, Taiwan); these places are included here, as reported by the students.

## REFERENCES

Andrade, M. S. (2006), 'International students in English-speaking universities: adjustment factors', *Journal of Research in International Education*, 5(2), 131–54.

Boyatzis, R. (1998), *Transforming Qualitative Information: Thematic Analysis and Code Development*, Thousand Oaks, CA: Sage.

Braun, V., and V. Clarke (2006), 'Using thematic analysis in psychology', *Qualitative Research in Psychology*, 3(2), 77–101.

Brown, L. (2008), *The Adjustment Journey of International Postgraduate Students at a University in England*, Unpublished doctoral thesis, Bournemouth University, UK.

Capraro, R. M. (2007), 'Significance level', in N. J. Salkind (ed.), *Encyclopaedia of Measurement and Statistics*, Thousand Oaks, CA: Sage, pp. 889–91.

Chirkov, V. I., S. Safdar, J. de Guzman and K. Playford (2008), 'Further examining the role motivation to study abroad plays in the adaptation of international students in Canada', *International Journal of Intercultural Relations*, 32(5), 427–40.

Chirkov, V. I., M. Vansteenkiste, R. Tao and M. Lynch (2007), 'The role of motivation to study abroad in the adaptation of international students: a self-determination theory approach', *International Journal of Intercultural Relations*, 31(2), 199–222.

Creswell, J., and V. Plano (2007), *Designing and Conducting Mixed Methods Research*, Thousand Oaks, CA: Sage.

Denzin, N. K., and Y. S. Lincoln (1998), *Collecting and Interpreting Qualitative Methods*, Thousand Oaks, CA: Sage.

Diener, E., R. A. Emmons, R. J. Larsen and S. Griffin (1985). 'The Satisfaction with Life Scale', *Journal of Personality Assessment*, 49, 71–5.

Diener, E., E. M. Suh, R. E. Lucas and H. L. Smith (1999), 'Subjective well-being: three decades of progress', *Psychological Bulletin*, 125(2), 276–302.

Field, A. (2005), *Discovering Statistics Using SPSS*, 2nd edn, London: Sage.

Furnham, A., and S. Bochner (1982), 'Social difficulty in a foreign culture: an empirical analysis of culture shock', in S. Bochner (ed.), *Cultures in Contact: Studies in Cross-cultural Interaction*, Oxford: Pergamon, pp. 161–98.

Goodwin, C. J. (2010), *Research in Psychology: Methods and Design*, 6th edn, Hoboken, NJ: John Wiley.

Hannan, A. (2007), *Using Interviews in Education Research*. Available at: <http://cecs6200.pbworks.com/w/file/fetch/69409200/Using%20Interviews%20in%20Education%20Research.pdf> (last accessed 13 December 2018).

Hesse-Biber, S. N. (2010), *Mixed Methods Research: Merging Theory with Practice*, New York: Guilford Press.

Holloway, I., and S. Wheeler (2002), *Qualitative Research in Nursing*, Oxford: Blackwell.

Leimeister, S. (2009), *IT Outsourcing Governance: Client Types and Their Management Strategies*, Wiesbaden: Gabler.

MacIntyre, P. D., R. Clément, Z. Dörnyei and K. A. Noels (1998), 'Conceptualizing willingness to communicate in a L2: a situational model of L2 confidence and affiliation', *The Modern Language Journal*, 82(4), 545–62.

MacIntyre, P. D., R. Clément and K. A. Noels (1997), 'Biases in self-ratings of second language proficiency: the role of language anxiety', *Language Learning*, 47(2), 265–87.

Mason, J. (2002), *Qualitative Researching*, 2nd edn, London: Sage.

Ong, A. S. J., and C. Ward (2005), 'The construction and validation of a social support measure for sojourners: the Index of Sojourner Social Support (ISSS) Scale', *Journal of Cross-Cultural Psychology*, 36(6), 637–61.

Pashaeizad, H. (2010), 'A glance at the characteristics of mixed methods and importance of its applications in LIS researches', in A. Katsirikou and C. H. Skiadas (eds), *Qualitative and Quantitative Methods in Libraries: Theory and Applications: Proceedings of the International Conference on QQML2009*, Singapore: World Scientific, pp. 6–19.

RAND Mental Health Inventory (2018). Available at: <https://www.rand.org/health/surveys_tools/mos/mental-health.html> (last accessed 12 December 2018).

Rauscher, L., and B. H. Greenfield (2009), 'Advancements in contemporary physical therapy research: use of mixed methods designs', *Physical Therapy*, 89, 91–100.

Rosenthal, D. A., V. J. Russell and G. J. Thomson (2006), *A Growing Experience: The Health and Well-Being of International Students at the University of Melbourne*. Available at: <https://services.unimelb.edu.au/__data/assets/pdf_file/0011/358436/GrowingExperience.pdf> (last accessed 13 December 2018).

Sam, D. L. (2000), 'Satisfaction with life among international students: an exploratory study', *Social Indicators Research*, 53(3), 315–37.

Tabachnick, G. G., and L. S. Fidell (2007), *Experimental Designs Using ANOVA*, Belmont, CA: Duxbury.

UKCISA (2018), *International Student Statistics: UK Higher Education*. Available at: <https://www.ukcisa.org.uk/Research--Policy/Statistics/International-student-statistics-UK-higher-education> (last accessed 13 December 2018).

van Oudenhoven, J. P., and K. I. van der Zee (2002), 'Predicting multicultural effectiveness of international students: the Multicultural Personality Questionnaire', *International Journal of Intercultural Relations*, 26(6), 679–94.

Ward, C., S. Bochner and A. Furnham (2001), *The Psychology of Culture Shock*, 2nd edn, Hove: Routledge.

Ward, C., and A. Kennedy (1999), 'The measurement of sociocultural adaptation', *International Journal of Intercultural Relations*, 23(4), 659–77.

Ying, Y., and H. Liese (1994), 'Initial adjustment of Taiwan students to the U.S.: the impact of post-arrival variables', *Journal of Cross-Cultural Psychology*, 25(4), 466–77.

Young, T. J., and A. Schartner (2014), 'The effects of cross-cultural communication education on international students' adjustment and adaptation', *Journal of Multilingual and Multicultural Development*, 35(6), 547–62.

Young, T. J., P. G. Sercombe, I. Sachdev, R. Naeb and A. Schartner (2013), 'Success factors for international postgraduate students' adjustment: exploring the roles of intercultural competence, language proficiency, social contact and social support', *European Journal of Higher Education*, 3, 151–71.

Zhou, Y., and J. Todman (2009), 'Patterns of adaptation of Chinese postgraduate students in the United Kingdom', *Journal of Studies in International Education*, 13(4), 467–86.

# PART II

## 4

# ACADEMIC ADJUSTMENT AND ADAPTATION

In this chapter, we discuss and integrate interview and survey-based data related to the academic adjustment and adaptation of ISs. This includes adjustments to the demands of academic life in the new environment, such as styles of learning and teaching at the host university, as well as academic achievement as an outcome measure.

The following research questions are addressed in this chapter:

1. How do English language ability, knowledge about the host country, prior overseas experience, autonomy in the decision to study abroad, intercultural competence, social contact and social support relate to different aspects of academic achievement?
2. What are the dynamics and patterns of student sojourners' academic adjustment over time?

Below, we first present descriptive data related to our academic adaptation measures (4.1), before presenting qualitative data capturing dynamics and patterns of academic adjustment over time (4.2). We then detail quantitative data on the relationship between a range of contributory factors and different aspects of academic achievement (4.3), and end with a brief conclusion and implications for research and practice (4.4).

## 4.1 DESCRIPTIVE STATISTICS OF ACADEMIC ADAPTATION

A majority of studies on student sojourner adjustment and adaptation have focused on either psychological or sociocultural aspects. Relatively few studies have investigated the academic adjustment domain in detail (Bastien et al. 2018), which is surprising, given its central importance to students, and little has been written about measurable academic outcomes of a study sojourn abroad (Morrison et al. 2005). Fine-grained descriptions of academic achievement are especially sparse in the literature. In addition to an overall degree GPA, we therefore included separate measures for the taught component and the more student-led research element of the degree, respectively (cf. Young et al. 2013). We hoped that this would allow for a more nuanced perspective on academic achievement than has usually been the case. It also reflected the reality of one-year taught postgraduate programmes in the UK, which typically include a large taught component of lectures and seminars, and a student-led independent research project carried out over the summer months, each usually accounting for, respectively, two-thirds and one-third of the assessed element of the degree.

For the students in our sample, mean GPAs for all three academic achievement indicators were within the UK degree classification 'pass with merit', which typically refers to GPAs of between 60 and 69 per cent. Despite considerable variation across the sample, this indicates that, on the whole, students performed well in both their assessed coursework and their research dissertations (Table 4.1).

Students in the interviewee sample had slightly higher GPAs than the larger sample (Table 4.2) but this difference was not statistically significant. We could therefore

Table 4.1 Measures of central tendency for academic achievement

| | Taught GPA (N = 142) | Research GPA (N = 140) | Degree GPA (N = 140) |
|---|---|---|---|
| M | 63.18 | 63.10 | 63.20 |
| SD | 5.83 | 7.84 | 6.08 |
| Min. | 41.2 | 35.0 | 42.9 |
| Max. | 76.7 | 78.0 | 77.1 |

Note: GPA, grade point average; M, mean; SD, standard deviation.

Table 4.2 Interviewees' academic achievement scores

| Student | Age | Country of origin | Sex | Overall GPA | Taught GPA | Research GPA |
|---|---|---|---|---|---|---|
| 1 | 22 | Romania | F | 67.80 | 67.20 | 69.00 |
| 2 | 22 | Turkey | F | 69.20 | 67.80 | 72.00 |
| 3 | 23 | Malaysia | F | 63.40 | 64.70 | 61.00 |
| 4 | 23 | Italy | F | 68.20 | 67.80 | 69.00 |
| 5 | 26 | Germany | F | 69.00 | 68.00 | 71.00 |
| 6 | 23 | Lithuania | M | 66.10 | 67.20 | 64.00 |
| 7 | 26 | Indonesia | F | 63.00 | 65.00 | 59.00 |
| 8 | 27 | Finland | F | 70.10 | 69.70 | 71.00 |
| 9 | 24 | Romania | F | 68.80 | 69.70 | 67.00 |
| 10 | 25 | Mexico | M | 70.20 | 68.30 | 74.00 |
| 11 | 28 | Indonesia | F | 60.90 | 60.80 | 61.00 |
| 12 | 23 | USA | M | 69.70 | 69.00 | 71.00 |
| 13 | 26 | USA | F | 66.00 | 63.50 | 71.00 |
| 14 | 24 | Slovakia | F | 63.60 | 62.80 | 65.00 |
| 15 | 23 | China | F | 57.10 | 54.30 | 55.00 |
| 16 | 23 | China | M | 53.90 | 54.40 | 53.00 |
| 17 | 23 | Latvia | F | 68.10 | 69.70 | 65.00 |
| 18 | 24 | China | F | 59.00 | 61.50 | 54.00 |
| **TOTAL** | | | | **65.23** | **65.01** | **65.11** |

Note: F = female; GPA = grade point average; male = male.

assume that the interviewees were broadly representative of the wider cohort in terms of their academic achievement.

We were also interested in students' subjective experience of academic adaptation and included two measures to this effect in our self-report survey at Time 2 (see Chapter 3 for details). The first was self-rated academic adaptation, for which the mean score was 3.92 (standard deviation [SD] = .63, Min. = 2.22, Max. = 5.00), indicating that students generally felt well adjusted to the academic host environment nine months into the sojourn. Analysis showed that the items 'Dealing with academic staff' (M = 4.13, SD = .80) and 'Dealing with administrative staff' (M = 4.42, SD = .77) were rated highest, while 'Writing academic essays' (M = 3.41, SD = .91, 54 per cent self-rated at the midpoint or below) and 'Reading academic texts' (M = 3.66, SD = .96, 38 per cent) had the lowest mean scores. The second subjective measure was satisfaction with academic achievement, for which the mean score was 3.26 (SD = .71, Min. = 1.00, Max. = 5.00). Only about half (48 per cent) self-rated above the mid-point of the scale (that is, 4–5), indicating that a fairly large proportion of the group were not fully satisfied with their academic achievement.

Group comparisons showed that students who had attended English language courses prior to commencing their degree programme had a significantly lower overall degree GPA mean score (59.20, SD = 5.18) than those who did not access this kind of support (M = 65.32, SD = 5.46), $t(133) = -6.47$, $p < .001$. This suggests that students who started off with lower English language attainment were less likely to perform well on their degree programme than their peers who did not need this kind of support. We also found that students with prior overseas experience performed significantly better on the degree overall (M = 64.57, SD = 5.60) than those without this kind of prior experience (M = 62.06, SD = 6.25), $t(141) = -2.53$, $p = .013$. It may well be that prior experience of studying and/or living in another country offset some of the acculturative stress for these students, thereby easing their adjustment and allowing them to focus on their academic performance, a point put forward by Melnick and colleagues (2011), who found a positive association between prior cross-cultural experiences of a sample of Asian postgraduate students in the USA and their subsequent academic achievement.

In sum, descriptive analysis of our academic adaptation measures suggested that students in our sample performed well on both the taught and the student-led components of their degree programme. Both English language ability and previous overseas experience appeared to have an impact on the degree of academic achievement. Next, we wanted to ascertain further the impact of a set of contributory factors on academic adaptation.

## 4.2 ACADEMIC ADJUSTMENT OVER TIME

The qualitative data we present below capture academic adjustment as experienced by the students in our sample. Here, we summarise key themes emerging from the interviewees' accounts as they were going through the experience of adjusting to the *modus operandi* at their host university. Themes are supported by verbatim examples.

### 4.2.1 TIME 1: THE EARLY SOJOURN STAGES

Student accounts from the first interview round were largely anticipatory in nature, as they had little, if any, first-hand experience of learning and teaching at the host university. Overall, students seemed positive about their upcoming year and the prospect of studying at a British university.

> I think if I carry that same work ethic that I had in undergrad into here I think I'll do just fine. (US student, female)
>
> I'm thinking that I will put a lot of time into the study so I shouldn't have actual problems. (Romanian student, female)

The small amount of classroom experience they had had at this point was experienced by most interviewees as positive, most especially interactions they had with academic staff.

> In Latvia it's more accepted that the teacher will explain you things and they are universal, you don't question them and it's also here your professors ask you for your opinion and you can say whatever you want [...] I like the system here more. I feel more comfortable here. (Latvian student, female)

The multinational and multilingual make-up of their degree cohort was highlighted by most interviewees as positive and exciting, although there was some disappointment about the apparent lack of domestic students on the course.

> I really like that it's an international environment but also I would like that more British people would be in the programme. (Romanian student, female)

Although students seemed highly motivated and optimistic about their prospective academic experience, we also found in the corpus a fair amount of problematising and negative comments. These mostly related to students' doubts about their own abilities, both linguistically and otherwise, and how this might have an impact on their academic achievement. A lack of confidence in their English language abilities was especially apparent in the data.

> I'm not sure I will get an excellent score because of the limited language ability. (Chinese student, female)

The prospect of studying in a foreign language was daunting to many students. The essay-based nature of much of the coursework and related reading seemed challenging to many students in our sample, as illustrated in the following exchange with a female Chinese student:

> Y: [...] in this course we should read a lot of books but we all feel it's very hard to read book because we should look up the words all the time and then translate

> into Chinese and to think in Chinese but maybe it will have a difference in English way maybe, so maybe there are some differences.
> I: Like a different meaning?
> Y: Yeah, maybe we will have some misunderstanding, maybe. And it always take a long time for us to read even one page, and maybe we will spend one hour in reading just one page.

Several students reported feeling 'nervous' or 'worried' about the essay-based nature of much of the expected coursework and the prospect of writing academic essays in a second language.

> I'm worried that I might not have this good level of academic writing. (Latvian student, female)

Comparisons between prior experiences in their home countries and 'new' conventions at the host university were common.

> I'm not really good in academic writing, so I'm just worried about that, and because back home it's very exam-oriented in a way that everything relies on exams. (Malaysian student, female)
> We just read, read, read and then we take the exam orally. We don't really write since we leave school, so academically speaking if I think about this year ahead I'm really worried about writing essays and that's it. (Italian student, female)

The limited classroom time and the prospect of independent study were also identified as a concern, in particular by students who were used to a more teacher-directed academic model.

> I'm used to be supported. This is very different [...] everything you should do by yourself. (Chinese student, male)

Some pointed to limited opportunities for social contact:

> We don't have many courses in MA, so we cannot have a chance to know many people. We cannot see each other very frequently, so we cannot be close friends. (Turkish student, male)
> People are much on their own [...] I haven't had any occasions yet to become friends with someone maybe because of that thing that all the system is based on the individual. (Italian student, female)

In sum, during the first interview round, students were unable to comment on specific aspects of their academic adjustment and comments thus remained anticipatory or limited to initial experiences of learning and teaching at the host university. Overall, there was a fair amount of doubt and uncertainty among students about their own English language abilities and how this might affect their academic performance, especially regarding reading and writing. None the less, our general impression was that students were looking forward to the year ahead and demonstrated a largely positive outlook.

### 4.2.2 TIME 2: FIVE MONTHS INTO THE PROGRAMME

By the time of the second interview round, our interviewees were about halfway through the taught element of their degree programme. Five months into their sojourn, they were now able to comment in more detail on their academic experiences, which, by and large, we felt were positive. As the interviews took place before students had received much, if any, formal feedback on coursework, there was little comment on actual academic performance. But, on the whole, our data suggested that students felt satisfied with their academic adjustment and many expressed more confidence in their abilities, both academic and linguistic. The following comments were typical of the sample:

> I think I've adjusted quite well. (Romanian student, female)
> I feel I adjusted well and I'm doing the right things, I'm fitting in. (Romanian student, female)
> As time goes by I think I found it much easier than before because I can understand most of the knowledge teacher told us. (Chinese student, female)

However, for some, operating in a second language remained a challenge, especially in the classroom:

> Sometimes when I want to say something I get confused and lost, I just keep thinking 'Well how do I say this in English?' (Indonesian student, female)

Students were now able to comment on more specific aspects of academic adjustment, such as essay writing and other types of assessment. Whilst some students appeared to struggle with unfamiliar academic conventions, such as plagiarism and literature citations, by and large it seemed that students felt they had coped well with assessed coursework thus far.

> The assignments were not bad. It took much time but it was ok. (Lithuanian student, male)
> They say that you are expected to critically analyse a topic […] I'm a bit confused what they are expecting from me. (Turkish student, male)
> I forgot to put page number and quotation mark, so they said my assignment is what it's called irregularity […] I didn't do that intentionally. (Indonesian student, female)

Experiences of group work assignments were very varied, with some students describing it as a valuable and positive exercise while others experienced it as frustrating. Those who encountered difficulties commented on communication problems, compounded by apparent variations in English language abilities, and distribution of workload, which was perceived as unfair. In this respect, our findings confirmed those of Spencer-Oatey and Dauber (2017).

> When you cannot communicate and also you think there are free riders in your group it is very difficult and you feel it is not fair. (Romanian student, female)
>
> Sometimes I feel like a teacher in those groups because they don't know any basic situations with terms so it wasn't good for me. (Turkish student, male)

Classroom discussions were highlighted by many students as beneficial and, although daunting to those who were used to less interactive teaching approaches, most students seemed keen and motivated to take part.

> It's very interactive, everybody speaks up, so sometimes that motivates me to do the same thing because I think 'Ok, if they can do it then I can do it.' (Indonesian student, female)
>
> It's like a discussion [...] you never feel that you can't ask a question or participate at any time throughout the lecture. (US student, male)

The large amount of independent self-study required of students remained a challenge for some, although it was also described as 'beneficial'.

> A lot of things that people have to do are like on their own, so reading and writing [...] I haven't had much chance to like create groups to work together. (Italian student, female)

Comments on interactions with university staff were uniformly positive, with students highlighting the approachability of the former and the seemingly 'close' relationship between students and staff.

> Teachers are very kind. This is different from China. In China we should do everything, follow the teacher and follow their command [...] here we can have our own thoughts and our own ideas [...] teachers are more like friends. I think it's very good. (Chinese student, female)

Our second interview round suggested that students felt, by and large, well adjusted to the academic environment. They reported more confidence in their own linguistic and academic abilities and generally expressed a fairly high level of satisfaction with their academic experiences so far. Where problematising or negative comments were noticeable, this was mostly related to difficulties encountered during group assignments and unfamiliar academic conventions related to essay writing. Although students were not yet able to comment on their actual academic performance, it appears that they coped well with coursework thus far, even if the time leading up to hand-in dates was experienced as stressful. Overall, we were able to conclude fairly confidently that, five months into the degree programme, students' own sense of academic adjustment was overwhelmingly positive.

### 4.2.3 TIME 3: NINE MONTHS INTO THE PROGRAMME

Academic adjustment appeared to continue to follow an upward trajectory for most students in our sample. By the time of the third interview round, the students had completed the taught component of their programme and had received feedback on assessed coursework. This meant that they were now able to comment on their actual academic performance. Overwhelmingly, comments on academic adjustment were positive, with several interviewees noticing an improvement between the first and second semesters. It appeared that students now felt comfortable with the *modus operandi* at their host university, and confidence in their own abilities continued to improve.

> I feel that I really progressed academically this semester. I feel my papers are a lot better and I kind of grasped how exactly UK writing is and what exactly they are looking for. (US student, male)
> I feel better than the first semester because I am more familiar with how to study, how to write my assignment. (Chinese student, female)

But the pressures of competing deadlines for assessed coursework, compounded by an expectation that students should largely study independently, still proved difficult for some interviewees.

> Everybody is just giving so much time and everybody expects to do everything on your own. It's a bit different from our country, so I struggled with managing time. Maybe that's the basic thing I learned – I have to manage my time on my own without somebody else pushing me. (Turkish student, male)

Those who were initially less confident with their English language abilities now reported increased satisfaction, especially regarding their reading and writing skills.

> I'm proud that my reading speed has increased a lot, and assignments don't feel so difficult to write anymore. (Finnish student, female)
> I learned some academic words and I always read, search the literature review. I think writing has improved but for speaking I think almost the same. (Chinese student, male)

Comments on academic performance were mixed. While some students felt they had exceeded their own expectations, others expressed a sense of disappointment with the grades they received.

> Academically I was a bit surprised. I expected I can do much better but certainly I need to change things when I continue with PhD, so I had some problems with adjusting to academic life. (Turkish student, male)

> Actually I still not very satisfied with my academic performance. (Chinese student, female)

What was most noticeable during the third interview round was that the students' focus appeared to shift from academic experiences to more general outcomes of study abroad, with many describing the experience of studying on an international degree programme as transformative. Comments related not so much to academic aspects but rather to the acquisition of broader, transferable communication skills. One Chinese student reported feeling 'more confident' and 'more willing to communicate with others', while another appeared to have overcome her reluctance to approach others:

> Before I come here I'm very nervous, I don't dare to speak to strangers, to people I'm not familiar with but now I can find a topic or I can speak with them. (Chinese student, female)

Finally, students reported a general sense of more cultural awareness and open-mindedness, which appeared to have been prompted partly by the content of their degree programme and partly by first-hand experiences of intercultural encounters.

> I have learned how similar people are coming from so different cultures. (Romanian student, female)
> Don't try to judge, criticise, because you understand that it's different and they are people just like you. (Lithuanian student, male)

The data from our third interview round suggest that students' own sense of academic adjustment remained positive, with an apparent steady improvement over time for most interviewees. It seems that the more time students spent at the host university, the better they became at adopting and applying newly acquired conventions and skills. The experience of studying at the host university was overwhelmingly described as positive, with many highlighting the transformative nature of a study sojourn abroad, most especially in intercultural terms. The degree of satisfaction with academic achievement, perhaps not surprisingly, varied across the group, with some students seemingly content with their performance and other feeling they could have done better.

## 4.3 ASSOCIATIONS BETWEEN CONTRIBUTORY FACTORS AND ACADEMIC ADAPTATION

This section presents results regarding associations between contributory factors (see Chapter 2 for details) and our academic achievement measures. For each contributory factor, a correlation analysis was performed, followed by a linear single or multiple regression analysis using the enter method.

### 4.3.1 ENGLISH LANGUAGE ABILITY

We measured students' English language ability at both entry (Time 1) and exit point (Time 2). The Time 1 measure emerged as a significant predictor of the taught GPA, $\beta = .30$, $t(126) = 3.47$, $p < .01$, and explained 9 per cent of the variance in the data, $F(1, 126) = 12.01$, $p = .001$. Next, it emerged as a significant predictor of the research GPA, $\beta = .25$, $t(124) = 2.87$, $p < .01$, and explained 6 per cent of the variance in the data, $F(1, 124) = 8.24$, $p = .005$. Finally, it predicted the overall degree GPA, $\beta = .30$, $t(124) = 3.47$, $p < .01$, and explained 9 per cent of the variance in the data, $F(1, 124) = 12.02$, $p = .001$.

We found an even closer association with the Time 2 measure. Firstly, it predicted the taught GPA, $\beta = .48$, $t(129) = 6.19$, $p < .001$, and explained 23 per cent of the variance in the data. Secondly, it predicted the research GPA, $\beta = .47$, $t(127) = 5.95$, $p < .001$, and explained 22 per cent of the variance in the data. Thirdly, it predicted the overall degree GPA, $\beta = .51$, $t(127) = 6.63$, $p < .001$, and explained 26 per cent of the variance in the data.

These results were in line with our own expectations and confirm and extend in scope the findings of our previous study of a similar student sojourner group (Young et al. 2013). Although the variance explained by the Time 1 measure was modest (between 6 and 9 per cent), the Time 2 measure was able to explain a considerable degree of the variance in academic achievement (between 22 and 26 per cent).

Prior research on the relationship between English language ability and academic achievement has largely focused on standardised test scores as predictive variables (e.g. TOEFL or IELTS), and findings from this body of work are somewhat inconclusive. Some studies found no significant relationship between ISs' TOEFL scores and subsequent GPAs (e.g. Light et al. 1987; Melnick et al. 2011), while others did report significant associations. For example, a USA-based study of seventy-seven first-year undergraduate students reported a significant correlation between students' English language ability and their GPAs (Stoynoff 1997). Our results suggest that, above and beyond standardised test scores, students' own sense of their communicative skills and confidence in using the language appear to play an important role in their academic achievement.

### 4.3.2 KNOWLEDGE ABOUT THE UK

Pre-sojourn knowledge about the UK correlated significantly with the taught GPA ($r = .21$, $p < .05$), the research GPA ($r = .29$, $p < .01$) and the overall degree GPA ($r = .25$, $p < .05$), indicating that students with greater levels of knowledge about their host country are likely to perform better academically. Indeed, simple linear regression analyses showed that knowledge about the UK was a significant predictor of academic achievement. Firstly, it significantly predicted the taught GPA, $\beta = .21$, $t(139) = 2.51$, $p < .05$, and explained 4 per cent of the variance in the data, $F(1, 139) = 6.28$, $p = .013$. Secondly, it significantly predicted the research GPA, $\beta = .29$, $t(137) = 3.55$, $p < .01$, and explained 8 per cent of the variance in the data, $F(1, 137) = 12.63$, $p = .001$. Thirdly, it significantly predicted the overall degree

GPA, $\beta = .25$, $t(137) = 3.06$, $p < .01$, and explained 6 per cent of the variance in the data, $F(1, 137) = 9.34$, $p = .003$.

Although pre-sojourn knowledge about the UK was able to predict academic achievement only to a modest extent (between 4 and 8 per cent of the variance explained), our results provide some indication that students who acquire knowledge about the host country prior to their arrival are more likely to perform well academically. It seems plausible that those students who familiarised themselves with the academic conventions of the host university prior to arrival, most especially assessment practices, have more accurate expectations and are thus better able to adjust to the new academic environment (Caligiuri et al. 2001). Our findings mirror those of Chapman and colleagues (1988), who found that knowledge about the US educational environment predicted the academic achievement of international postgraduate students.

### 4.3.3 AUTONOMY IN THE DECISION TO STUDY ABROAD

We found that the RAI and most of the self-regulation subscales correlated significantly with all three academic achievement measures (Table 4.3).

Linear regression analyses showed that autonomy in the decision to study abroad was highly predictive of all three academic achievement indicators. Firstly, it significantly predicted the taught GPA, $\beta = .34$, $t(139) = 4.32$, $p < .01$, and explained 12 per cent of the variance in the data, $F(1, 139) = 18.64$, $p < .001$. Secondly, it significantly predicted the research GPA, $\beta = .38$, $t(137) = 4.79$, $p < .01$, and explained 14 per cent of the variance in the data, $F(1, 137) = 22.95$, $p < .001$. Thirdly, it significantly predicted the overall degree GPA, $\beta = .38$, $t(137) = 4.77$, $p < .01$, and explained 14 per cent of the variance in the data, $F(1, 137) = 22.73$, $p < .001$. This suggests that those students who felt that they stood behind their decision to study abroad were also likely to perform well academically.

Our findings here are in line with those of Chirkov and colleagues (2007), who have previously found that the RAI predicted academic motivation of Chinese ISs at a Canadian university (18 per cent of the variance explained). In a follow-up study, they found no significant associations between the RAI and academic success (Chirkov et al. 2008). However, the researchers in this investigation used a broad self-report measure of academic success rather than actual academic achievement

Table 4.3 Bivariate correlations between the Relative Autonomy Index and academic achievement

| | RAI | INTRI | IDENT | INTRO | EXTER |
|---|---|---|---|---|---|
| Taught GPA | .34** | .24** | .03 | −.24** | −.31** |
| Research GPA | .38** | .26** | .000 | −.33** | −.31** |
| Degree GPA | .38** | .26** | .02 | −.30** | −.33** |

Note: **significant at p < .01 (two-tailed); EXTER = external regulation; GPA, grade point average; IDENT = identified regulation; INTRI = intrinsic motivation, INTRO = introjected regulation; RAI = Relative Autonomy Index.

scores. The present study was the first to investigate the relationship between the RAI and subsequent actual performance on assessed academic work measured in GPAs.

### 4.3.4 INTERCULTURAL COMPETENCE

Three dimensions of intercultural competence (IC) correlated significantly with all three academic achievement measures: these dimensions were cultural empathy, social initiative and flexibility (Table 4.4).

Next, multiple regression analyses yielded statistically significant models for variance in academic achievement in relation to IC. The models contributed to between 21 and 25 per cent of the variance in the data. Coefficient results showed that the main predictors of academic achievement were cultural empathy, open-mindedness and flexibility. These three dimensions were significantly associated with all three academic achievement measures. Social initiative was significantly associated with the research and degree GPA. Emotional stability was marginally associated with the taught GPA (Table 4.5).

Table 4.4 Bivariate correlations between intercultural competence and academic achievement

| | CE | OM | SI | ES | FL |
|---|---|---|---|---|---|
| Taught GPA | .37** | .13 | .22** | −.11 | .22** |
| Research GPA | .34** | .12 | .32** | .004 | .29** |
| Degree GPA | .38** | .14 | .28** | −.06 | .26** |

Note: **significant at p < .01 (two-tailed); CE = cultural empathy; ES = emotional stability; FL = flexibility; GPA, grade point average; OM = open-mindedness; SI = social initiative.

Table 4.5 Regression analysis of intercultural competence and academic achievement

| | Taught GPA | | Research GPA | | Degree GPA | |
|---|---|---|---|---|---|---|
| | $\beta$ | $t$ | $\beta$ | $t$ | $\beta$ | $t$ |
| Mean CE | .42 | 4.09** | .39 | 3.92** | .43 | 4.33** |
| Mean OM | −.26 | −2.17* | −.41 | −3.46** | −.34 | −2.87** |
| Mean SI | .17 | 1.52 | .34 | 3.14** | .25 | 2.30* |
| Mean ES | −.17 | −1.94^ | −.07 | −.80 | −.13 | −1.51 |
| Mean FL | .18 | 2.11* | .20 | 2.36* | .20 | 2.36* |
| $R^2$ | 0.21 | | 0.25 | | 0.25 | |
| Adjusted $R^2$ | 0.19 | | 0.22 | | 0.22 | |
| F(df) | 7.40 (5, 136) | | 9.00 (5, 134) | | 8.88 (5, 134) | |
| Sig. | p < .001 | | p < .001 | | p < .001 | |

Note: **significant at the 99 per cent level; *significant at the 95 per cent level; ^significant at the 90 per cent level; CE = cultural empathy; ES = emotional stability; FL = flexibility; GPA, grade point average; OM = open-mindedness; SI = social initiative.

The MPQ subscales were able to explain a considerable degree of the variance in academic achievement (between 21 and 25 per cent), suggesting a close link between IC and academic achievement. This is broadly in line with our previous study of ISs' adaptation, in which the MPQ subscales explained between 14 and 26 per cent of the variance in the data (Young et al. 2013). Prior to this report, few studies had tested the predictive validity of the MPQ subscales for academic achievement. In an early study, van Oudenhoven and van der Zee (2002) found the MPQ subscales to be slightly predictive of academic achievement among a sample of students at an international business school in the Netherlands (7 per cent of the variance), although a very broad measure of academic performance was used in their study.

It is not surprising that students who scored highly on cultural empathy and flexibility were also likely to perform well academically. It seems plausible that the ability to empathise with people from other 'cultural groups' might help students to adjust to unfamiliar learning and teaching styles at the host university, including assessment procedures. Moreover, as familiar norms and practices of academic study might no longer be appropriate in the new environment (van Oudenhoven and van der Zee 2002), the ability to learn from experiences and adjust behaviour accordingly (that is, flexibility) might aid students in their academic adjustment, possibly resulting in higher academic achievement. The finding that open-mindedness showed a negative beta-value is puzzling, as it seems likely that open-minded individuals would find it easier to adjust to new academic environments. However, the negative beta-weight for OM must be interpreted with caution, in view of its non-significant correlation with the academic achievement measures. We found similar results for cultural empathy and open-mindedness in our earlier study, but did not find a significant association between flexibility and academic achievement (cf. Young et al. 2013).

Our results further showed that social initiative was significantly associated with the research GPA and the overall degree GPA. One possible explanation for this finding is that proactive students are perhaps more likely to look up information on the academic conventions of the host university. Also, students who tend to approach social situations in an active way are perhaps more likely to work with others and to form study groups with their peers, possibly resulting in higher academic achievement. Moreover, it seems plausible that the ability to take the initiative was a useful prerequisite for the, largely student-guided, research element of the degree, which required a great deal of independence.

Finally, there are indications in the data that the less emotionally stable students were, the higher their academic achievement on the taught degree element. This finding mirrors results reported by van Oudenhoven and van der Zee (2002), who suggest that emotionally unstable individuals who worry about many things are likely to put more effort into passing assessments, thereby possibly resulting in higher academic achievement. The relationship between emotional stability and mean taught GPA was weak, though, and further research is needed to ascertain this dynamic.

### 4.3.5 SOCIAL CONTACT

We found significant correlations between degree of social contact with different groups and academic achievement (Table 4.6). Degree of contact with co-nationals and with non-co-national ISs correlated significantly with all three academic achievement measures. The former showed negative correlations, indicating that the more contact students had with co-nationals, the worse they performed academically. The latter showed positive correlations, suggesting that the more students mixed with 'international' peers, the better they performed academically.

Degree of social contact was able to explain between 20 and 24 per cent of the variance in academic achievement, and degree of contact with non-co-national ISs was the main predictor for all three academic achievement measures (Table 4.7).

Our findings highlight the importance of social interaction and friendship networks for student sojourners' academic success and, again, are in line with our earlier study, although the variance explained there was somewhat lower (between 13 and 15 per cent; see Young et al. 2013). These findings serve to highlight the importance of links among student sojourners during their time abroad and provides further insights into the importance of an 'international community of practice' (Montgomery and McDowell 2009).

Table 4.6 Bivariate correlations between social contact and academic achievement

| | SC-BS | SC-CN | SC-IN | SC-LC |
|---|---|---|---|---|
| Taught GPA | .14 | –.21* | .43** | .10 |
| Research GPA | .16 | –.21* | .45** | .14 |
| Degree GPA | .20* | –.22** | .48** | .14 |

Note: **significant at $p < .01$; *significant at $p < .05$ (two-tailed); GPA = grade point average; SC-BS = social contact with British students; SC-CN = contact with co-nationals; SC-IN = contact with non-co-national international students; SC-LC = contact with local community.

Table 4.7 Regression analysis of social contact and academic achievement

| | Taught GPA | | Research GPA | | Degree GPA | |
|---|---|---|---|---|---|---|
| | $\beta$ | $t$ | $\beta$ | $t$ | $\beta$ | $t$ |
| SC-BS | .07 | .87 | .07 | .89 | .08 | .99 |
| SC-CN | –.08 | –.99 | –.08 | –.99 | –.08 | –1.03 |
| SC-IN | .40 | 4.84** | .41 | 4.98** | .44 | 5.46** |
| SC-LC | –.03 | –.32 | .01 | .10 | –.01 | –.07 |
| $R^2$ | 0.20 | | 0.21 | | 0.24 | |
| Adjusted $R^2$ | 0.17 | | 0.19 | | 0.22 | |
| F(df) | 8.43 (4, 137) | | 9.17 (4, 135) | | 10.78 (4, 135) | |
| Sig. | $p < .001$ | | $p < .001$ | | $p < .001$ | |

Note: **significant at the 99 per cent level; GPA = grade point average; SC-BS = social contact with British students; SC-CN = contact with co-nationals; SC-IN = contact with non-co-national international students; SC-LC = contact with local community.

Table 4.8 Regression analysis of social support and academic achievement

| | Taught GPA | | Research GPA | | Degree GPA | |
|---|---|---|---|---|---|---|
| | *β* | *t* | *β* | *t* | *β* | *t* |
| SC-BS | .33 | 3.12** | .26 | 2.44* | .33 | 3.08** |
| SC-CN | –.11 | –1.05 | –.12 | –1.08 | –.12 | –1.10 |
| $R^2$ | 0.07 | | 0.04 | | 0.07 | |
| Adjusted $R^2$ | 0.06 | | 0.03 | | 0.06 | |
| F(df) | 5.56 (2, 139) | | 3.14 (2, 137) | | 5.33 (2, 137) | |
| Sig. | 0.005 | | 0.046 | | 0.006 | |

Note: **significant at the 99 per cent level, *significant at the 95 per cent level; GPA = grade point average; SC-BS = social contact with British students; SC-CN = contact with co-nationals; SS-IN = instrumental social support; SS-SE = socio-emotional social support.

## 4.3.6 SOCIAL SUPPORT

Our analysis showed that the socio-emotional subscale correlated significantly with academic achievement on the taught element (r = .26, p < .01), on the research element (r = .19, p < .05) and the overall degree GPA (r = .25, p < .01). No significant association was found with the instrumental support subscale. Multiple regression analyses revealed that social support modestly predicted academic achievement (between 4 and 7 per cent of the variance explained). Socio-emotional support emerged as the main predictor for all three academic achievement measures (Table 4.8).

In our earlier study we found no significant relationship between social support and academic achievement (cf. Young et al. 2013), but the present findings point to a close relationship between emotional support and social companionship (Ong and Ward 2005) on the one hand, and academic achievement on the other. Most studies on the impact of social support on academic achievement to date have been conducted with 'home' students in their first year of university. Findings have been inconclusive, with some studies reporting a positive relationship between social support and students' GPAs (DeBerard et al. 2004; Robbins et al. 2004) and others finding no impact at all (Grayson 2003; Nicpon et al. 2006).

Our study was unusual, in that it employed a differentiated measure of actual academic achievement as opposed to broader self-report measures (e.g. van der Zee and van Oudenhoven 2002; Chirkov et al. 2008). We found that academic success for ISs undertaking one-year taught postgraduate degrees in the UK can be explained by both pre- and in-sojourn factors. Based on our findings, we can fairly confidently conclude that a 'successful' student sojourner is likely to be somebody who fulfils some, and ideally all, of the following: firstly, they have the ability to speak the host language well; secondly, they have a fair bit of knowledge about the host country; and thirdly, they will most likely to have made the decision to study abroad independently from others. They are also likely to exhibit high levels of cultural empathy and flexibility, to have strong international networks and to be able to access, and then experience, high levels of socio-emotional support (Figure 4.1).

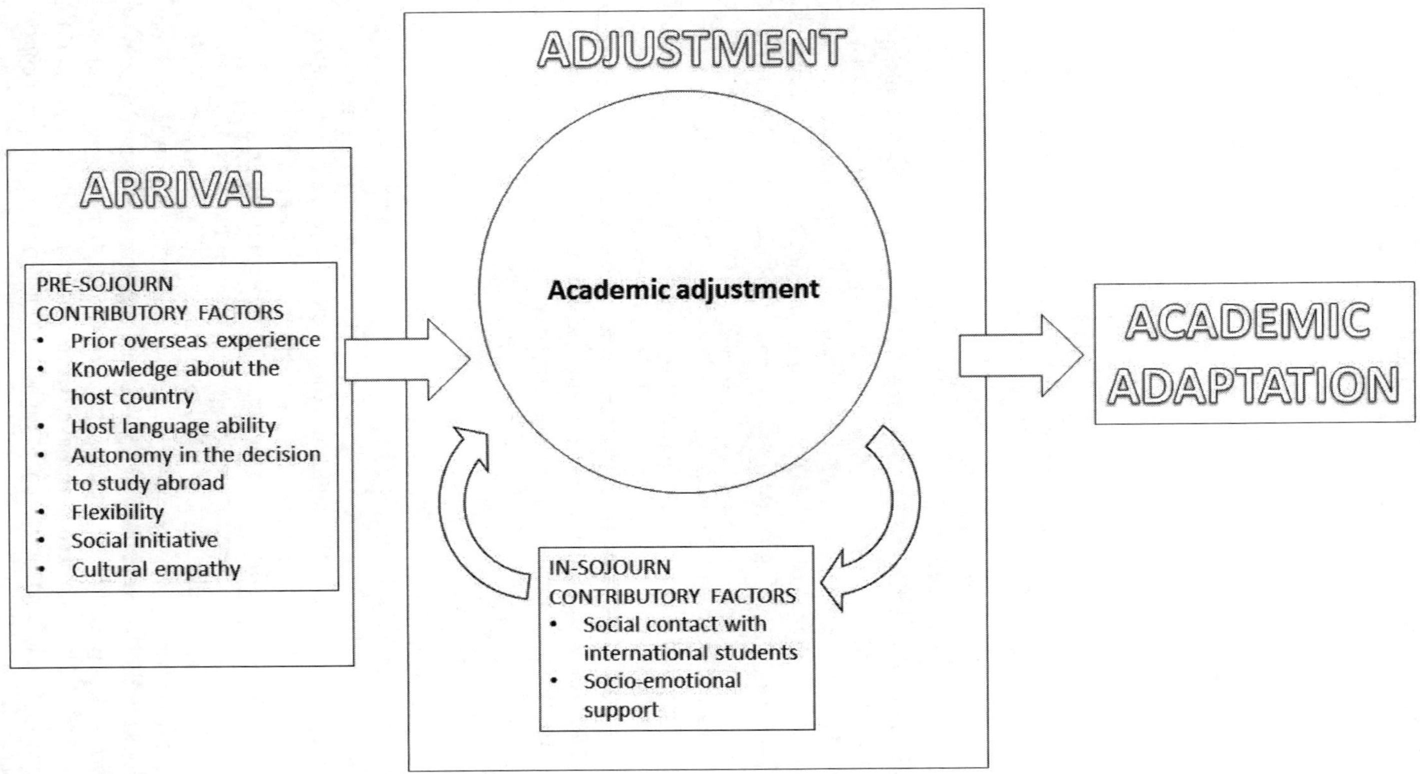


*Figure 4.1 Significant associations between contributory factors and academic adaptation*

In the following section we explore experiential academic adjustment over time from the perspective of the students themselves, as they were going through the experience of the transition to 'international' study.

## 4.4 CONCLUSION

An academic qualification is a key outcome of an international study sojourn (Spencer-Oatey and Xiong 2006), yet, surprisingly, relatively few studies to date have explored academic adjustment and adaptation in depth. In this chapter, we aimed to investigate the latter from a mixed-methods perspective, focusing on measurable academic outcomes as well as on students' 'lived' experiences at their host university. We were interested in factors that could predict academic achievement and the temporal patterns of academic adjustment over time as experienced by the students. We can draw several tentative conclusions from the data presented above.

Firstly, our data suggest that, very broadly, the individuals in our sample were 'successful' students and most achieved a good academic outcome, albeit not always to their own satisfaction. The achievement of our sample was actually broadly in line with that of the cohorts of which they were part. We can therefore perhaps conclude that findings in relation to their academic adaptation and adjustment might be broadly in line, at least, with those of students following similar programmes (see also Young and Schartner 2014). Our analysis showed that the degree of academic success is probably predicted by a range of factors, both pre-sojourn and in-sojourn. At the pre-sojourn level, prior overseas experience, good command of the host language, or English if this is the language of instruction, a degree of prior knowledge about the host country and autonomy in the decision to study abroad seem to make it more likely that students will perform well academically. A high level of intercultural competence, especially cultural empathy and flexibility, also appears to influence academic achievement positively. In line with previous studies, we found that social contacts developed during the sojourn were crucial to academic success but, unlike much of the prior research, we did not find any evidence of ties with host nationals playing an important role. Instead, it was contact with other non-co-national ISs that determined the degree of academic achievement in our data. We also found that socio-emotional support was more important for academic achievement than instrumental support.

Secondly, our qualitative data showed that, while students experienced academic adjustment in diverse and nuanced ways, a general temporal pattern did emerge. The students in our sample appeared to experience most adjustment difficulties in the early sojourn stages, when they were least familiar with the *modus operandi* at the host university. This was reflected in a large number of 'problematising' and 'negative' comments in the first interview round relative to the second and third. The most crucial factors aiding academic adjustment in our sample were evidently time and experience. It was noticeable that the more exposure students had to the academic host environment and the more they experienced its 'ways of doing things', the better they felt they were adjusting. This clearly shows that the frequently cited U-curve

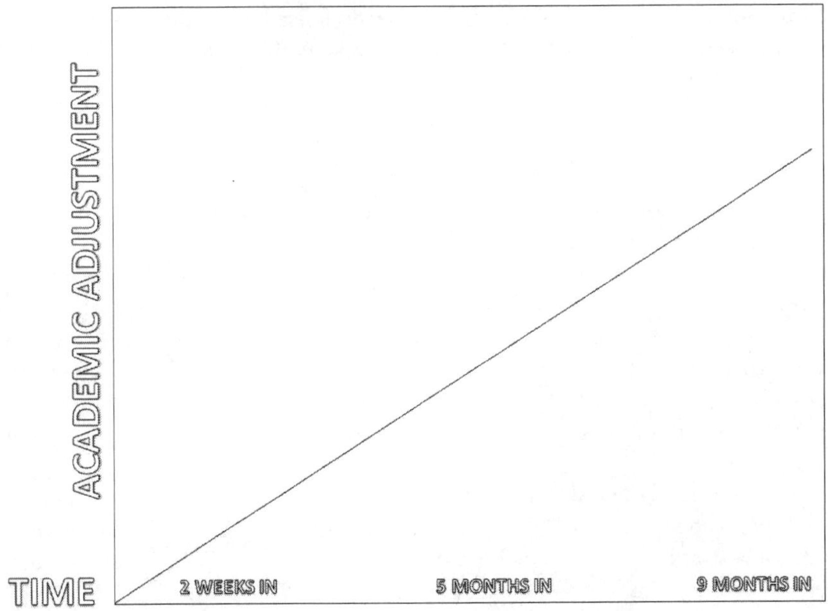


*Figure 4.2 Academic adjustment trajectory of students in this study*

model of adjustment (see Chapter 2) was not applicable to the academic domain in our data. Instead, academic adjustment here is best captured as a relatively steady ascending learning curve (Figure 4.2).

At a conceptual level, our findings serve to confirm that both the culture-learning and social skills paradigm, as well as stress and coping frameworks, can be useful in the study of academic adjustment. More commonly used to describe sociocultural adjustment (cf. Ward et al. 2001), culture-learning models are, we feel, very relevant when conceptualising academic adjustment. We found evidence that acquiring the conventions of the academic host environment was crucial to students' academic success. The more adept they became at learning and applying these, the better their own sense of academic adjustment. Additionally, and most especially in the early sojourn stages, an ability to cope with stress, triggered by the transition to an unfamiliar academic environment, was crucial to students' sense of adjustment. Our data strongly suggest that positive appraisal of academic challenges or 'optimistic coping' (Ryan and Twibell 2000) can determine how well ISs adjust and, ultimately, how well they perform.

## REFERENCES

Bastien, G., T. Seifen-Adkins and L. R. Johnson (2018), 'Striving for success: academic adjustment of international students in the U.S.', *Journal of International Students*, 8(2), 1198–219.

Caligiuri, P. M., J. Philips, M. Lazarova, I. Tarique and P. Burgi (2001), 'The theory of met expectations applied to expatriate adjustment: the role of cross-cultural training', *International Journal of Human Resource Management*, 12(3), 357–72.

Chapman, D., T. Y. Wan and M. Xu (1988), 'Academic adjustment of international students in American universities', *Education and Research*, 6(2), 96–10.

Chirkov, V. I., S. Safdar, J. de Guzman and K. Playford (2008), 'Further examining the role motivation to study abroad plays in the adaptation of international students in Canada', *International Journal of Intercultural Relations*, 32(5), 427–40.

Chirkov, V. I., M. Vansteenkiste, R. Tao and M. Lynch (2007), 'The role of motivation to study abroad in the adaptation of international students: a self-determination theory approach', *International Journal of Intercultural Relations*, 31(2), 199–222.

DeBerard, M., G. Spielmans and D. Julka (2004) 'Predictors of academic achievement and retention among college freshmen: a longitudinal study', *College Student Journal*, 38, 66–80.

Grayson, J. (2003), 'The consequences of early adjustment to university', *Higher Education*, 46, 411–29.

Light, R. L., M. Xu and J. Mossop (1987), 'English proficiency and academic performance of international students', *TESOL Quarterly*, 21(2), 251–61.

Melnick, G. A., G. Kaur and G. Yu (2011), 'Social integration and academic outcomes: the case of an international public policy and management program', *Journal of Public Affairs Education*, 17(4), 569–84.

Montgomery, C., and L. McDowell (2009), 'Social networks and the international student experience: a community of practice?', *Journal of Studies in International Education*, 13(4), 455–66.

Morrison, J., B. Merrick, S. Higgs and J. Le Metais (2005), 'Researching the performance of international students in the UK', *Studies in Higher Education*, 30(3), 327–37.

Nicpon, M., L. Huser, E. Blanks, S. Sollenberger, C. Befort and S. Kurpius (2006), 'The relationship of loneliness and social support with college freshmen's academic performance and persistence', *Journal of College Student Retention: Research, Theory and Practice*, 8(3), 345–58.

Ong, A. S. J., and C. Ward (2005), 'The construction and validation of a social support measure for sojourners: the Index of Sojourner Social Support (ISSS) Scale' *Journal of Cross-Cultural Psychology*, 36(6), 637–61.

Robbins, S. B., K. Lauver, H. Le, D. Davis, R. Langley and A. Carlstrom (2004), 'Do psychosocial and study skill factors predict college outcomes? A meta-analysis', *Psychological Bulletin*, 130(2), 261–88.

Ryan, M. E., and R. S. Twibell (2000), 'Concerns, values, stress, coping, health and educational outcomes of college students who studied abroad', *International Journal of Intercultural Relations*, 24, 409–35.

Spencer-Oatey, H., and D. Dauber (2017), 'The gains and pains of mixed national group work at university', *Journal of Multilingual and Multicultural Development*, 38(3), 219–36.

Spencer-Oatey, H., and Z. Xiong (2006), 'Chinese students' psychological and sociocultural adjustments to Britain: an empirical study', *Language, Culture and Curriculum*, 19(1), 38–53.

Stoynoff, S. (1997), 'Factors associated with international students' academic achievement', *Journal of Instructional Psychology*, 24(1), 56–68.

van Oudenhoven, J. P., and K. I. van der Zee (2002), 'Predicting multicultural effectiveness of international students: the Multicultural Personality Questionnaire', *International Journal of Intercultural Relations*, 26(6), 679–94.

Ward, C., S. Bochner and A. Furnham (2001), *The Psychology of Culture Shock*, 2nd edn, Hove: Routledge.

Young, T. J., and A. Schartner (2014), 'The effects of cross-cultural communication education on international students' adjustment and adaptation', *Journal of Multilingual and Multicultural Development*, 35(6), 547–62.

Young, T. J., P. G. Sercombe, I. Sachdev, R. Naeb and A. Schartner (2013), 'Success factors for international postgraduate students' adjustment: exploring the roles of intercultural competence, language proficiency, social contact and social support', *European Journal of Higher Education*, 3, 151–71.

# 5

# PSYCHOLOGICAL ADJUSTMENT AND ADAPTATION

In this chapter, we present and integrate interview and survey-based data related to the psychological adjustment and adaptation of ISs. For this conceptual domain, our focus was on students' psychological adjustment over time, as well as on the outcomes of these processes, self-rated, using two indicators: psychological wellbeing (PWB) and satisfaction with life (SWL). These two indicators are commonly distinguished when used to measure sojourners' psychological responses to the host environment (Ward et al. 2004), and it was hoped that bringing them together would give a fuller and more rounded picture of our student participants' psychological adaptation to life and study in the new environment.

The following research questions are addressed in this chapter:

1. What are the dynamics and patterns of student sojourners' psychological adjustment over time?
2. How do English language ability, knowledge about the host country, prior overseas experience, autonomy in the decision to study abroad, intercultural competence, social contact and social support relate to psychological adaptation?

Below, we first present descriptive data related to the two psychological adaptation measures (5.1). We then detail qualitative findings and representative data from each interview stage and responses to the open survey questions in order to address research question 1, above (5.2). We then explore associations between the quantitative data relating to the relationships between a range of contributory factors and the outcome variables, to address research question 2 (5.3). We end the chapter with a brief conclusion that summarises and integrates our findings in respect of psychological adjustment and adaptation (5.4).

## 5.1 DESCRIPTIVE STATISTICS OF PSYCHOLOGICAL ADAPTATION

As noted above, psychological adaptation was conceptualised and measured in terms of PWB and SWL. As with English language ability (ELA), intercultural competence (IC) and knowledge about the host society (the UK, KNW), these two measures were included in both the Time 1 and Time 2 surveys to monitor changes in individuals

Table 5.1 Descriptive statistics for psychological wellbeing and satisfaction with life

| Variables | M | SD | Min. | Max. | α |
|---|---|---|---|---|---|
| PWB Time 1 | 3.60 | .61 | 1.55 | 5.00 | .86 |
| PWB Time 2 | 3.54 | .55 | 1.82 | 4.91 | .86 |
| SWL Time 1 | 3.46 | .66 | 1.80 | 5.00 | .87 |
| SWL Time 2 | 3.48 | .77 | 1.60 | 5.00 | .87 |

Note: M = mean; PWB = psychological wellbeing; SD = standard deviation; SWL = satisfaction with life.

Table 5.2 Distribution of scores on the Satisfaction with Life Scale (SWLS)

| Score on the SWLS | Frequency | Percentage |
|---|---|---|
| 21–25 (extremely satisfied) | 30 | 21.4% |
| 16–20 (satisfied) | 67 | 46.5% |
| 15 (average) | 7 | 4.9% |
| 10–14 (dissatisfied) | 36 | 25.1% |
| 5–9 (extremely dissatisfied) | 3 | 2.1% |

Table 5.3 Interviewees' psychological wellbeing and satisfaction with life scores over time

| Variables | N | M | SD | Min. | Max. |
|---|---|---|---|---|---|
| PWB Time 1 | 16 | 3.57 | .51 | 2.73 | 4.45 |
| PWB Time 2 | 20 | 3.61 | .55 | 2.63 | 4.81 |
| PWB Time 3 | 20 | 3.59 | .53 | 2.55 | 4.27 |
| SWL Time 1 | 16 | 3.59 | .45 | 2.60 | 4.20 |
| SWL Time 2 | 20 | 3.77 | .71 | 1.80 | 4.80 |
| SWL Time 3 | 20 | 3.69 | .60 | 2.20 | 4.80 |

Note: M = mean; N = number; PWB = psychological wellbeing; SD = standard deviation; SWL = satisfaction with life.

over time. Table 5.1 displays descriptive statistics for PWB and SWL. An important finding was that we found no statistically significant differences for the mean scores between Time 1 and Time 2 for the group as a whole.

Scores from Diener and colleagues' (1985) Satisfaction with Life Scale (SWLS) can range from 5 to 25. The distribution of scores for the respondents is shown in Table 5.2. The majority of students were either 'satisfied' or 'extremely satisfied' with their life in the host environment at Time 2, indicating that 'life is enjoyable and the major domains of life are going well' (Diener 2006: 1).

The interviewees completed measures for PWB and SWL at all three interview rounds. Table 5.3 displays the relevant descriptive statistics. Paired-sample t-tests showed that differences in mean scores over time were not statistically significant, indicating that PWB and SWL remained relatively stable over time. As we will see in Section 5.2 below, the interview findings did provide considerably more detail and, perhaps, a more nuanced perspective on this.

There was a significant correlation between SWL and PWB ($r = .49$, $p < .01$), which is not uncommon (cf. Lewthwaite 1996). This correlation provides evidence that students who feel happy are also likely to exhibit greater lifer satisfaction. This is perhaps not surprising but none the less provides useful confirmatory evidence of the relationships between these factors.

In sum, scores for PWB and SWL at Time 2 were generally high, indicating that, overall, students were happy and satisfied with life in the host environment. Mean scores were slightly higher than in a comparable previous sample of student sojourners in the UK (cf. Young et al. 2013), although Young and colleagues (2013) took the measure mid-sojourn when students were perhaps less well adjusted. The data also revealed that two demographic variables were significantly associated with psychological adaptation. Independent-samples t-tests also showed that the MA ALT students reported lower SWL scores (M = 3.25, SD = .71) than the MA CCC students (M = 3.55, SD = .77), $t(141) = 2.01$, $p = .046$). It may be possible that the explicit intercultural training that the CCC students received might have aided their adjustment to life and study in the UK and could have resulted in higher SWL scores (Young and Schartner 2014), or that perhaps these students were already predisposed towards better adjustment, given their choice of programme. Finally, it was noteworthy that those students who had undertaken English language pre-sessional courses at the host university reported lower SWL scores (M = 3.27, SD = .72) than students who had not needed such language development support (M = 3.55, SD = .78), $t(132) = -2.04$, $p = .043$, indicating an association between host language ability prior to the programme commencing and later SWL in the new environment. As we will see (and have seen), this link between language, adjustment and adaptation is a persistent theme rising out of our investigations.

## 5.2 PSYCHOLOGICAL ADJUSTMENT OVER TIME

To give a clearer idea of the adjustment trajectories of our student participants, qualitative data here are presented in relation to different stages of their sojourn in roughly chronological order. Firstly, we summarise and give representative examples of the pre-arrival stage (5.2.1), then of the first few weeks in the UK (5.2.2), then five months into the one-year programmes (5.2.3), and then nine months into these one-year programmes (5.2.4). This is followed with a brief discussion about the psychological adjustment of our participants over time (5.2.5) before we end this section with a conclusion and a summary response to research question 1 (5.2.6).

### 5.2.1 PRE-ARRIVAL

The majority of comments on students' own wellbeing in the pre-arrival stage was of a 'problematising' or 'negative' nature related to our analytical framework. None the less, there was considerable variation among participants, and individual accounts of the pre-arrival stage ranged from the highly positive to the highly negative. The nature and intensity of emotions experienced before leaving home varied greatly by individual. Some students reported feeling at ease and 'ready' to start a new chapter in their lives:

> I was already ready to leave my country, so practically I was partying a lot, doing a lot of parties with my friends and everything and just telling everyone that I would never come back and stay in Europe forever. (Mexican student, male)
> I was ready to go. (Finnish student, female)
> I think I was really excited, I don't think I was nervous or anxious or anything like that. (US student, female)

Others felt overwhelmed by the prospects of leaving home:

> It felt like 'Ok, I'm leaving' and then 'Oh my God, I'm gonna leave this country and it's gonna be so far away' and then it felt even worse. I felt even more sad when I got my visa. (Indonesian student, female)

Most students described the weeks leading up to departure from home as a time of mixed emotions. The following words were used by interviewees in the first interview round to describe feelings about departure from the home country: 'stressed', 'excited', 'anxious', 'unreal', 'scared', 'nervous' and 'depressing'. The vocabulary used by interviewees pointed to a jittery and unsettled state of mind as a number of interviewees reported being 'torn' between feelings of excitement and anxiety:

> [...] anxiety if I was making the right decision but also excited because of the possibilities that could lie ahead. (US student, male)
> [...] I was quite scared but at the same time I was really excited [...] (Italian student, female)
> I was very nervous and very anxious but excited as well. (German student, female)

The organisational and administrative aspects of preparing for study abroad put some students under stress: in particular, issues related to visa procedures and English language requirements, as illustrated below.

> The visa procedure took my most of time and the packing. It was a bit rush so I don't want to remember that. (Turkish student, male)
> I have to have 7 on my IELTS. It took me three times to get 7. (Indonesian student, female)
> My situation was quite complex because I came short 0.5 points in the writing section in IELTS. I had to retake it and just all the documents I had to send. It was very urgent. I was in a rush really. (Lithuanian student, male)

For others, financial concerns about tuition fees and living costs emerged as a significant stress factor:

> I'm paying the international fee and I'm paying it from my personal savings and it's unbelievable. This amount is unbelievable and that's nothing about the other costs here with the accommodation and with the pocket money. (Turkish student, female)

The data also indicated that the prospects of losing familiar social support systems seemed to have a great impact on students' wellbeing in the pre-arrival stage, in particular as departure drew closer. Saying goodbye to family members and friends at the airport was a difficult moment for most participants:

> When I was at the airport in Romania I started crying when I left my parents [...] I think it was the only moment when I was thinking 'Why do I want to do this?' (Romanian student, female)
>
> [...] actually leaving Malaysia was very hard. I mean I was on board and I was crying, so it was difficult. (Malaysian student, female)
>
> [...] when I had to say goodbye to my father it was really hard, then waiting to get on the plane my phone kept ringing and my friends were trying to say goodbye once more even though we already said goodbye and that made it harder for me [...] (Romanian student, female)

However, in some cases, it was the parents who struggled most to cope with the departure of their children:

> Whenever I saw my mum's face she was about to cry. (Turkish student, female)
>
> It was difficult to say goodbye to my mum. She was very worried before I actually got on the plane. (Latvian student, female)

Most students in the sample travelled to the UK by themselves, and some, especially those who travelled long distances, described their journey to the UK as 'lonely' and 'sad':

> I arrived in Dubai and it's little bit lonely because I don't have any friends [...] I just went to the mosque and I pray. (Indonesian student, female)
>
> [...] I felt so sad. I cried on the plane because I was alone. I heard that some students from Indonesia they came here with their friends, other students probably, but I was alone. (Indonesian student, female)

Finally, some interviewees worried that their religious background might provoke negative reactions on the part of the host society:

> [...] sometimes I think that because of Islamophobia they may be irritated [...] (Turkish student, male)
>
> I was quite worried [...] after the whole 9/11 thing because I am a Muslim so people back home always say 'Are you sure, you want to go all the way there and

> study because you know how they treat you guys over there' [...] (Malaysian student, female)

However, students who had concerns about discrimination and adverse reactions also commented positively on its absence while in the UK:

> [...] when I say I don't eat pork, they never show a kind of negative reaction. (Turkish student, male)
> [...] we can't generalise because you won't know it until you go and actually experience it and yeah I mean Newcastle has been really, really kind to me, thank God. (Malaysian student, female)

### 5.2.2 THE FIRST FEW WEEKS IN THE UK (TIME 1)

Overall, the data related to students' first few weeks in the UK indicated that participants experienced a range of emotions concerning the academic and sociocultural environment they were experiencing for the first time and the familiar world they had left behind. Although 'negative' and 'problematising' comments dominated in the first interview round, a number of students also showed a positive orientation towards their own psychological adjustment and seemed optimistic and upbeat about their ability to cope with academic demands and day-to-day life in the UK. Previous travel experience, strong motivation to study in the UK, intrinsic attraction to the UK, and personal attitude towards the sojourn combined to alleviate nervousness:

> I was quite scared but the thing is that I've already had an experience abroad on my own in a country. (Italian student, female)
> I think I'll do just fine because I'm a very optimistic person. (Romanian student, female)
> I am always happy when I am in the UK (Turkish student, female)
> [...] wanting to actually be in this kind of environment and country it sort of pushes me to try to do well, try to be OK, try to fit in and everything. (Malaysian student, female)

One student from the USA attributed her lack of nervousness to the forethought and planning she had put into the sojourn:

> [...] I knew this is something I really wanted to do. This wasn't like an emotional decision where I just decided to go study abroad. I started this process back in January, so I think I had emotionally, physically, mentally prepared myself for a long time for it.

She felt psychologically ready to enter the new environment, which also contributed to a confident and positive outlook. Pre-arrival preparation and the acquisition of information and knowledge about the new environment in advance helped to reduce anxiety and increase confidence among participants. Students prepared for their sojourn in a number of ways. One Romanian student, for example, watched films about the host city to familiarise herself with the new environment in advance:

> […] I was trying to build up in my mind an enthusiasm for leaving so I was looking for movies about [*name of host city*]

Others prepared for the academic aspect of their sojourn, although these efforts were often restricted to researching course requirements and professors on the internet:

> I researched the different professors that were in the programme here, so I kind of read up on them a little bit, read what the expectations were […] (US student, female)

On the whole, only few students prepared specifically for their studies prior to departure from home:

> I did some research concerning the university and what I'm going to study. I saw the pre-reading list but I didn't read any book from it. (Romanian student, female)
> […] I don't have anything prepare about my studies […] I don't know what kind of teaching style here so I didn't prepare anything about study. (Indonesian student, female)

Two Chinese interviewees attended a six-week pre-sessional English language course at the host university prior to the start of their degree programme. Both students pointed to a lack of confidence in their own English language abilities at Time 1 despite undergoing this training:

> I don't know how to conquer barriers about language […] it's hard for me to communicate with other people. (Chinese student, female)
> […] I'm not very confident about my English. (Chinese student, female)

With some exceptions, students prepared in largely practical manners for their sojourn: packing, organising travel and making visa arrangements, looking up information about the host city and university on the internet, and buying warm clothes for the 'cold' British weather dominated the pre-departure preparations.

Overall, the main topics of concern to the students, in rough order of frequency, were: English language difficulties, loneliness and homesickness, the weather, financial concerns, future career prospects and loss/lack of familial support. In the first interview round, there was a relatively high level of concern in the interviewee group over the twin needs of having to cope in an English-speaking environment and having to meet the demands of the degree programme. Findings indicated a link between foreign language use and feelings of anxiety and nervousness. A number of interviewees felt that language proficiency would affect their ability to cope with the demands of their course, including following lectures, academic reading, classroom discussions and assessed written work:

> It's hard for me to read or to listen to the teacher to get information [...] (Chinese student, female)
> All the books are in English and everybody speaks English so well, I'm gonna have to catch up with it. (Indonesian student, female)

The academic demands of the degree programme were a source of great concern for some interviewees, who felt they were inadequately prepared for the essay-based nature of their course. Fear of failure was preoccupying during the first interview round, with the importance of academic progress and success reflected in a number of comments:

> I will just probably have to kind of do the work that I can do and not think about failing because that's something that I fear, and I know that I'm not gonna fail because I always push myself but it's just this irrational fear. (Finnish student, female)
> I am worried about not being able to complete the programme because otherwise when you come back to Turkey, like you have to pay for the money, that's the problem. So I am a little bit under stress that I should complete it successfully. (Turkish student, male)
> I'm hoping to get really, really, really good marks for all the assignments and everything. (Malaysian student, female)

A number of students felt that their English language competence might have an impact on their ability to navigate day-do-day life in host environment. Participants who were second-language users of English expressed concern about their ability to communicate with British people and 'native speakers' in general. Interviewees reported feeling 'nervous', 'stressed' and 'scared' about using English on a daily basis, and some perceived their English language ability as inadequate, pointing to a lack of confidence in their own abilities:

> I don't have enough confidence in myself because I think my English is still not good enough for communicate. (Indonesian student, female)

Negotiation of everyday communication episodes was a cause for concern for a number of interviewees: in particular, interactions with British people. One student from Turkey, for example, was preoccupied with a sense that his behaviour might be inappropriate in interactions with host nationals, and felt that he lacked the knowledge to interpret social cues of the host community. He was also concerned about understanding British accents:

> I have sometimes difficulty in understanding other accents, including British accent. That's the basic concern for me. This is the most different. Sometimes I

> don't know how to react or how to behave in certain situations so I hope I will learn. (Turkish student, male)

The social implications of not being able to communicate effectively in English were also emphasised by other interviewees, who felt that their English language ability might impact negatively on relationship formation with British people on campus and in the wider community:

> I sometimes get very nervous and I don't have intonation [...] sometimes I speak very in a dull way so I am sometimes worried about this because I may seem a boring person. (Turkish student, male)

Some students were conscious that language ability would affect their ability to adjust to the new environment:

> If I can conquer the barriers of language, maybe everything will be easier than before. (Chinese student, female)

Confidence and concern over language ability varied considerably in the interviewee sample. Some interviewees did not express any concern about English language ability, but rather pointed to the 'exciting' opportunity of studying in English and reported feeling at ease about this:

> I'm excited about the opportunity to study [...] in English. It's a new thing for me. (Romanian student, female)
> [...] I think that I can speak English fluently and have no problems at all. (Turkish student, female)
> [...] everything is in English, but I think I will have the ability to do it. (Romanian student, female)

Missing home was a common theme emerging from conversation with interviewees, who repeatedly described the first few days in the new environment as, in some way, 'difficult'. Instances of problems with sleeping and with homesickness seemed to occur frequently in the initial sojourn stage, particularly during the very first night spent in the UK:

> [...] at night I'm very homesick because it's the first night I spent here. (Chinese student, female)
> I was still jetlagged, so I would sleep around 7pm, but then I would wake up at 3 or 4am in the morning. It's still dark and nobody was awake. (Indonesian student, female)
> The night was pretty rough just because I couldn't sleep and I was like 'Man, what am I doing?' I think that was probably the worst I had as far as homesickness. (US student, male)

With no access to the support structures enjoyed at home, some students turned to 'virtual' support via online communication tools such as Skype:

> [...] I couldn't sleep. I just called my mother and my boyfriend and I cried. I just couldn't sleep and I just slept maybe two hours. (Indonesian student, female)
>
> I made phone calls all the time to my family member, to my friends and busy with connect to the computer because I want to go to ... send e-mails [...] (Chinese student, female)

For some students, homesickness was compounded by feelings of isolation and loneliness:

> [...] when I went to bed I always felt that I was in a plane or [...] in a stranger's house because this was my own house and I was just like by myself and nobody in the house, nothing. (Turkish student, female)
>
> And then the first one month I was here, I was really homesick [...] I was just feeling lonely in my room, 'Oh my God, I'm so far away!' (Indonesian student, female)

Initial experiences of homesickness and isolation were profound enough for some students to lead them to contemplate returning home. Students recalled thinking 'one year is just too long' (Indonesian student, female) and 'I want to buy a ticket tomorrow and go back' (Chinese student, male). Shortly after arrival in the UK, one student from Turkey packed her bags and was ready to cut her sojourn short:

> I was always on the telephone saying that I want to go back for sure, and I even once I packed my stuff and went to the airport.

Despite some initial distress, all interviewees emphasised that their wellbeing improved rapidly once classes had started and they had the opportunity to interact with their peers. This highlights the crucial role of social ties and social support for psychological adjustment, a point we will return to often, below.

A number of students commented on the importance of a family support system for PWB. The temporary loss of this support network caused some students to feel 'sad', 'concerned' or 'nervous'. Feelings of homesickness seemed particularly strong among those whose dependents at home were a source of concern – students who had left partners and children in their home countries seemed to struggle with the loss of a close family unit:

> Currently my wife and children are still in the US. This has led to a great deal more sadness in my life than is usual. (Student from the US, male, Time 1 survey)
>
> I am mindful of my husband, children and business in Barbados and concerned that everything remains well in my absence. (Student from Barbados, female, Time 1 survey)

Given that the postgraduate student population is typically older than the undergraduate student body, it is perhaps not surprising that several participants were married with children, and that concern about those left behind was a common theme for these students. One student reported that her family had not supported her decision to undertake postgraduate study abroad.

> My family did not support me coming to England for my master's. They were upset that I was 'leaving them' and felt like I could get a fine job in the USA without a master's. I worry that when I graduate I will not be able to get a job and they'll say I told you so. (Student from the USA, female, Time 1 survey)

A further topic of concern was the climate in the host country. Comments about the 'cold' and 'rainy' British weather were common across the sample but especially salient to those from places with warmer climates:

> The snow, I've never lived in the snow [...] I've never had to walk in it [...] that's probably the only thing that I'm nervous about, being cold. (US student, female)
> [...] when I arrived at the accommodation it was raining and I was thinking 'Oh, did I make the right decision to come to a really rainy place?' because I'm a person that is very fond of summer. (Romanian student, female)

The next concerns for students were related to the costly nature of an academic sojourn. References to costs associated with an academic sojourn were common right across the sample and a number of students reported feeling anxious about their finances and expenses:

> My savings are going to be finished in about January. (Slovakian student, female)
> I'm also worried about budgeting my money; make sure that I'm going to be successful with that. (US student, male)
> If only I didn't have to pay for my flat instalment. (Student from Macau, male, Time 1 survey)

Some students emphasised the importance of finding part-time work in order to cope with the financial implications of study abroad:

> I very much hope I will get a part-time job, not to cover all my expenses but some of them, and I think this is a goal for me but also I'm a little bit worried that it might not happen. (Romanian student, female)

Next, several interviewees expressed concerns about future career prospects. Students' comments related largely to the ability to re-enter the job market successfully and to build a career along the desired path:

> I'm nervous about landing a career after I'm finished. (US student, male)
> At the moment I'm a bit scared to enter the job market [...] I just hope that I will be really prepared for the job market. (German student, female)
> I'm worried that maybe I finish my degree and graduate and I will just have to go back home and not get this job and not travel a lot. (Latvian student, female)

One interviewee felt 'nervous' about the UK visa policy and felt that his plans to find work in the UK after completion of his master's degree were threatened by current immigration policy:

> There are difference between the European students and the international students. I don't want to immigrate but I want to stay here a little longer because maybe one year and a half is a little short. This is what I'm a little worried about. (Chinese student, male)

This student from China belonged to a cohort of students who could not qualify for a so-called post-study work visa, as the UK government had abolished this arrangement in the previous year. It had previously been possible for overseas graduates of British universities to work in the UK for up to two years upon completion of their studies.

Two further issues with potential implications for PWB were problematised by the students: living arrangements in the host country and mid-sojourn visits to the home country. Some students felt that mid-sojourn visits to their home countries might impact negatively on their wellbeing and could 'interrupt' their psychological adjustment:

> I feel that if I go home for a month, like if I went home for Christmas and in March for a month that would screw me. Going home and then I've comforted there for a month and then either missing here or not wanting to come back [...] I just don't wanna mess with where I'm at too much and the adjustment. (US student, male)

Despite these concerns, this student did eventually return to the USA for Christmas and Easter. Furthermore, the nature of living arrangements in the UK seemed to be crucial for students' wellbeing, as the account below exemplifies. This was the only student in the sample who lived by herself. In the first interview, she explained that 'personal space is my luxury', and felt that she needed a quiet environment in order to keep up with the demands of postgraduate study. None the less, she highlighted the disadvantages of living alone and seemed to struggle to cope with living by herself:

> It's a little bit hard because I have started to speak with the mirror and with the walls sometimes because I am not used to this. (Turkish student, female)

She attempted to compensate for this lack of company through 'virtual' contact with friends and family in her home country, Turkey:

> […] the technology is really good nowadays with the Skype and all of these telephone cheap calls. Whenever I want, I can call my family or my friends and it's not that much far away.

The importance of 'virtual' social media contact with home was also emphasised by other interviewees and was seen as crucial for PWB. For example, one student from the USA felt that daily e-contact with her family in California enabled her to 'feel part of their lives' and sharing her experienced with family members helped her to adjust to the new surroundings:

> I talk to my family every single day for probably three hours a day, so I think that is a big push for me because they know exactly everything that's going on with me day to day, and I know exactly what's going on with my family day to day […] I'm so close to them and so … adapting and adjusting has been fine […]

Others also highlighted the importance of close interpersonal relationships for PWB. In particular, partners living in the UK were identified as a reliable and crucial source for emotional support:

> I have a lot of support of him [the boyfriend] and obviously my friend is living with me, so I think I'll be fine with that background. (German student, female)
>
> I think I'll do fine because I have a close relationship with my parents and we talk on Skype daily and also my boyfriend lives quite close […] (Romanian student, female)

As noted above, feelings of excitement were present in the initial sojourn stage and a number of interviewees showed a positive orientation towards their own psychological adjustment. None the less, positive feelings of initial excitement seemed to be outweighed by more negative experiences of stress, anxiety, homesickness and loneliness for a majority of our participants.

It seems clear that transition acted as a trigger for stress for most participants, and the data revealed a general trend of insecurity and decreased emotional stability in the initial sojourn stage. The weeks before departure from home were generally described as a time of mixed emotions, as students were torn between feelings of excitement and anxiety. The first few days in the new environment were experienced as difficult by many participants, especially the first night, which was characterised for some by difficulties sleeping and a longing for home. However, it must be noted that transition was not a uniform experience, as students differed in their experience of initial acculturative stress. Some felt at ease during the pre-arrival stage and the first few weeks in the host country, and demonstrated a confident and optimistic outlook at Time 1, while others were overwhelmed by the experience of leaving home and entering an unfamiliar environment.

To summarise, as we note above, key issues of concern identified by the students in the first data-collection stage included English language difficulties, the weather

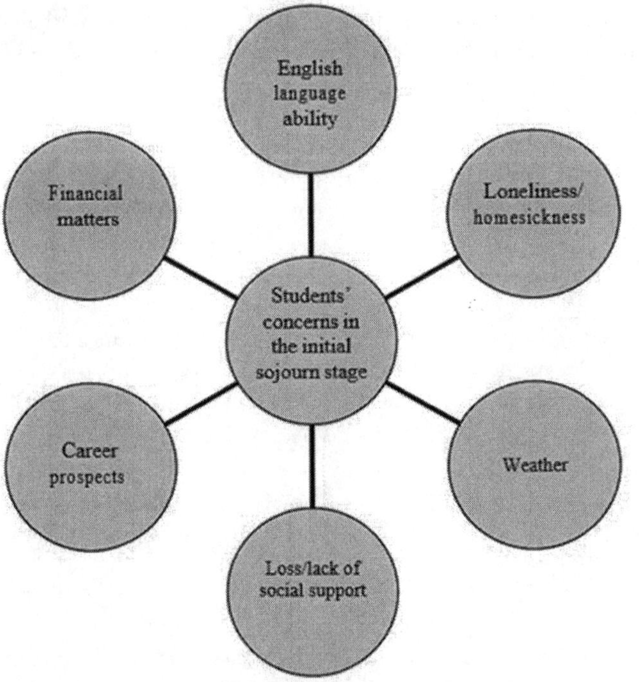


*Figure 5.1 Students' concerns in the initial sojourn stage*

in the UK, costs associated with the sojourn, career prospects and loss/lack of familial support. The importance of interpersonal relationships for PWB and the crucial role of 'virtual' contact with home were highlighted by a number of students. Participants' accounts of their experiences in the initial sojourn stage are captured in Figure 5.1.

### 5.2.3 FIVE MONTHS INTO THE PROGRAMME (TIME 2)

The second interview round took place when students were five months into the programme. Overall, there was little comment on PWB at Time 2 but, on the whole, students seemed to feel better five months into the sojourn compared to the first few weeks in the UK, confirmed by the more frequent use of positively connoted words such as 'happy', 'nice' and 'good' across the sample. After some initial acculturative stress during the early stage of the sojourn, many students demonstrated a more relaxed demeanour during the second interview round, reporting increased confidence and satisfaction with their life in the UK:

> I've been feeling good about myself, bit more confident than before coming here. I started to get used to living alone because this was a first for me and I was a bit

> anxious in the beginning but now I feel good, I don't know, I've been feeling like this is right for me [...] (Romanian student, female)
> Didn't think I would be as ok as I am being away from home for this long, but I'm totally fine. (US student, female)
> It took some physical and mental maybe some efforts but now I feel that I'm already, like, where I have to be. (Lithuanian student, male)

Overall, homesickness seemed to be most intense in the initial sojourn stage (as suggested in many models of sojourner adjustment) and diminished over time as students formed a network of friends among their peer group. None the less, at significant times – for example, at night, at Christmas and during busy assessment periods – a longing for home tended to resurface and intensify for some participants:

> Sometimes it is a little bit difficult, especially at night because I miss my friends and family from home. It gets a little bit lonely but not too much. (Latvian student, female)
> I have friends there, so I spent Christmas with them. It was nice, it was very nice but yeah I think it was the first time I really missed the family atmosphere, I don't know, the traditions and the meals. (Romanian student, female)
> I think the more time you have to think, the more homesick you can get, so I've been trying to keep myself as busy as I can. (US student, male)

Although there was some initial doubt about the implications of mid-sojourn home visits for psychological adjustment (as noted in the section above), trips to the home country during the Christmas vacation seemed to have a positive effect on student wellbeing in some cases:

> It's a short break but I think I needed it. (Malaysian student, female)
> I thought that it would be better to go back and see my family [...] I just wanted to relax with my family who looks after me and cooks and, you know, nice house, nice people and I just relaxed. (Turkish student, female)
> I went home to see my family and that was really nice. I think I missed my family a lot, so that was a nice like step in between. (German student, female)
> [...] I was able to go home for a month which was really great because I got to share my experiences back home, and then you know get that sense of home and family and everything, and kind of rejuvenate me for the next six, eight months. (US student, female)

By the second interview round, most students had formed stable friendships with their peers, and a number of interviewees commented positively on the support generated by these newly formed relationships:

> They are very supportive, I don't know, we talk all the time and try to give advice about anything. Advice about, I don't know, school projects, advice about places to go and where to go, events. (Romanian student, female)

> Turkish friends, like we come together, we are from the same scholarship, so we have the same problems, so we sometimes talk about it. And academic support, we always talk about my department friends. (Turkish student, male)

The majority of 'negative' and 'problematising' comments at Time 2 were related to academic aspects of the sojourn in the UK, as students had experienced the intensive assignment schedule typical of a British one-year master's programme. Although students seemed generally to cope reasonably well with the demands of academic writing, it was experienced as a time-consuming and stressful process, indicating a link between emotional wellbeing and academic workload (see Chapter 7):

> [...] most of the things were written assignment in the first semester, so you had to do a lot and it was your first semester. It made me depressive. (Turkish student, female)
>
> I also had the pressure of writing all the assignments [...] it really wasn't that good I guess. (Latvian student, female)

At Time 2, participants were anxiously awaiting their first feedback on assessed work, so this was an issue of great importance to them and generated a number of comments in the interviews. Many interviewees seemed to feel insecure about their academic performance, illustrated in the use of words such as 'stressed out', 'worried' and 'nervous':

> I was stressing out a bit 'cause I didn't really know, and still don't know how well I'm doing in my assessments [...] I don't know what exactly the lecturers expect in my assignments, so I guess I was kind of nervous and felt a bit under pressure about writing my essays because cause I was never sure if it will be good enough or not. (German student, female)
>
> It's between happy and also a little bit worried about my marks I guess. So it's a mix of lots of feelings. (Indonesian student, female)
>
> Feeling nervous of my result. You know the first time I came I wanted to become, like make my parents proud of me and wanna become like excellent (Indonesian student, female)

Apart from the academic aspects of study abroad, the cold weather during the winter months remained a dominant topic of conversation and some students pointed to the implications of the 'depressing' British weather for their psychological and physical wellbeing:

> [...] the weather is a problem. Yeah, I was frustrated, depressed, angry and at the same time, yeah I mean, weather was making me very, very depressive because in the mornings, I mean it's nine o' clock, it's dark, three o' clock, it's dark and because I come from, like, a place which is always sunny, first it affected me a lot. (Turkish student, female)

Future job prospects equally remained a source of concern for several participants. Students were conscious that the MA degree alone would not guarantee successful entry into the job market, and part-time work and internships were becoming an increasingly pressing priority for students by Time 2:

> I have to start working or, I don't know, do something so that's basically my main issue [...] (Slovakian student, female)
>
> I want to find some opportunities to like volunteer or internship, so this is the most difficult for me because I should write my CV and you know the competition is very fierce because I want to grasp every chance to improve. (Chinese student, male)

Despite the generally positive tenor of comment on psychological adjustment at Time 2, some interviewees experienced feelings of loneliness and homesickness, especially during the Christmas period. The main topic of salience for students' wellbeing at Time 2 was a sense of academic achievement. Students experienced the busy assignment period as 'stressful' and 'depressing', and were anxiously awaiting their first feedback on assessed work.

### 5.2.4 NINE MONTHS INTO THE PROGRAMME (TIME 3)

By Time 3, students were nine months into their programme and were thus able to reflect on their own adjustment trajectories over a time encompassing all of the taught element, and much of the research element, of their programmes. From the students' accounts, two key findings emerged. Firstly, it was impressed on us strongly that there was no such thing as *the* IS psychological experience. Participants experienced cross-cultural transition in distinct and nuanced ways, demonstrating the complexity of reactions to an IS sojourn, and the individuality and distinctiveness of the general experience. Some students described their sojourn as 'wavy' (Slovakian student, female) and as a period of 'ups and downs' (Romanian student, female), while others reflected more positively on their overall sense of wellbeing.

> [...] I thought I would have more trouble kind of being away [from home]. (US student, male)

Secondly, despite considerable variation between individuals, a general trend for psychological adjustment could nevertheless be discerned from the data. Students' accounts of their experiences and wellbeing throughout the sojourn strongly suggest that, very commonly, the initial sojourn stage was a time of stress, anxiety and nervousness. Feelings of loneliness and homesickness were greatest during this time, as students had to cope with the loss of familiar support systems and had only limited meaningful relationships in the UK:

> I think at the very beginning it was the greatest shock because obviously you don't have anyone at the very beginning, your support system is not built up yet and everything is new. (US student, female)

As the sojourn progressed, students' wellbeing generally seemed to improve, as they were able to build a supportive network of friends and got used to life and study in the UK:

> I didn't really have any like psychological or like real intense adjustment or like loss of social support network issues because I think you develop friendships here that replace your social support network so I think that was a big help with my adjustment. (US student, male)
> […] I started to go to class and then I meet many people and then I just started to adapt to the people, to the environment and everything. (Indonesian student, female)

By Time 2, instances of homesickness had become considerably less frequent, and by Time 3, they had disappeared altogether. On the whole, it seemed that the longer students were exposed to the new environment, the happier they felt:

> When I arrived in October I was so scared but I feel much more self- confident now and happier in general. (Italian student, female, Time 2 survey)
> […] if I scale 1–10, now it's like 7, 8 compared to 2 or 3 the first time I came here. (Indonesian student, female)
> […] it was a big difference between the beginning and the end because as you get used to, you feel different. When you come you are very quite sensitive, more sensitive. (Lithuanian student, male)

The data provided little evidence for a U-curve trajectory (Lysgaard 1955) with a 'honeymoon' stage of early euphoria (Oberg 1960), although some interviewees described the early stages of their sojourn as 'exciting', 'interesting' and 'new':

> To begin with, the first months when I was very happy because everything was so interesting and new. New people, new places. Also I had a lot of energy. (Romanian student, female)
> […] initially it was really nice because it was a very different city and we like hanged around a lot. (Turkish student, male)

Findings also suggest that although students' psychological adjustment improved as time progressed, their overall wellbeing remained variable and was, at times, influenced by factors as varied as the weather or the demands of postgraduate study. A number of interviewees reported difficulties with adjusting to the weather and repeatedly described it as 'depressing':

> The first like two, three months I was really thinking about turning back but I now know the reason. It was not because I hated the school or the culture, it was because of the weather […] it was raining, raining and I just felt like just shouting at someone or doing nothing because the weather affects me a lot. (Turkish student, female)

> Maybe go to somewhere sunny otherwise you will be depressed. (Turkish student, male)

There was strong evidence for a link between academic aspects of study abroad and PWB. Busy assessment periods seemed to have an impact on students' wellbeing throughout the course of the sojourn and a number of interviewees repeatedly described these time periods as 'depressing' and 'stressful':

> [...] Christmas and January with assignment period, it was like a low period that I had. Not a bad mood but I got a little bit depressive. I don't know, maybe because I didn't go home, maybe because I was so busy with the assignments, so it was like a darker period. (Romanian student, female)
> I'm a bit stressed with the exams and the assignments because they are all concentrated in this month mainly, so yeah it's a very intense period of my life. (Romanian student, female)

Nonetheless, most students did report relatively steady academic adjustment (see Chapter 3, above), which also seemed to reflect positively on their PWB. Over time, students reported feeling 'less stressed' and 'more comfortable' with academic study in the UK:

> I would say that at the beginning I panicked with uni work so I was really stressed but then things got better so under that aspect. (Italian student female)
> I was very worried about studies in the beginning but I kind of feel rather comfortable with it now or confident. (Latvian student, female)

Students were also more anxious, as they were waiting for feedback on assessed work, and some interviewees reported 'feeling better' once they had received input from assessors:

> It's torturing me that the grades are taking so long. (German student, female)
> After I know the exam result I feel much better. (Chinese student, female)

Future career prospects were a source of concern for students throughout their sojourn, but towards the end of their time in the UK some students appeared particularly anxious about the future:

> [...] one of the things that have made me a bit worried is the fact that I'm not sure what's gonna happen [...] in the long term I have so many uncertainties and this sometimes has caused me a bit of a trouble [...] (Romanian student, female)

As their time abroad drew to a close, students also seemed to feel increasingly 'sad' about leaving the UK and the friends they had made there. Reflecting on her state of mind in the last few weeks of her sojourn, one student from Finland reported feeling 'nostalgic about the year and sad to leave friends'.

### 5.2.5 PSYCHOLOGICAL ADJUSTMENT OVER TIME

Given the range of sojourner literature on 'culture shock' (e.g. Ward et al. 2001) and the popularity of associated models such as the U-curve (Lysgaard 1955), it might be expected that ISs experience high levels of anxiety and stress. A look at the earlier literature does indeed paint a rather bleaker picture of student sojourners' physical and mental health than the one we found. In a 1967 paper, L. Ward argued for the existence of a 'foreign-student syndrome', characterised by depression, vague physical symptoms and a withdrawn interaction style (cited in Furnham 2004). Similarly, a 1992 study by Janca and Helzer reported severe psychological breakdowns among ISs in the former Yugoslavia, characterised by paranoia and depression, symptoms that the researchers took as evidence for 'maladaptation to the new living conditions' (Janca and Helzer 1992: 287). More recently, it is still widely reported that student sojourners experience more stress and anxiety than their local peers (Hechanova-Alampay et al. 2002); however, the assumption that the experience of study abroad results in poor general mental health is being increasingly challenged. It is worth emphasising that the experience of study abroad ultimately leaves many students positively disposed to their host university, the host city and the host country as a whole. Negative experiences and difficulties in the early sojourn stages are generally soon overcome and most students recall mainly positive experiences (Furnham 2004).

In this study, although students reported various degrees of frustration and insecurities, especially in the initial sojourn stage, overall there was little indication that profound threats to their wellbeing had occurred at any stage. This is similar to Brenner's (2003) findings on the psychological adjustment of US students sojourning abroad and, indeed, our own 2013 study of a similar student cohort (Young et al. 2013). The vast majority of students in the present study reported a positive sense of wellbeing and satisfaction throughout the sojourn, although the initial sojourn stage (including the weeks leading up to departure from home) was experienced by many as difficult. This is in line with previous research in the UK and Australia (e.g. Brown and Holloway 2008; Khawaja and Stallman 2011), and stands in direct opposition to the notion of early 'honeymoon' euphoria suggested in the U-curve model (see Lysgaard 1955; Oberg 1960).

Schreier and Abramovitch (1996) distinguish between initial and ongoing concerns, a useful typology that can be applied to this study. The new situation, perhaps not surprisingly, did cause some anxiety among the students, and issues surrounding language confidence, academic stressors, loneliness and homesickness were salient in the early sojourn weeks, while frustration with some aspects of the host environment (such as the weather) was present throughout the sojourn. However, at no stage did this lead to deeper psychological problems or pathological symptoms such as depression (with perhaps one exception, where one student genuinely considered returning home at one point early in the sojourn). This finding stands in contrast to Brown's (2008a) ethnographic study of postgraduate student sojourners in the UK, which reported evidence for more intense psychological and physiological reactions, such as emotionality, tearfulness, insomnia, anxiety, loss of appetite and depression.

Overall, the findings indicate that students' psychological adjustment remained variable over time (cf. Ward et al. 1998), although, again overall, it did seem to improve as the sojourn progressed, as reflected in students' accounts of increased confidence. Instances of homesickness and sadness were most salient in the initial sojourn stage and seemed to subside over time. After a period of initial doubts and insecurities, students' psychological adjustment generally followed a path of improvement (see Figure 5.2 later), although a slight drop was recorded approximately 3–4 months into the sojourn, when students became homesick over Christmas time and had to deal with their first assessed academic assignments. From the start of the second semester onwards, psychological adjustment seemed to level off, perhaps as a consequence of students having become more effective 'cultural learners' (Ward et al. 2001). None the less, academic stressors and aspects of the host environment such as the weather continued to have an impact on students' wellbeing throughout, albeit not to a great extent.

The finding that psychological adjustment difficulties were most pronounced in the early sojourn weeks does not coincide with the 'honeymoon' phase of euphoria suggested in the U-curve model (Lysgaard 1955), but is in line with more recent research that depicts the initial sojourn stages as a time of stress and nervousness (e.g. Ward and Kennedy 1996a, 1996b; Brown 2008b; Brown and Holloway 2008). The findings further correspond to Ward and colleagues' (2001) conceptualisation of psychological adjustment, suggesting that student sojourners' wellbeing is likely to be lowest when life changes are greatest while coping resources (that is, social ties and social support in the host country) are limited. Similar to the pattern found in this study, research commonly reports a decrease in psychological adjustment between departure from home and arrival in the host country (Ying and Liese 1991; Brown and Holloway 2008), followed by fairly swift improvement in the first few months of the sojourn (Ward and Kennedy 1996b).

Consistent with previous literature, building social ties appeared to buffer stress (e.g. Furukawa 1997). Students who had left partners or children in their home countries expressed a sense of loneliness and concern for the wellbeing of their family members, exemplifying the effect of loss of social ties on student sojourner wellbeing. For others, living costs and tuition fees in the host country were of concern.

Although financial means might be a considerable concern for university students in general (Rosenthal et al. 2006), those coming from abroad are likely to face higher tuition fees and costs of living than in their own country. Consistent with prior studies, some students sought part-time work in order to compensate for their financial expenses in the host country (cf. Li and Kaye 1998; Roberts et al. 1999).

By far the greatest amount of stress was prompted by the transition into an unfamiliar academic environment. Concerns in the early stages related largely to perceived English language ability and its impact on academic success, as well as unfamiliar academic conventions of essay-writing and self-directed learning. However, worries about academic aspects decreased steadily over time as students developed what Brown (2008a) calls 'academic cultural competence' and reported growing ease in coping with the demands of their degree programme. This highlights the role of culture-learning in psychological adjustment, indicating that the more students learned about their academic host environment, the better they felt psychologically, as discussed below. None the less there was a slight drop in psychological adjustment as students confronted their first assessment period around Christmas. This finding points to a correlation between adjustment to the academic environment and student wellbeing, as suggested by Zhou and Todman (2009), a link that we further explore in Chapter 7 of this book.

Although the demands of postgraduate study, such as busy assignment periods, continued to trigger some stress from time to time, this did not seem to have a significant impact on students' general sense of wellbeing and life satisfaction, which remained fairly constant throughout the sojourn. This is sustained by the questionnaire results, which showed no significant differences in the PWB and SWL scores between the different measurement points in time (as noted above), further indicating that psychological adjustment seemed to follow a relatively steady path after some initial acculturative stress upon arrival. It might be that knowing that their sojourn in the UK was temporary may have had an impact on how psychologically affected students became (Brenner 2003).

Overall, findings from the interviews indicate that students viewed their sojourn as a learning process, describing it as a growth-facilitating experience. At the onset of their sojourn, some students felt relatively incompetent, doubting their own academic, linguistic and social abilities. They did not yet feel that they had sufficient knowledge and experience to respond appropriately to the demands of the host environment, and this lack of confidence seemed to hinder their adjustment (cf. Lewthwaite 1996). However, over time, these students acknowledged that much had been learned through consistent exposure to the host environment. Learning the characteristics of the host environment (Furnham and Bochner 1982, 1986) led to increased confidence among the students and was seen as paramount for their own sense of psychological adjustment. Thus, it seems that students' wellbeing and SWL improved as a direct function of acquiring knowledge and skills that enabled them to function effectively in the (academic) host environment (Ward et al. 2001). This suggests that culture-learning can perhaps be considered a coping response to acculturative stress. In light of this finding, it makes sense to recognise the complementarity of the culture-learning and the stress and coping framework, rather than viewing them as completely separate constructs (Ward et al. 2001).

What is apparent in the present research is that students reported few really substantial difficulties, and very little evidence was found of persistent psychological difficulties. However, it should be noted that this sample was characterised by a number of factors that may have eased their transition into the host environment. One such factor is the supportive environment created by strong non-compatriot friendships among the cohort, which could have worked as a coping mechanism during cross-cultural transition. Social mixing with 'international' peers (that is, non-co-national ISs) was positively related to students' sense of psychological adjustment. The study showed that a sense of social connectedness was fundamental to the students' wellbeing: the interview data highlight the importance of contact with others and, most especially, of social support derived from international peers for students' own sense of psychological adjustment. Furthermore, the quantitative questionnaire results showed that students had a strong sense of social support – more than half of the participants scored above the mid-point of the five-point scale for social support (Chapter 4) – and nobody in the interviewee sample reported feeling isolated at any point in the sojourn.

Another possible explanation for the relatively smooth psychological adjustment across the sample could be the focus on international postgraduate students, who are likely to be older than undergraduate peers and thus perhaps better able to deal with acculturative stress, although findings on the relationship between age and adjustment are ambiguous (Ward et al. 2001). Students' educational background may also have played a role: all participants had previously completed at least an undergraduate degree and it might therefore be possible that this prepared them for some of the stress encountered in the host environment, although not necessarily for local learning and teaching practices and the specific demands of postgraduate study (Garson 2005; Luxon and Peelo 2009). Generally, prior education is associated with better adaptation and lower levels of stress due to its link to resources such as culture-specific knowledge and skills (Ward et al. 2001). It could also be that the students in this study were particularly well prepared for their sojourn, as many reported previous overseas experience (8 of 20 interviewees). Research suggests that students with prior overseas experience encounter fewer adjustment difficulties and less acculturative stress, and exhibit greater SWL (e.g. Bochner et al. 1986; Rohrlich and Martin 1991), although no significant difference in PWB and SWL was found between students with and without prior overseas experience in this study (see Chapter 4). It is generally believed that students with prior overseas experience may learn how to cope with reactions to living in an unfamiliar environment, although prior sojourns abroad do not necessarily always prevent acculturative stress (Furnham 2004).

### 5.2.6 SUMMARY

To sum up this section, our first research question asked about the dynamics and patterns of student sojourners' psychological adjustment over time. We found that three interrelated processes seemed integral to the psychological adjustment of the students in this study:

1. Temporal factor: we found diminishing psychological difficulties as the sojourn progressed.
2. Coping: we saw lots of evidence of the use of coping mechanisms being used for dealing with acculturative stress, including social contact and social support.
3. Culture-learning: across the sample we saw the acquisition of relevant knowledge and skills, which led to increased confidence.

The general trajectory of students' psychological adjustment is represented in Figure 5.2.

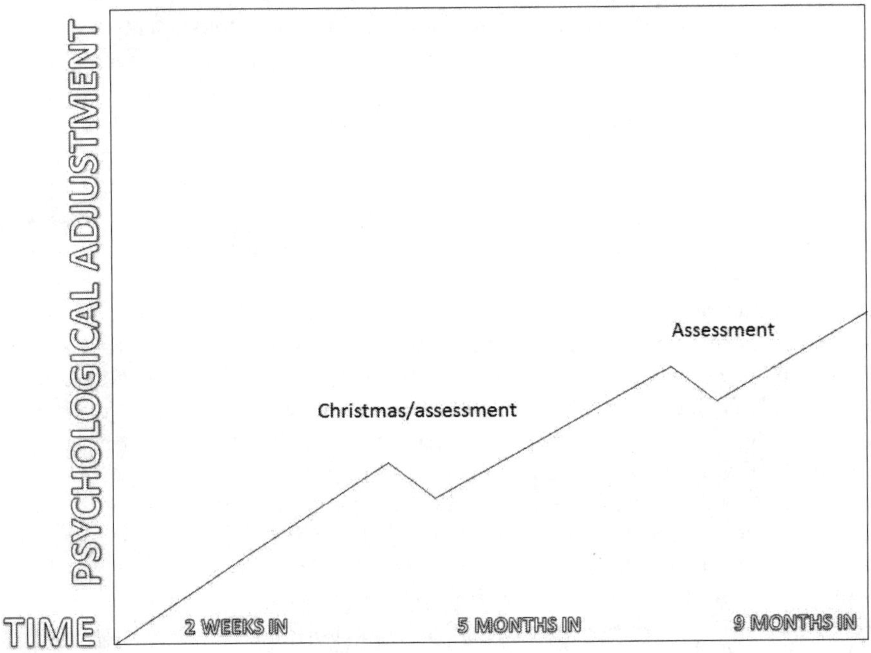


*Figure 5.2 Psychological adjustment over time*

## 5.3 ASSOCIATIONS BETWEEN CONTRIBUTORY FACTORS AND PSYCHOLOGICAL ADAPTATION

This section presents the quantitative data exploring associations between the contributory factors and the psychological adaptation indicators, PWB and SWL. It addresses our second research focus for this chapter: how English language ability, knowledge about the host country, prior overseas experience, autonomy in the decision to study abroad, intercultural competence, social contact and social support relate to psychological adaptation.

### 5.3.1 ENGLISH LANGUAGE ABILITY

English language ability measured at Time 1 (ELA T1) correlated significantly with SWL ($r$ =.21, $p < .05$); no significant correlation was found with PWB. A linear regression analysis revealed that ELA T1 was a significant predictor of SWL, $\beta = .21$, $t(127) = 2.41$, $p = .018$, and explained 4 per cent of the variance in the data, $F(1, 127) = 5.78$, $p = .018$, $R^2 = .04$, adjusted $R^2 = .04$. ELA measured at Time 2 correlated significantly with both SWL ($r = .45$, $p < .01$) and PWB ($r = .20$, $p < .05$). Linear regression analyses revealed that ELA T2 was a significant predictor of SWL (20 per cent of the variance explained) and of PWB (4 per cent) (Table 5.4).

Table 5.4 Regression analysis of English language ability at Time 2 and psychological adaptation

| | SWL | | PWB | |
|---|---|---|---|---|
| | *β* | *t* | *β* | *t* |
| ELA T2 | .45 | 5.72** | .20 | 2.34* |
| $R^2$ | 0.20 | | 0.04 | |
| Adjusted $R^2$ | 0.20 | | 0.03 | |
| F(df) | 32.75 (1, 130) | | 5.46 (1, 130) | |
| Sig. | $p < .001$ | | 0.021 | |

Note: **significant at the 99 per cent level; *significant at the 95 per cent level; ELA T2 = English language ability measured at Time 2; PWB = psychological wellbeing; SWL = satisfaction with life.

Table 5.5 Regression analysis of the Relative Autonomy Index and psychological adaptation

| | SWL | | PWB | |
|---|---|---|---|---|
| | *β* | *t* | *β* | *t* |
| RAI | .37 | 4.73** | .26 | 3.14** |
| $R^2$ | 0.14 | | 0.07 | |
| Adjusted $R^2$ | 0.13 | | 0.06 | |
| F(df) | 22.36 (1, 140) | | 9.86 (1, 140) | |
| Sig. | $p < .001$ | | 0.002 | |

Note: **significant at the 99 per cent level; PWB = psychological wellbeing; RAI = Relative Autonomy Index; SWL = satisfaction with life.

### 5.3.2 KNOWLEDGE ABOUT THE UK

A significant positive correlation was found between knowledge about the UK (KNW) and SWL ($r = .20$, $p < .05$). The correlation between KNW and PWB ($r = .23$), was not statistically significant. A linear regression analysis showed that KNW was a significant predictor of SWL, $\beta = .20$, $t(140) = 2.39$, $p = .018$, contributing to 4 per cent of the variance in the data, $F(1, 140) = 5.72$, $p = .018$, $R^2 = .04$, adjusted $R^2 = .03$.

### 5.3.3 AUTONOMY IN THE DECISION TO STUDY ABROAD

The Relative Autonomy Index (RAI) was entered into multiple linear regression models with SWL and PWB as outcome variables. The models were statistically significant and contributed to 14 per cent of the variance in SWL and to 7 per cent of the variance in PWB (Table 5.5).

Table 5.6 Bivariate correlations between intercultural competence and psychological adaptation

| | IC T1 | |
|---|---|---|
| | PWB | SWL |
| CE | .14 | .42** |
| OM | .26** | .33** |
| SI | .27** | .42** |
| ES | .43** | .29** |
| FL | .11 | .24** |

Note: **significant at $p < .01$ (two-tailed); CE = cultural empathy; ES = emotional stability; FL = flexibility; IC T1 = intercultural competence measured at Time 1; OM = open-mindedness; PWB = psychological wellbeing; SI = social initiative; SWL = satisfaction with life.

### 5.3.4 INTERCULTURAL COMPETENCE

Aspects of intercultural competence (IC) correlated positively with the psychological adaptation indices (Table 5.6). Multiple regression analyses using the enter method yielded statistically significant models for variance in SWL and PWB in relation to IC. First, the four IC subscales were entered in a multiple regression model with SWL as the outcome variable. A highly significant model emerged, contributing to 28 per cent of the variance in the data. Analysis of coefficients showed that cultural empathy (CE), social initiative (SI) and emotional stability (ES) were significant predictors of SWL. CE was the strongest predictor, followed by SI and ES (Table 5.7). Next, the IC subscales were entered into a multiple regression model with PWB as the outcome variable. Another highly significant model emerged, contributing to 21 per cent of the variance in the data. Analysis of coefficients showed that ES was a significant predictor of PWB (Table 5.7).

### 5.3.5 SOCIAL CONTACT

We found significant positive correlations between SWL and contact with British students ($r = .26$, $p < .01$), with non-co-national ISs ($r = .47$, $p < .01$) and with members of the local community ($r = .25$, $p < .01$); no significant correlations were found between degree of social contact and PWB. To explore the relationship between degree of social contact and SWL further, a multiple regression analysis was conducted. The model was highly significant and contributed to 26 per cent of the variance in the data. Analysis of coefficients showed that degree of contact with non-co-national ISs was the main predictor of SWL. Contact with British students was marginally associated with SWL (Table 5.8).

Table 5.7 Regression analysis of intercultural competence and psychological adaptation

| | SWL | | PWB | |
|---|---|---|---|---|
| | $\beta$ | $t$ | $\beta$ | $t$ |
| Mean CE | .37 | 3.80** | .04 | .41 |
| Mean OM | –.15 | –1.33 | .06 | .52 |
| Mean SI | .26 | 2.46* | .11 | 1.04 |
| Mean ES | .21 | 2.63* | .40 | 4.64** |
| Mean FL | .02 | .23 | –.11 | –1.21 |
| $R^2$ | 0.28 | | 0.21 | |
| Adjusted $R^2$ | 0.25 | | 0.18 | |
| F(df) | 10.56 (5, 137) | | 7.30 (5, 137) | |
| Sig. | p < .001 | | p < .001 | |

Note: **significant at the 99 per cent level; *significant at the 95 per cent level; CE = cultural empathy; ES = emotional stability; FL = flexibility; OM = open-mindedness; PWB = psychological wellbeing; SI = social initiative; SWL = satisfaction with life.

Table 5.8 Regression analysis of social contact and satisfaction with life

| | SWL | |
|---|---|---|
| | $\beta$ | $t$ |
| SC-BS | .14 | 1.69^ |
| SC-CN | .04 | .54 |
| SC-IN | .43 | 5.43** |
| SC-LC | .11 | 1.33 |
| $R^2$ | 0.26 | |
| Adjusted $R^2$ | 0.24 | |
| F(df) | 11.92 (4, 138) | |
| Sig. | p < .001 | |

Note: **significant at the 99 per cent level; ^significant at the 90 per cent level; SC-BS = social contact with British students; SC-CN = social contact with co-nationals; SC-IN = social contact with contact with non-co-national international students; SC-LC = social contact with local community; SWL = satisfaction with life.

### 5.3.6 SOCIAL SUPPORT

Significant positive correlations were found between the social support (SS) subscales and both psychological adaptation indicators (Table 5.9). A multiple regression analysis showed that the two subscales accounted for 12 per cent of the variance in SWL. Analysis of coefficients showed that socio-emotional support was a significant predictor of SWL (Table 5.10). An analysis of variance (ANOVA) yielded no significant association between the SS subscales and PWB.

Table 5.9 Bivariate correlations between social support and psychological adaptation

| | Socio-emotional SS | Instrumental SS |
|---|---|---|
| PWB | .17* | .17* |
| SWL | .34** | .25** |

Note: **significant at p < .01; *significant at p < .05 (two-tailed); PWB = psychological wellbeing; SS = social support; SWL = satisfaction with life.

Table 5.10 Regression analysis of social support and satisfaction with life

| | SWL | |
|---|---|---|
| | $\beta$ | *t* |
| SS-SE | .31 | 3.06** |
| SS-IN | .05 | .47 |
| $R^2$ | 0.12 | |
| Adjusted $R^2$ | 0.11 | |
| F(df) | 9.43 (2, 140) | |
| Sig. | p < .001 | |

Note: **significant at the 99 per cent level; SS-IN = instrumental social support; SS-SE = socio-emotional social support; SWL = satisfaction with life.

### 5.3.7 SUMMARY AND DISCUSSION OF THE QUANTITATIVE FINDINGS

Our research question in relation to contributory factors asked how, respectively, students' English language ability, knowledge about the host country, prior overseas experience, autonomy in the decision to study abroad, intercultural competence, social contact and social support relate to their psychological adaptation. As with our qualitative data, detailed in Section 5.2, above, psychological adaptation was defined in terms of students' satisfaction with life and their sense of psychological wellbeing. Our investigation confirmed a variety of contributory factors for student sojourners' psychological adaptation. Overall, the contributory variables were better able to predict satisfaction with life than psychological wellbeing. This suggests that the contributory factors were better able to predict the more cognitive aspects of subjective wellbeing rather than the emotional aspects. The findings indicate that there are some characteristics that make students sojourners more likely to adjust well psychologically to the host environment: students exhibiting high levels of satisfaction with life after nine months of study in the host country are likely to be language-proficient, emotionally stable and proactive, and to have high levels of cultural empathy. They are also likely to have made the decision to study abroad independently from others, to have high levels of self-perceived knowledge about the host country, and to have high levels of social contact with non-co-national ISs and socio-emotional support in the host country. Students exhibiting high levels of psychological wellbeing after nine months of study in the host country are likely to

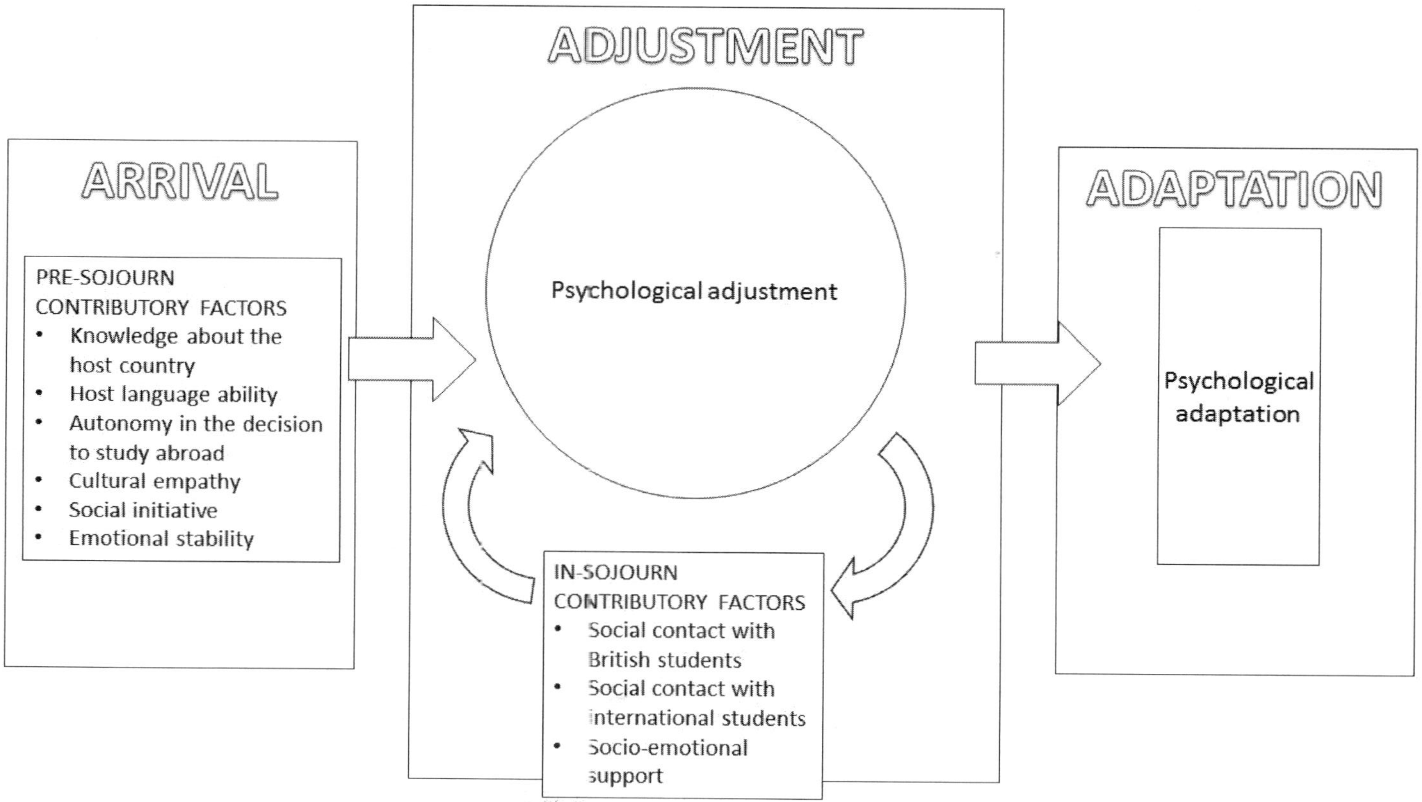


*Figure 5.3 Significant associations between contributory factors and psychological adaptation*

be emotionally stable and to have made the decision to study abroad independently from others (Figure 5.3).

## 5.4 CONCLUSION

It is useful in concluding this chapter to reiterate, and attempt some integration of, our findings with regard to research questions 1 and 2. We found, as a descriptive quantitative measure, that neither satisfaction with life nor psychological wellbeing showed any significant change over time. Our qualitative findings in respect of research question 1 related to the dynamics and patterns of psychological adjustment. They actually indicated diminishing levels of psychological difficulties over the sojourn as a common feature, as well as much use of coping mechanisms by our participants, and considerable evidence of culture-learning by them as they progressed through their degree. Our quantitative findings related to factors – situated at some level and to some extent 'within', or exhibited by, our participants – that might help to predict their degree of psychological adaptation, especially in terms of a sense of their satisfaction with life in the new environment. Among factors exhibited before their sojourn, more independence in the decision to study and more knowledge about the host society were important predictors of this sense of satisfaction during the sojourn. In terms of qualities and characteristics, people reporting more satisfaction with life in the new environment tended to be more English language-proficient and to be more emotionally stable, more proactive in terms of reaching out to others and able to exhibit high levels of empathy with cultural 'others'. We also found associations between another aspect of psychological adaptation – psychological wellbeing at different points of the sojourn – and the degree of independence in deciding to undertake the programme, and the degree of emotional stability reported by our participants, reinforcing the centrality and importance of these factors.

Taken together, findings in respect of research questions 1 and 2 serve to give us a rounded picture of our student participants as people undergoing transition into and through a new intercultural experience. We have identified a number of factors that are likely to make the process psychologically rewarding. We did find that the general experience of the sojourn seemed psychologically rewarding for most. This was even more the case if the individual could exhibit individual agency and had qualities that tended to promote successful interaction, both with the demands of their studies and with other people from a variety of backgrounds. The 'tools' to facilitate such interactions – linguistic, intercultural-competent and emotional – seemed clearly evident across both qualitative and quantities datasets.

## REFERENCES

Bochner, S., N. Hutnik and A. Furnham (1986), 'The friendship patterns of overseas and host students in an Oxford student residence', *Journal of Social Psychology*, 125, 689–94.

Brenner, B. R. (2003), *A Study of Self-awareness, Self-efficacy, and Sojourner Adjustment over Time*, Unpublished doctoral thesis, University of Maryland, USA.

Brown, L. (2008a), *The Adjustment Journey of International Postgraduate Students at a University in England*, Unpublished doctoral thesis, Bournemouth University, UK.

Brown, L. (2008b), 'The incidence of study-related stress in international students in the initial stage of the international sojourn', *Journal of Studies in International Education*, 12(1), 5–28.

Brown, L., and I. Holloway (2008), 'The initial stage of the international sojourn: excitement or culture shock?', *British Journal of Guidance and Counselling*, 36(1), 33–49.

Diener, E., R. A. Emmons, R. J. Larsen and S. Griffin, (1985), 'The Satisfaction with Life Scale', *Journal of Personality Assessment*, 49, 71–5.

Diener, E. (2006), *Understanding Scores on the Satisfaction with Life Scale*. Available at: <http://labs.psychology.illinois.edu/~ediener/Documents/Understanding%20SWLS%20 Scores.pdf> (last accessed 13 December 2018).

Furnham, A. (2004), 'Foreign students: education and culture shock', *Psychologist*, 17(1), 16–19.

Furnham, A., and S. Bochner (1982), 'Social difficulty in a foreign culture: an empirical analysis of culture shock', in S. Bochner (ed.), *Cultures in Contact: Studies in Cross-cultural Interaction*, Oxford: Pergamon, pp. 161–98.

Furnham, A., and S. Bochner (1986), *Culture Shock: Psychological Reactions to Unfamiliar Environments*, London: Methuen.

Furukawa, T. (1997), 'Sojourner adjustment', *Journal of Nervous and Mental Diseases*, 185, 263–8.

Garson, B. (2005), 'Teaching abroad: a cross-cultural journey', *Journal for Education and Business*, 80(6), 322–6.

Hechanova-Alampay, R., T. A. Beehr, N. D. Christiansen and R. K. van Horn (2002), 'Adjustment and strain among domestic and international student sojourners: a longitudinal study', *School Psychology International*, 23(4), 458–74.

Janca, A., and J. E. Helzer (1992), 'Psychiatric morbidity of foreign students in Yugoslavia: a 25 year retrospective analysis', *International Journal of Social Psychiatry*, 38(4), 287–92.

Khawaja, N. G., and H. M. Stallman (2011), 'Understanding the coping strategies of international students: a qualitative approach', *Australian Journal of Guidance and Counselling*, 21(2), 203–24.

Lewthwaite, M. (1996), 'A study of international students' perspectives on cross-cultural adaptation', *International Journal for the Advancement of Counselling*, 19(2), 167–85.

Li, R. Y., and M. Kaye (1998), 'Understanding overseas students' concerns and problems', *Journal of Higher Education Policy and Management*, 20, 41–50.

Luxon, T., and M. Peelo (2009), 'Academic sojourners, teaching and internationalisation: the experience of non-UK staff in a British university', *Teaching in Higher Education*, 14(6), 649–59.

Lysgaard, S. (1955), 'Adjustment in a foreign society: Norwegian Fulbright grantees visiting the United States', *International Social Science Bulletin*, 7, 45–51.

Oberg, K. (1960), 'Cultural shock: adjustment to new cultural environments', *Practical Anthropology*, 7, 177–82.

Roberts, R., J. Golding, T. Towell and I. Weinreib (1999),'The effects of economic circumstances on British students' mental and physical health', *Journal of American College Health*, 48, 103–9.

Rohrlich, B. F., and J. N. Martin (1991), 'Host country and reentry adjustment of student sojourners', *International Journal of Intercultural Relations*, 15(2), 163–82.

Rosenthal, D. A., V. J. Russell and G. J. Thomson (2006), *A Growing Experience: The Health and Well-Being of International Students at the University of Melbourne*. Available at:

<https://services.unimelb.edu.au/__data/assets/pdf_file/0011/358436/GrowingExperience.pdf> (last accessed 13 December 2018).

Schreier, A. R., and H. Abramovitch (1996), 'American medical students in Israel: stress and coping', *Medical Education*, 30, 445–52.

Ward, C., S. Bochner and A. Furnham (2001), *The Psychology of Culture Shock*, 2nd edn, Hove: Routledge.

Ward C., and A. Kennedy (1996a), 'Before and after cross-cultural transition: a study of New Zealand volunteers on field assignments', in H. Grad, A. Blanco and J. Georgas (eds), *Key Issues in Cross-cultural Psychology*, Lisse: Swets & Zeitlinger, pp. 138–54.

Ward, C., and A. Kennedy (1996b), 'Crossing cultures: the relationship between psychological and sociocultural dimensions of cross-cultural adjustment', in J. Pandey, D. Sinha and D. P. S. Bhawuk (eds), *Asian Contributions to Cross-cultural Psychology*, New Delhi: Sage, pp. 289–306.

Ward, C., C. Leong and M. Low (2004), 'Personality and sojourner adjustment: an exploration of the Big Five and the cultural fit proposition', *Journal of Cross-Cultural Psychology*, 35, 137–51.

Ward, C., Y. Okura, A. Kennedy and T. Kojima (1998), 'The U-curve on trial: a longitudinal study of psychological and sociocultural adjustment during cross-cultural transition', *International Journal of Intercultural Relations*, 22(3), 277–91.

Ying, Y.-W., and L. H. Liese (1991), 'Emotional well-being of Taiwan students in the U.S.: an examination of pre- to post-arrival differential', *International Journal of Intercultural Relations*, 15(3), 345–66.

Young, T. J., and A. Schartner (2014), 'The effects of cross-cultural communication education on international students' adjustment and adaptation', *Journal of Multilingual and Multicultural Development*, 35(6), 547–62.

Young, T. J., P. G. Sercombe, I. Sachdev, R. Naeb and A. Schartner (2013), 'Success factors for international postgraduate students' adjustment: exploring the roles of intercultural competence, language proficiency, social contact and social support', *European Journal of Higher Education*, 3, 151–71.

Zhou, Y., and J. Todman (2009), 'Patterns of adaptation of Chinese postgraduate students in the United Kingdom', *Journal of Studies in International Education*, 13(4), 467–86.

# 6
# SOCIOCULTURAL ADJUSTMENT AND ADAPTATION

In this chapter, we discuss and integrate interview and survey-based data related to the sociocultural adjustment and adaptation of ISs. Below, we first present descriptive data regarding our sociocultural adaptation measure. We then present qualitative data (6.1), which we hope provide a fine-grained and nuanced picture of participants' 'lived' sociocultural experiences of 'fitting into' the host environment. We then present quantitative data (6.2), which we hope illustrate which factors might contribute to sociocultural adaptation over time.

The following research questions are addressed in this chapter:

1. What are the dynamics and patterns of student sojourners' sociocultural adjustment over time?
2. How do English language ability, knowledge about the host country, prior overseas experience, autonomy in the decision to study abroad, intercultural competence, social contact and social support relate to different aspects of sociocultural adaptation?

Our sociocultural adaption measure, the Sociocultural Adaptation Scale (SCAS), is detailed in Chapter 3. The overall mean score was high at 4.05 (SD = .45, Min. = 2.61, Max. = 5), indicating that, nine months into their programme of study, the majority of participants felt well adjusted to the new sociocultural environment. Of the individual items, 'Making British friends' (M = 3.15, SD = 1.05) and 'Understanding the local accent' (M = 3.13, SD = 1.00) had the lowest mean scores, indicating that students experienced the greatest difficulties in these areas (see also Table 6.1).

Table 6.1 Sociocultural Adaptation Scale items rated as most difficult by respondents

| Item | % of respondents reporting either 'extreme difficulty' or 'great difficulty' |
|---|---|
| Understanding the local accent | 27.4% |
| Making British friends | 26.4% |
| Seeing things from a British person's point of view | 20.4% |
| Meeting people from the local community | 20.2% |

'Making friends with people from your own country' (M = 4.62, SD = .80) and 'Going into restaurants and cafes' (M = 4.69, SD = .63) were rated highest.

## 6.1 SOCIOCULTURAL ADJUSTMENT OVER TIME

Ward and colleagues (2001) situate sociocultural adjustment within a culture-learning and social skills framework and place great importance on the sojourners' ability to learn about the host culture and to interact with host nationals. According to this conceptualisation, sociocultural adjustment difficulties are expected to be at their peak in the initial sojourn stage, when the sojourner has the least familiarity with and knowledge about the host society and when meaningful relationships with host nationals are still limited. The sociocultural adjustment trajectory is described by Ward and colleagues as an ascending curve representing a learning process (that is, the acquisition of culturally relevant knowledge and skills) over time. This learning curve is anticipated to be rapid in the early stages of the sojourn and is subsequently expected to level off as the sojourner becomes increasingly familiar with the host society (Ward et al. 1998). We were interested to see whether this trajectory would fit the experiences of students in our study.

Data were collected through a series of individual semi-structured interviews at three time stages: two weeks into the programme of study (Time 1), five months into the programme (Time 2) and nine months into the programme (Time 3). Findings are presented in chronological order below.

### 6.1.1 TWO WEEKS INTO THE PROGRAMME (TIME 1)

Students' comments at this early stage were largely related to initial first-hand experiences in the new environment. Overall, they generally showed a positive orientation towards the host environment and their own sociocultural adjustment. This was reflected in positive comments about initial encounters with British people and in students' general motivation to explore the new environment – curiosity about aspects of life in the UK and a desire to learn more about 'UK culture' were expressed by many students, including references to history, travel, the arts, popular culture and sports. A desire to learn about the host city and to interact with local residents was frequently expressed. The latter was often perceived as a useful tool to 'adapt' and 'get used to the UK life'.

> I would like to meet with local people more because I think they represent the culture, British culture better. (Turkish student, male)
>
> It would be nice just to get to know more about this area and more about the culture. (German student, female)

Interviewees' accounts of initial first-hand encounters with local people were, for the most part, positive, albeit mainly focused on formulaic, transactional interactions and small-talk, as illustrated in this comment by a student from Germany:

> I love that people are not as scared to talk to each other. So far when I waited for the bus I almost always had a tiny conversation with someone or a shop-assistant who talked to you. (German student, female)

Many students used their own country of origin as a frame of reference when commenting on initial encounters with locals:

> During daytime every person on the street will smile at you. It is not usual in China. (Chinese student, female)
> It seems that they are warm people. I had some problems in Lithuania because people are not eager to help you, just different characters. Here people are more open. (Lithuanian student, male)

Initial problems were mostly related to a lack of familiarity with the 'difficult' local accent, which took students by surprise. A number of interviewees also reported difficulties relating to younger local residents. Teenagers in particular were described as 'rude', and students appeared reluctant to approach younger people, especially if this was outside the campus environment:

> I am afraid to talk with them. They made their hair in colourful so I don't think they are friendly to talk with. (Chinese student, female)

A reluctance to socialise with younger British people tended to be accompanied by comments about the role of alcohol in social activities, best illustrated in this exchange with an Italian student:

> Student: [...] for what concerns the young people as well, they are really different from what I'm used to.
> Interviewer: Could you give me an example?
> Student: Well, the approach of young people when they go out for example. I mean I am not always in my own house, not even in Italy, for sure, but I mean here I feel like people just go out to drink.

This was a typical response, as several students expressed concern about engaging in activities that involved drinking alcohol, which was described as 'strange' by one student from Lithuania. Others struggled to adjust to the vibrant nightlife in the host city and felt anxious when walking home at night:

> There are many, many drunk people so I am afraid of them. (Turkish student, male)
> During night I'm a little afraid because drunk people. (Chinese student, female)

Some students appeared to struggle with unfamiliar norms for social interaction, especially regarding how relationships are formed, commenting on the 'individualistic' nature of people.

> In our culture if we know each other we have contact and making some relationship but in here if for example I meet you today and, like, we talk and after that finish, you know, so that's kind of new for me. (Indonesian student, female)

Others commented on politeness norms, such as one student from Finland who expressed unease about the pervasiveness of 'small-talk':

> That kind of English politeness is something that I find a bit difficult to adjust to [...] in Finland, if you say sorry once that's enough [...] politeness or small talk is not necessarily the thing that we master in Finland. (Finnish student, female)

In the early sojourn stages, comments about 'missing' familiar foods and the 'different' food culture were common and comparisons were frequently made with food in the home country:

> The food is a little bit problematic here for me [...] I find it a little bit greasy and everything is like in sandwich or, I don't know, hamburgers. (Turkish student, female)
>
> I'm still not very happy about all the food [...] I do miss bakeries. I don't know what to do without bakeries so far. (German student, female)

For some students, special dietary requirements constrained the food choices available to them, resulting in extra efforts to obtain suitable products:

> I'm Muslim and I need to eat Halal food and it took about 40 minutes by walk to go to [an area in the host city known for multicultural food] so and it cost more money to get there. (Indonesian student, female)

Several students reported bringing food items with them to the UK:

> Maryland seafood seasoning like I had to bring it and hot sauce and American peanut butter. So I brought that just because I knew that was stuff I would miss. (US student, male)
>
> I brought some Chinese traditional food and Chinese ingredients because my friends told me it's very important here – you have to cook yourself (Chinese student, male)

Finally, comments about the 'cold' and 'rainy' weather were common in the early sojourn stages, with students from warmer climates in particular expressing concern about the winter months to come, as illustrated in this remark by a student from Malaysia:

> It's so different for me because Malaysia is really, really hot and we don't really have winter and cold. (Malaysian student, female)

Some students prepared in advance for what they thought would be a cold winter, like this student from California:

> I went out and bought a lot of like coats and scarves and stuff like that that I had never really bought before. (US student, female)

Students' comments on sociocultural adjustment two weeks into the sojourn included frequent comparisons between the host environment and their home countries, as well as between pre-arrival expectations and realities encountered in the new surroundings. Although initial experiences in the host environment varied by individual, there were many commonalties and similar concerns, in particular related to the practicalities of living abroad, such as dealing with differences in climate, food and interaction with local people.

### 6.1.2 FIVE MONTHS INTO THE PROGRAMME (TIME 2)

By the time the second wave of interviews took place, students had been at their host university for approximately five months. They were now able to comment in greater detail on their experiences of living in the host environment and of interacting with people. Comments related to sociocultural adjustment were, on the whole, positive, with many students reporting feeling more familiar with the host environment, having settled into a familiar routine, as described by a student from the US:

> I don't really have any issues throughout my day as I might have had in October [...] how to go to the grocery store effectively, I know how to use the buses effectively, the metro, you know. In a pub, I know to go up to the bar and order food and drinks [...] I'm learning the norms of society. I think I've pretty much gotten most of them. (US student, male)

Most accounts of social interactions were of a similar positive nature, with communication being described as 'easy' and students reporting to be spending more time mixing with others. A number of interviewees who were not first-language English speakers reported improvements in their English language ability and increased confidence when interacting with local people:

> I think I have learnt some basic vocabulary in daily life [...] the street terminology or the things you use in daily life. (Turkish student, male)
> I definitely learned to understand English native speakers better because at the beginning it was frightening. (Latvian student, female)

Although interactions with local people still remained largely limited to brief service encounters, these were described as positive experiences, with several students recalling instances of pleasant conversations with strangers:

> In the street you can just have a chat with someone, like waiting in front of the shop maybe. They are open to this, they don't mind it. (Turkish student, male)

Local people were described as 'friendly', 'helpful' and 'open-minded', although some students appeared to struggle with what they described as 'British politeness':

> Maybe I expected their politeness to be authentic but a lot of times I felt that it's just a crust, it's not real. (Finnish student, female)

Students' perceptions of the host society had become more nuanced by the second interview round, as they were increasingly differentiating between different groups of people. Comments were varied, ranging from the highly positive for some groups to the highly negative for others. Interactions with people at the host university, including academic, administrative and support services staff, were described as highly positive. Similarly, service encounters in banks, supermarkets and the local transport system were evaluated favourably.

> When I go shopping or go to the supermarket or other places they always very kind and always say 'thank you' many times, so I feel very happy. (Chinese student, female)

Students showed a particularly positive orientation towards older people, who were described as 'polite', whereas perceptions of younger people remained rather negative, as illustrated in the comment below by a Romanian student:

> I have a very contrastive opinion about the young British people and the more mature and I think the mature are very responsible and polite and the young ones are very crazy and party people. (Romanian student, female)

Students continued to comment on the pervasiveness of alcohol in the social activities of younger people. While some of these comments were fairly neutral, others pointed to a lack of suitable places to socialise:

> During the night, not just weekends, like there's drunk people everywhere, I don't know it's just shocking for me because they really like shouting, yelling. (Indonesian student, female)
>
> There's no other choice here like only pub and club that open at night but if you go to Indonesia you can go to a restaurant, you can go to the café. (Indonesian student, female)
>
> They are partying every day. I mean Mexican people, we are known for doing parties all the time […] but here it's amazing, I mean even Mondays they are partying. (Mexican student, male)

Five months into their sojourn, students also commented on the impact of academic workload on social activities, with several students highlighting the challenges associated with balancing academic study with life in a new environment.

> I had to manage everything on my own, like house rents [...] everything is new for me, just everything, buying daily food and stuff like that, just everything, and at the same time I have to keep up with the studies. (Indonesian student, female)

A number of students continued to struggle to adjust to the local climate and gave accounts of prolonged periods of illness throughout the winter months and the impact this had on their physical and psychological wellbeing:

> I don't really like the weather because it always makes me sick. (Latvian student, female)
>
> Weather was making me very, very depressive because in the mornings, I mean it's nine o' clock – it's dark, three o' clock – it's dark and because I come from like a place which is always sunny. (Turkish student, female)

Finally, students reported greater familiarity with British foods, although some remained critical of local eating habits:

> I prefer my own food culture. I miss certain ingredients, I miss certain ways food is prepared so I'd say I'm not really agreeing with, like, having crisps as a part of your healthy diet is a good choice. (German student, female)

Five months into their sojourn most interviewees reported feeling well adjusted to the new environment and, overall, they appeared to be able to cope effectively with daily life in the host city. Certain aspects of the local life remained a challenge, most especially the weather and perceived pervasiveness of a 'drinking culture'.

### 6.1.3 NINE MONTHS INTO THE PROGRAMME (TIME 3)

By the third interview round, students were approximately nine months into their sojourn and now commented overwhelmingly positively on their sociocultural adjustment. 'Fitting in' was described as 'easy', and students reported feeling 'comfortable' and 'used to' life in the host environment. In fact, some students appeared to have exceeded their own expectations:

> I was surprised mostly of myself and about my ability to adapt to new surroundings and to make strong social networks in such a short time. (Finnish student, female)

Overall, comparison between the host environments and students' home countries were considerably less frequent in the third interview round. After nine months in the host environment, most had developed a clear daily routine and were generally more focused on their day-to-day activities, rather than comparing life in the UK to previous experiences in their home countries. Most interviewees now viewed their lives in the UK as 'normal':

> I feel like I'm just living my life here [...] it's kind of like this is the life I live and back home is my old life, but I didn't feel like that last year, but now I feel like that. (US student, male)

It seems that, very broadly, sociocultural adjustment improved gradually as the sojourn progressed. Over time, students acquired the skills and knowledge necessary to function effectively in the host environment. Interviewees' own accounts provide evidence that most adjustment difficulties were experienced in the early sojourn stages, when students had only limited meaningful interpersonal relationships and were not yet familiar with more specific aspects of life in the host environment, such as where to shop and where to socialise.

> I think at the very beginning it was the greatest shock because obviously you don't have anyone at the very beginning, [...] but after the first couple of weeks I think I was really able to adapt, and ever since then it's been pretty much the same. (US student, female)

However, several interviewees described a sense of having 'missed out' on opportunities to socialise, as the demands of academic study inhibited them from fully immersing themselves in the host environment:

> I was very much focused on my academic performance and finding a job for when I finished. Actually I wasn't enjoying myself that much, but now I am more [...] I started realising 'Oh, I've been missing out on this!' (Romanian student, female)

As students were approaching the end of their sojourn, the focus in their accounts shifted from adjustment issues to outcomes of living abroad. Students overwhelmingly described their experience as positive and many stated that they would 'do it again':

> I think it's a great experience [...] if I could go back I would probably spend more time abroad. (German student, female)
> I can tell everyone at home that this is a wonderful experience and everyone should just go. (Indonesian student, female)

A number of interviewees also commented on the transformative nature of study abroad. After living away from family members and familiar surroundings for a period of time, often at a great distance, students reported increased self-confidence and life skills, and a greater sense of independence:

> I can cook myself, I should control my time, everything. In China, my parents always take care for me but now I care for myself. I think I enjoy the freedom, enjoy the abroad life. (Chinese student, male)

Orientations towards British people remained, on the whole, positive, although comments on interactions with host nationals were less frequent by the time of the third interview round, with most students appearing to have settled into mixed-nationality 'international' friendship groups. Nine months into the sojourn, British people still remained on the periphery of students' social lives, restricted largely to brief service encounters. Although negative comments on younger British people decreased markedly from Time 2 to Time 3, the vibrant nightlife and pervasiveness of alcohol were still commented on:

> Concerning the young people, this was a cultural shock [...] I cannot believe it when I see how many people just lay down on the asphalt being very, very drunk. (Romanian student, female)
> What I don't necessarily agree with, but maybe that's just me, is like the drinking and going out culture – I can't take it [...] it's very, very hard to get used to and very hard to not be judgemental (...) (German student, female)

Some felt that differences in the ways people socialise prevented them from forming close bonds with local students of their age group.

> I feel some barriers and it's quite difficult how they behave, huge difference compared to my country. (Lithuanian student, male)

Finally, adjustment to the weather remained a topic of importance to students, as it appeared to affect students' wellbeing throughout their sojourn:

> Maybe go to somewhere sunny otherwise you will be depressed. (Turkish student, male)
> I wish weather was better because it's just constant topic of frustration. (Latvian student, female)

### 6.1.4 SUMMARY AND DISCUSSION

The overwhelming impression from analysis of the data presented above is that students gradually developed a routine in daily life tasks (such as where to shop and where to eat) as the sojourn progressed. Over the three interview stages, all students reported progress in sociocultural adjustment over time and a sense of generally successful accommodation to the new sociocultural environment. While sociocultural difficulties appeared to be greatest in the early weeks of the sojourn and gradually alleviated as the sojourn progressed, much in line with Ward and colleagues' (2001) proposed ascending curve, we found the trajectory not to be quite as linear (see Figure 6.1 later). There were areas in which adjustment was seen as less successful, most notably in the quantity and perceived quality of interactions with local people, as discussed further below. Thus sociocultural adjustment, although generally improving over time, can be seen through our data as a long and potentially uneven process (Coles and Swami 2012), with significant individual variation across students (see also Wright and Schartner 2013). As such, it may involve more than merely the acquisition of new culture-specific knowledge and skills emphasised in cultural learning models (Furnham and Bochner 1986; Ward 2004); coping approaches are also needed to deal with more difficult sociocultural experiences.

Overall, we were able to discern two key differences between Ward and colleagues' (2001) model and the pattern uncovered in our data. Firstly, sociocultural adjustment was not determined by culture-learning as a result of host national contact. Students in our study managed to achieve relatively high levels of apparent sociocultural adaptation, even without the extensive host national contact that is so central to culture-learning models. Instead, 'international' friendships fulfilled an important social function, corroborating findings from previous studies (e.g. Montgomery 2010). Students gradually adjusted to the new sociocultural environment through interaction with significant others who were also going through the 'international student experience' rather than through the acquisition of knowledge and skills from members of the host society (see also Young et al. 2013). 'Culture-learning', at least in our data, seemed to take place within an 'international community of practice', as suggested by Montgomery and McDowell (2009), and it is therefore important for this aspect to be acknowledged in culture-learning models of sociocultural adjustment. In sum, conceptualisations of sociocultural adjustment require a more complex and nuanced perspective than the one offered by the original culture-learning model, taking into account the interactions student sojourners have with their international peers, and thereby placing less emphasis on the importance of host national contact in this process (Schartner 2015).

The second key finding was that some adjustment difficulties did not alleviate over time, and an initial stage of rapid adjustment, as suggested by Ward and colleagues (2001), could not be clearly discerned in the data. Instead, the students' learning curve was found to go beyond the early sojourn stages without necessarily levelling off over time, and was also found to be more uneven than originally suggested by the culture-learning and social skills approach (Furnham and Bochner 1986). Most notably, perceived lack of meaningful contact with British people was a strong emergent theme throughout the three interview rounds. Paradoxically, students described British people as friendly and kind (in contrast to Tajfel and Dawson's 1965 book, *Disappointed Guests*, where British people were described as patronising, conservative and unfriendly), yet at the same time they found it difficult to instigate and sustain meaningful relationships with them. Motivations to interact with British people were strong, and students acknowledged the social and linguistic benefits of contact with the hosts, such as a perceived provision of cultural knowledge not available elsewhere. However, much to the students' perceived detriment, contact with British people was consistently described as short, superficial and formulaic, with interactions largely confined to service encounters where conversation beyond small-talk and standardised interaction was hardly possible. Our data suggest that the most important 'brokers' of the host culture were academic and administrative university staff, as well as students' house and flat mates. This finding is not unique to our research; nor is it specific to the UK context, with research from across anglophone countries reporting that ISs generally wish for more host interaction than they actually experience (Thomson et al. 2006; Khawaja and Stallman 2011; Yuan 2011). In one UK study, ISs reported that they had no British friends at all (UKCOSA 2004). Similar instances of ISs finding themselves 'friendless' have been reported from the USA (Fischer 2012).

Structural issues, such as the high IS intake on many UK postgraduate taught degrees (averaging 70 per cent, according to latest UKCISA figures, as noted in Chapter 1, above), makes social mixing with British students inherently more difficult. Additionally, some nationalities tend to be very predominant in certain programmes: for example, students from the People's Republic of China on UK business-related degrees at both undergraduate and postgraduate levels. This is also a result of ISs often choosing different degree programmes from their domestic peers (OECD 2012), making it more likely that 'international' enclaves co-exist in parallel with the host student community (Al-Sharideh and Goe 1998; Volet and Ang 1998).

Placement in 'international' accommodation can be equally problematic. Most students in this study shared cooking and living facilities with fellow sojourners rather than British peers, not least because on-campus accommodation for postgraduates often reflects the strongly 'international' make-up of the degree course cohorts. Research suggests that accommodation arrangements can be crucial for the development of intercultural contact (e.g. Kudo and Simkin 2003), and that placement in exclusively 'international' halls of residence can be counterproductive to the integration of student sojourners with the host community (Peacock and Harrison 2009).

So how can student sojourners' sense of social connectedness with host nationals be strengthened? One solution might be a more deliberate creation of social spaces where 'international' and 'home' can interact, including more proactive management of classrooms and housing (Sovic 2009; Coles and Swami 2012). ISs have reported wanting more institutional support in developing social ties on their course (e.g. Bartram 2007), so opportunities for interactions with local students could be usefully integrated into academic activities. Volet and Ang (1998: 9) note:

> Over the years, it has become clear that unless intercultural contact is engineered as part of formal study, social cohesion will not happen and all students will miss out on critical learning opportunities.

A possible challenge might be a reluctance on the part of 'home' students to instigate interaction with their international counterparts. While the latter are generally highly motivated to interact with local students, a perceived lack of reciprocal interest on the part of the former has been reported in a number of studies (e.g. Jacob and Greggo 2001; Hechanova-Alampay et al. 2002; Wright and Schartner 2013). This may well be a result of differences in the way leisure time is spent. As noted above, several students ascribed their lack of host contact to the night-time socialising and perceived 'drinking culture' of the local people, especially the young. The vibrant nightlife and perceived high level of alcohol consumption in the host city appeared unsettling for students, and many were reluctant to engage in social activities where alcohol was consumed in large quantities. This reluctance was further exacerbated by associated behaviours such as shouting and fighting, and unfamiliar dress styles. This was a strong emergent theme and persistent issue throughout the interview rounds with students repeatedly stating that British people 'drink too much'. This finding is in line with other UK-based research suggesting that ISs experience the alcohol consumption of local students as excessive, and that this was a source of dissatisfaction for the former (UKCOSA 2014; Brown 2008). An IS experience report commissioned by UNITE (2006) also concluded that ISs' alcohol consumption was markedly lower than that of their British peers (see also Vivancos et al. 2009).

Studies on the actual alcohol consumption of British students are, however, ambiguous (see Gill's 2002 review). Smart and Ogborne (2000) found that per capita consumption by British students was, in fact, lower than that of their peers in other European countries, and Hibell and colleagues (2009) reported a drop in alcohol consumption among British students. None the less, research on the general population has recently documented an unprecedented rise in heavy drinking among youngsters in the UK, most especially among young women (Plant and Plant 2006). A 2013 study commissioned by the Centre for Social Justice reported that alcohol dependence among British men was second in Western Europe, and alcohol dependence among British women higher than anywhere else in Europe. It was estimated that one in four adults in England drank to harmful levels. The same report also found a North–South divide in England and concluded that 26 of the 30 local authorities with the highest rate of alcohol-related hospital admissions were in the North of the country (BBC 2013), the setting of the present study. In a UK-based study by Peacock and Harrison (2009), British students themselves identified a distinct 'British drinking culture', which, it was felt, could create an alien and intimidating environment for ISs. The same authors further found that the social spaces frequented by British students were generally noisy environments, such as bars and nightclubs, which may pose additional barriers for social interaction (Harrison and Peacock 2008). Similarly, students in the present study pointed to a lack of suitable spaces to meet British students, echoing an observation made by Malaysian undergraduate students in the UK in a study by Coles and Swami (2012).

In sum, it seems that alcohol played a key part in the segregation of UK and ISs. This study clearly shows that student sojourners, from a multiplicity of countries, feel uncomfortable with the perceived over-consumption of alcohol in the UK. Host universities need to be aware that some ISs might associate public intoxication with aspects such as violence and intimidation (Harrison and Peacock 2008), and could offer alternative ways of social mixing at and beyond course level.

Aside from lack of host contact, two further prevailing adjustment issues were apparent in our data. The first related to language and communication. While students commented frequently on the friendliness and openness of local people, they appeared to struggle with what they described as 'British politeness', supporting the notion that a lack of shared cultural reference points (such as politeness norms) can affect communication (Harrison and Peacock 2008). Findings were similar to those reported in an Australian study by Volet and Tan-Quigley (1999), in which ISs struggled with small talk in their interactions with university administrative staff. Additionally, students had difficulty adjusting to different 'Englishes' encountered in the host environment, in particular the local accent. This is in line with research suggesting that students who have perhaps studied more formal English in their home countries find themselves struggling with the less formal language-in-use and the sociolinguistic skills needed to negotiate the host environment (Rosenthal et al. 2006).

A second persistent challenge was the weather conditions in the host city, such as rain, snow and shorter daylight hours, especially during the winter semester. Students repeatedly explained how the rainy and cold weather impacted negatively on their psychological wellbeing and resulted in recurrent physical illnesses and diminished outdoor activities. Pre-arrival information on and preparation for the British weather (for example, buying warm clothes) did little to reduce the effect of direct experience. These findings are not new and are supported in other research on ISs' adjustment (e.g. Maundeni 2001). The British weather has previously been identified as an obstacle to adjustment by student sojourners in Brown's (2008) longitudinal study.

The data presented above give an insight into students' 'lived' experiences of socio-cultural adjustment. It indicates that, nine months into their programme of study,

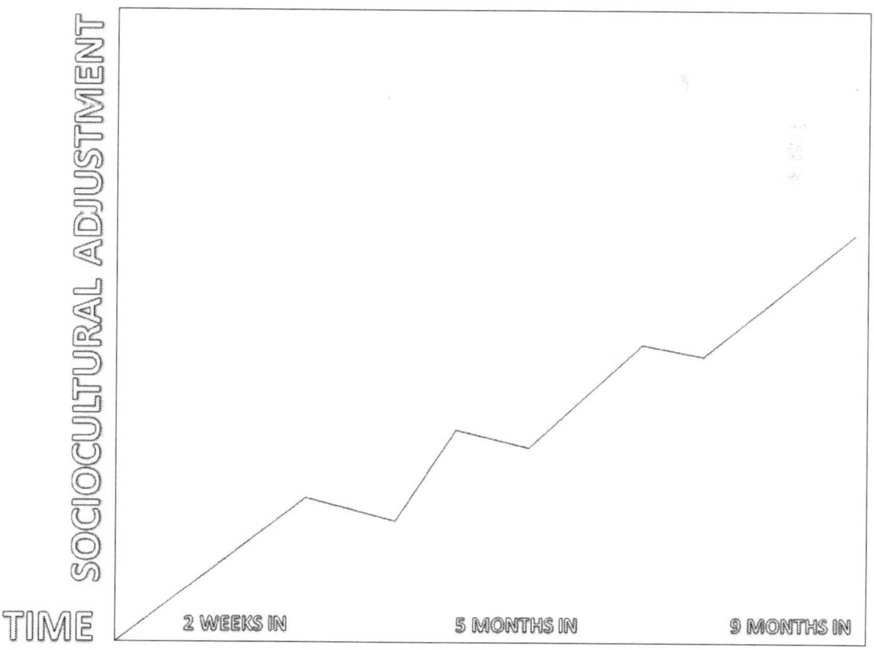


*Figure 6.1 Sociocultural adjustment amongst student sojourners over time*

students had, on the whole, adjusted well to the new environment. One could say that there was a general sense of 'success' and, whilst not a linear process, sociocultural adjustment did appear to follow an ascending curve, with better adjustment experienced towards the end of the sojourn (Figure 6.1).

Having presented students' own perspectives on sociocultural adjustment above, in the next section we provide data regarding the relationship between our sociocultural adaptation measure and various contributory factors.

## 6.2 CONTRIBUTORY FACTORS TO SOCIOCULTURAL ADAPTATION

One interest of our research was which factors, if any, might determine the degree of sociocultural adaptation achieved at the end of the sojourn. We therefore collected data on a range of possible contributory factors. This included English language ability, prior knowledge about the UK, prior overseas experience, motivation for study abroad, intercultural competence, social contact and social support. Our outcome measure was the Sociocultural Adaptation Scale (SCAS; see Chapter 3). In order to determine whether there was a relationship between the above factors and the outcome measure, we first conducted correlation analysis. This showed that there were statistically significant correlations between most contributory factors and the outcome measure. Subsequently, we performed a series of linear simple and multiple regression analyses to determine the predictive power of the contributory factors for sociocultural adaptation.

### 6.2.1 ENGLISH LANGUAGE ABILITY

We found no significant correlation between English Language Ability (ELA) measured at Time 1, but ELA measured at Time 2 correlated significantly with sociocultural adaptation ($r = .40$, $p < .001$). It was also a significant predictor of sociocultural adaptation, $\beta = .40$, $t = 5.04$, $p < .001$, and explained 16 per cent of the variance in the data, $F(1, 130) = 25.42$, p < .001, $R^2 = .16$, adjusted $R^2 = .16$.

### 6.2.2 KNOWLEDGE ABOUT THE UK

We found a moderately strong and significant correlation between knowledge about the UK (KNW) and sociocultural adaptation (r = .34. p < .001). A simple linear regression analysis showed that prior KNW explained 11 per cent of the variance in the outcome measure, $F(1, 140) = 17.68$, p < .001, $R^2 = .11$, adjusted $R^2 = .11$. Analysis of coefficients showed that prior knowledge about the UK was a significant predictor of sociocultural adaptation, $\beta = .34$, $t = 4.20$, p < .001.

### 6.2.3 AUTONOMY IN THE DECISION TO STUDY ABROAD

The SCAS correlated positively with intrinsic motivation for study abroad, and negatively with introjected and external motivation (Table 6.2). The Relative Autonomy Index (RAI) correlated positively with sociocultural adaptation.

Table 6.2 Bivariate correlations between autonomy in the decision to study abroad and sociocultural adaptation

| | RAI | INTRI | IDENT | INTRO | EXTER |
|---|---|---|---|---|---|
| SCAS | .45** | .31** | .12 | –.34** | –.38** |

Note: **significant at the 99 per cent level; EXTER = external regulation; IDENT = identified regulation; INTRI = intrinsic motivation, INTRO = introjected regulation; RAI = Relative Autonomy Index; SCAS = Sociocultural Adaptation Scale.

A simple linear regression analysis showed that the RAI was a significant predictor of sociocultural adaptation, $\beta = .45$, $t = 5.98$, $p < .001$, and explained 20 per cent of the variance in the data, $F(1, 140) = 35.70$, $p < .001$, $R^2 = .20$, adjusted $R^2 = .20$.

### 6.2.4 INTERCULTURAL COMPETENCE

Significant positive correlations were found between sociocultural adaptation and all five intercultural competence (IC) subscales (Table 6.3).

Next, the IC subscales were entered into a multiple linear regression model with sociocultural adaptation as the outcome variable. The model was highly significant and contributed to 29 per cent of the variance in the data. Analysis of coefficients showed that cultural empathy (CE), social initiative (SI) and emotional stability (ES) were significant predictors of sociocultural adaptation (Table 6.4).

### 6.2.5 SOCIAL CONTACT

Sociocultural adaptation correlated significantly with social contact with British students (SC-BS), $r = .23$, $p < .001$, with social contact with ISs (SC-IN), $r = .36$, $p < .001$, and with social contact with the local community (SC LC), $r = .18$, $p < .05$. A multiple regression analysis revealed that degree of social contact (SC) contributed to 16 per cent of the variance in the outcome measure. Analysis of coefficients showed that degree of contact with non-co-national ISs (SC-IN) was the main predictor of sociocultural adaptation. Contact with British students (SC-BS) was marginally predictive (Table 6.5).

Table 6.3 Bivariate correlations between intercultural competence and sociocultural adaptation

| | CE | OM | SI | ES | FL |
|---|---|---|---|---|---|
| SCAS | .33** | .36** | .48** | .35** | .28** |

Note: **significant at the 99 per cent level; CE = cultural empathy; ES = emotional stability; FL = flexibility; OM = open-mindedness; SCAS = Sociocultural Adaptation Scale; SI = social initiative.

Table 6.4 Regression analysis of intercultural competence and sociocultural adaptation

| | SCAS | |
|---|---|---|
| | $\beta$ | $t$ |
| CE | .19 | 2.00* |
| OM | –.08 | –.68 |
| SI | .35 | 3.32** |
| ES | .22 | 2.77** |
| FL | .03 | .40 |
| $R^2$ | 0.29 | |
| Adjusted $R^2$ | 0.26 | |
| F(df) | 11.20(5, 135) | |
| Sig. | $p < .001$ | |

Note: **significant at the 99 per cent level; *significant at the 95 per cent level; CE = cultural empathy; ES = emotional stability; FL = flexibility; OM = open-mindedness; SCAS = Sociocultural Adaptation Scale; SI = social initiative.

Table 6.5 Regression analysis of social contact and sociocultural adaptation

| | SCAS | |
|---|---|---|
| | $\beta$ | $t$ |
| SC-BS | .15 | 1.78^ |
| SC-CN | .04 | .43 |
| SC-IN | .33 | 3.95** |
| SC-LC | .05 | .59 |
| $R^2$ | 0.16 | |
| Adjusted $R^2$ | 0.14 | |
| F(df) | 6.63 (4, 138) | |
| Sig. | $p < .001$ | |

Note: **significant at the 99 per cent level; ^significant at the 90 per cent level; SCAS = Sociocultural Adaptation Scale; SC-BS = social contact with British students; SC-CN = contact with co-nationals; SC-IN = contact with non-co-national international students; SC-LC = contact with local community.

### 6.2.6 SOCIAL SUPPORT

Finally, we found a positive and significant correlation with both socio-emotional social support (SS-SE), $r = .33$, $p < .001$, and instrumental social support (SS-IN), $r = .17$, $p < .05$. A multiple regression analysis showed that the two social support subscales together explained 11 per cent of the variance in the outcome measure, but only socio-emotional support emerged as a significant predictor of sociocultural adaptation (Table 6.6). No significant relationship was found between prior overseas experience and sociocultural adaptation.

Table 6.6 Regression analysis of social support and sociocultural adaptation

| | SCAS | | |
|---|---|---|---|
| | $\beta$ | | $t$ |
| SS-SE | .36 | | 3.58** |
| SS-IN | –.06 | | –.60 |
| $R^2$ | | 0.11 | |
| Adjusted $R^2$ | | 0.10 | |
| F(df) | | 8.64 (2, 140) | |
| Sig. | | $p < .001$ | |

Note: **significant at the 99 per cent level; SCAS = Sociocultural Adaptation Scale; SS-SE = socio-emotional social support; SS-IN = instrumental social support.

### 6.2.7 SUMMARY AND DISCUSSION OF QUANTITATIVE FINDINGS

In sum, the data above suggest that students who experienced successful socio-cultural adaptation nine months into their programme of study were likely to feel language-proficient and knowledgeable about the UK, to have made the decision to study abroad independently of others, to be proactive and emotionally stable, and to have high levels of cultural empathy. They were also likely to mix with British students and non-co-national ISs, and to have high levels of socio-emotional support in the host environment (Figure 6.2). We discuss the findings in more detail below in relation to each contributory factor. Wherever possible, we also refer back to the interview data in order to integrate the findings.

**English language ability**

The findings suggest that students who felt more satisfied with their English language ability at Time 2 also reported better sociocultural adaptation. This association could be explained by the crucial role of language ability for social interaction (Swami 2009), which is an inherent part of sociocultural adjustment (Ward et al. 2001). The findings are in line with research suggesting a link between lack of language fluency and sociocultural adjustment difficulties (e.g. Schutz and Richards 2003; Yeh and Inose 2003). Confirmation of the crucial role of host language ability can also be found in the interview data. Findings suggest that students' confidence in using English improved over time and was essential for fulfilling everyday tasks and for interacting with others, two key indicators of sociocultural adaptation (Ward et al. 2001). It appears that proficiency in the host language and, most especially, confidence in one's ability to use the language enable ISs not only to carry out everyday tasks effectively (Yang et al. 2006) but also to interact successfully with others and establish meaningful relationships in the host environment, as language skills invariably affect the quantity and quality of intercultural interaction (Ward et al. 2004). Self-rated English language ability, measured at exit point rather than at entry point, was a significant predictor of sociocultural adaptation. It may well be that the measure at Time 1 was somewhat inaccurate, as students had little

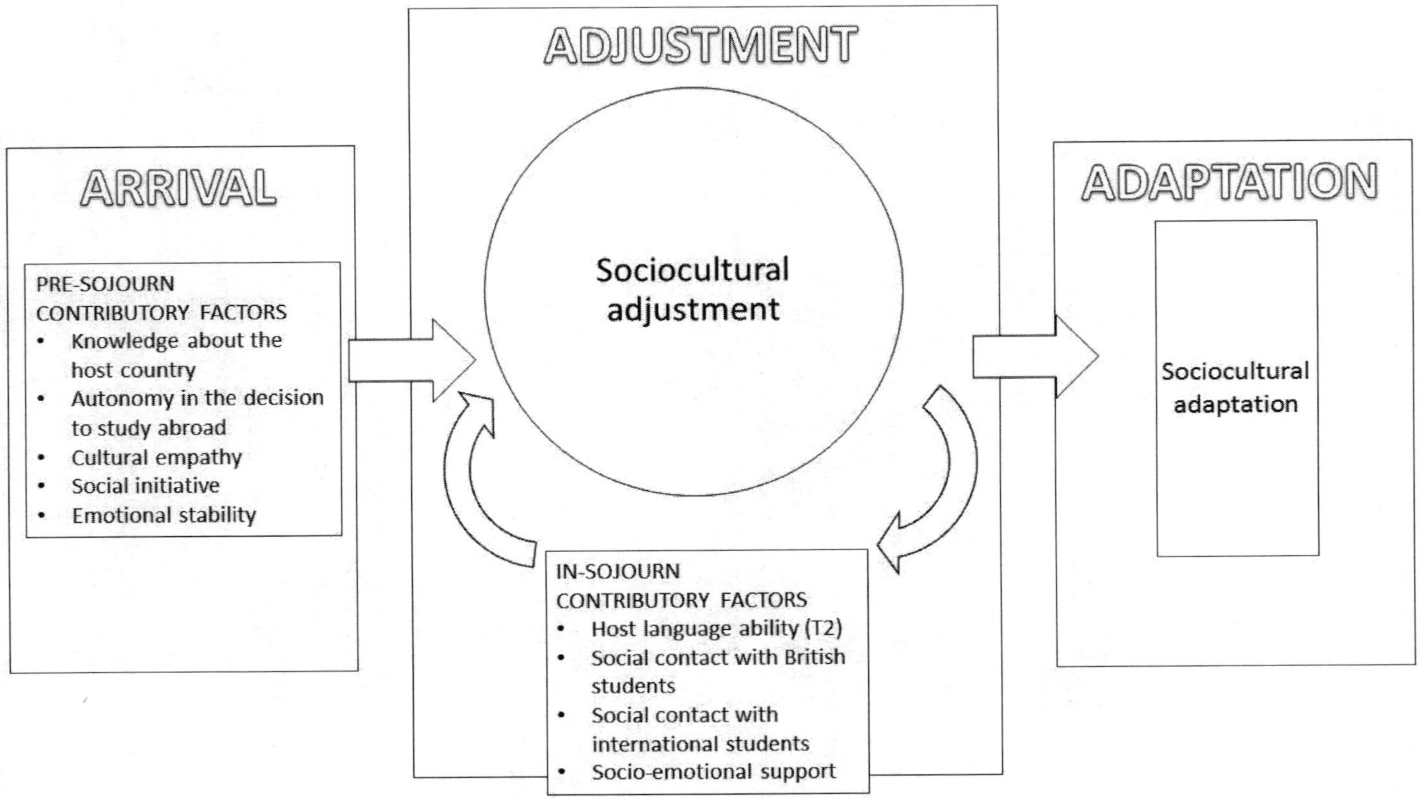


*Figure 6.2* *Significant associations between contributory factors and sociocultural adaptation (T2 = Time 2)*

experience of using English in an applied setting at this point. Future research could very usefully investigate the predictive power of a mid-sojourn host language ability measure.

**Knowledge about the UK**

Students who felt knowledgeable about the UK also reported high levels of sociocultural adaptation after nine months in the host country. This finding is in line with previous research, which has found sociocultural adaptation to be affected by 'cultural knowledge' (Black 1988; Ward et al. 1998), and points to the relevance of culture-learning approaches for the study of student sojourners' sociocultural adjustment and adaptation (Ward et al. 2001).

**Prior overseas experience**

No significant difference was found between students with prior overseas experience and those without, a somewhat surprising finding, as it is commonly assumed that exposure to a foreign country facilitates a social learning process whereby individuals learn to cope with unfamiliar cultural situations effectively (Begley and Shannon 2008). That is, people will interact with others from different backgrounds during their sojourn abroad and thus acquire new knowledge and intercultural skills (Lee and Sukoco 2010). It may be that previous experience of living in other countries may not necessarily be a prerequisite for subsequent sociocultural adaptation, as 'culture-specific skills' (Furnham and Bochner 1986) acquired in one location may not be appropriate in another location. Authors have suggested that prior exposure to the host country might have a more pertinent effect, as it allows sojourners to interact with host nationals and to acquire knowledge specific to the host environment (Gudmundsdottir 2012).

**Autonomy in the decision to study abroad**

The results indicate that the more students felt that they stood behind their decision to study in the UK, the more likely they were to report high levels of sociocultural adaptation nine months into the programme of study. This is in contrast to Chirkov and colleagues' (2007) study of Chinese student sojourners in Belgium and Canada, which found no significant association between relative autonomy in the decision to study abroad and subsequent sociocultural adaptation. Their study, however, employed a cross-sectional design and did not investigate predictive validity of the relative autonomy in the decision to study abroad over time. In a subsequent longitudinal study of IS samples in Canada, Chirkov and colleagues (2008) did find evidence for the predictive validity of relative autonomy in the decision to study abroad for sociocultural adaptation, although the variance in the data was lower than in the present study (10 per cent). It is important to emphasise that an intrinsic motivation for study abroad did not mean that students did not experience any sociocultural adjustment difficulties. The interview data indicate that even those who made their decision to study abroad independently from others and showed a strong personal attraction to the UK did struggle with sociocultural adjustment issues at some point in their sojourn, including aspects such as food, weather and relationship formation with members of the host community (see above).

**Intercultural competence**

We found a close association between sociocultural adaptation and intercultural competence. The amount of variance explained by the intercultural competence subscales together (29 per cent) was statistically significant and is comparable to the findings in prior research. For example, they previously accounted for 28 per cent of the variance in the sociocultural adaptation of Singaporean exchange students (Leong 2007) and for 26 per cent of the variance in peer social support of 'Western' expatriates in Taiwan (van Oudenhoven et al. 2003). More specifically, social initiative, emotional stability and cultural empathy emerged as significant predictors in our data, suggesting that students who scored highly on these aspects were also likely to report high levels of sociocultural adaptation after nine months in the host environment. Social initiative exhibited the strongest effect, which is in line with previous research where increased social initiative predicted a reduction in sociocultural difficulties among student sojourners (Leong 2007). The broader empirical literature further confirms the importance of proactive tendencies for intercultural communication and relationship-building (Black and Gregersen 1999), both of which are essential for sociocultural adaptation (Ward et al. 2001). Van Oudenhoven and van der Zee (2000), for example, found that social initiative was predictive of the extent to which university students in the Netherlands engaged in intercultural activities. According to the culture-learning approach, in order to achieve sociocultural adaptation, the student sojourner needs to interact with others in the host environment (Ward et al. 2001) and has to learn new social skills and behaviours in order to 'fit in' (Furnham and Bochner 1986). Thus, the tendency to approach social situations in an active way becomes a useful prerequisite for forming social relationships and for learning about the host environment (Li and Gasser 2005).

Emotional stability also contributed to better sociocultural adaptation. This is in line with stress and coping approaches to cross-cultural transition, which depict a sojourn abroad as a stressful life event that requires coping responses (Berry 2006). Indeed, contact with the unfamiliar host environment can have an intimidating and distressing effect on the student sojourner (Greenland and Brown 2005), thus emotional stability becomes crucial: emotionally stable individuals are probably more likely to appraise their transition into the host environment as less stressful (van Oudenhoven and van der Zee 2002) and are thus more likely to report higher levels of sociocultural adaptation.

Finally, cultural empathy emerged as a third crucial dimension in students' sociocultural adaptation. It has been linked to fewer sociocultural adjustment difficulties in previous research (Leong 2007). It seems that individuals who are able to empathise with members of different cultural groups are also more likely to establish a rapport with the host environment and to interact successfully with others, thereby acquiring the knowledge and skills necessary to function effectively in the host environment (Bochner 2006).

### Social contact

Our data suggest that social contact is a key contributory factor for sociocultural adaptation, most especially, it seems, contact with non-co-national ISs, which emerged as the main predictor. This finding stands in contrast to previous research, which has identified contact with host nationals as crucial for student sojourners' sociocultural adaptation (e.g. Ward et al. 1998; Li and Gasser 2005). From a culture-learning and social skills perspective, the degree of contact with host nationals is widely seen as an important predictor of sociocultural adaptation (Ward and Rana-Deuba 2000), as social mixing with host nationals is thought to allow student sojourners to acquire the 'culture-specific' skills and knowledge necessary to 'fit in' and function effectively in the host environment (Furnham and Bochner 1982; Bochner 2006). However, in our data, degree of contact with British students emerged as only a marginally significant predictor, and contact with the wider local community was not predictive. What is more, the interview data show that contact with host nationals remained at the periphery of students' social experience throughout the sojourn and thus did not play a central role in their sociocultural adjustment.

Although contact with non-co-national ISs seemed to compensate for the lack of host contact to some extent (cf. Young et al. 2013), the dearth of contact with Britons did result in regret and perceived detriment among the student sojourners. Host contact was seen as important for students' own sense of sociocultural adjustment in the interviews, and many students reported wanting more contact with British people in order to learn about 'British culture'. This does indicate that the students themselves attached great importance to learning about the 'host culture' from host nationals. However, our results show that students were able to achieve high levels of sociocultural adaptation despite a lack of host contact and without this form of culture-learning 'via host contact'.

### Social support

Social support was highly predictive of sociocultural adaptation, in particular socio-emotional support. This finding emphasises the quality of social contacts as an important dimension and mirrors previous research that points to a buffering effect of social support on acculturative stress (Smith and Khawaja 2011). Only recently have studies started to make a distinction between instrumental and socio-emotional support (e.g. Chavajay 2013). The importance of the latter is intriguing, as sociocultural adaptation is generally explored through a culture-learning lens (Ward et al. 2001). From this perspective, instrumental support is viewed as an important contributory factor associated with learning the knowledge and skills necessary to understand the host environment (Li and Gasser 2005; Bochner 2006). This view reflects the assumption that it is host nationals who provide student sojourners with instrumental support (Bochner et al. 1977; Furnham and Bochner 1986). While this might be true, to a certain extent, for university staff and service encounters off campus, the paucity of closer host contact reported in our data could mean that students did not receive the level of instrumental support generated through host ties alluded to in previous studies. It could be that instrumental support is not as central to sociocultural adaptation as previously thought, and that coping resources, in the form of socio-emotional support, might play a more crucial role, thus pointing to the relevance of stress and coping approaches (Berry 2006).

Overall, students' sense of 'successful' sociocultural adaptation is supported by our quantitative data. It shows that it is possible for student sojourners on one-year degree programmes to achieve high levels of sociocultural adaptation. The qualitative data have shown variations, both amongst students and over time, in terms of sociocultural adjustment trajectories over time. The quantitative data have, we hope, provided some insights as to which factors might be behind these variations.

## REFERENCES

Al-Sharideh, K. A., and W. R. Goe (1998), 'Ethnic communities within the university: an examination of factors influencing the personal adjustment of international students', *Research in Higher Education*, 39(6), 699–725.

Bartram B. (2007), 'The socio-cultural needs of international students in higher education: a comparison of staff and student views', *Journal of Studies in International Education*, 11(2), 205–14.

BBC (2013), *UK is Europe's 'Addictions Capital', Says Think Tank*, 1 September. Available at: <http://www.bbc.co.uk/news/uk-23913818> (last accessed 18 December 2018).

Begley, T., and L. Shannon (2008), 'The antecedents of a four-factor model of cultural intelligence', in S. Ang and L. Van Dyne (eds), *Handbook on Cultural Intelligence*, New York: M. E. Sharpe, pp. 41–55.

Berry, J. W. (2006), 'Acculturative stress', in P. T. P. Wong and L. C. S. Wong (eds), *Handbook of Multicultural Perspectives on Stress and Coping*, New York: Springer, pp. 287–98.

Black, J. S. (1988), 'Work role transitions: a study of American expatriate managers in Japan', *Journal of International Business Studies*, 19(2), 277–94.

Black, J. S., and H. B. Gregersen (1999), 'The right way to manage expats', *Harvard Business Review*, 77(2): 52–7.

Bochner, S. (2006), 'Sojourners', in D. L. Sam and J. W. Berry (eds), *The Cambridge Handbook of Acculturation Psychology*, Cambridge: Cambridge University Press, pp. 181–97.

Bochner, S., B. M. McLeod and A. Lin (1977), 'Friendship patterns of overseas students: a functional model', *International Journal of Psychology*, 12(4), 277–94.

Brown, L. (2008), *The Adjustment Journey of International Postgraduate Students at a University in England*, Unpublished doctoral thesis, Bournemouth University, UK.

Chavajay, J. (2013), 'Perceived social support among international students at a U.S. university', *Psychological Reports*, 112(2), 667–77.

Chirkov, V. I., M. Vansteenkiste, R. Tao and M. Lynch (2007), 'The role of motivation to study abroad in the adaptation of international students: a self-determination theory approach', *International Journal of Intercultural Relations*, 31(2), 199–222.

Chirkov, V. I., S. Safdar, J. de Guzman and K. Playford (2008), 'Further examining the role motivation to study abroad plays in the adaptation of international students in Canada', *International Journal of Intercultural Relations*, 32(5), 427–40.

Coles, R., and V. Swami (2012), 'The sociocultural adjustment trajectory of international university students and the role of university structures: a qualitative investigation', *Journal of Research in International Education*, 11(1), 87–100.

Fischer, K. (2012), 'Many foreign students are friendless in the U.S., study finds', *Higher Education Chronicle*, 14 June. Available at: <https://www.chronicle.com/article/Many-Foreign-Students-Find/132275> (last accessed 18 December 2018).

Furnham, A., and S. Bochner (1982), 'Social difficulty in a foreign culture: an empirical analysis of culture shock', in S. Bochner (ed.), *Cultures in Contact: Studies in Cross-cultural Interaction*, Oxford: Pergamon, pp. 161–98.

Furnham, A., and S. Bochner (1986), *Culture Shock: Psychological Reactions to Unfamiliar Environments*, London: Methuen.

Gill, J. (2002), 'Reported levels of alcohol consumption and binge drinking within the UK undergraduate student population over the last 25 years', *Alcohol and Alcoholism*, 37(2), 109–20.

Greenland, K., and R. Brown (2005), 'Acculturation and acculturative stress among Japanese students in the United Kingdom', *Journal of Social Psychology*, 145(4), 373–89.

Gudmundsdottir, S. (2012), 'The influence of prior living and working experience of Nordic expatriates on cultural adjustment in the United States', *International Journal of Humanities and Social Science*, 2(19), 87–92.

Harrison, N., and N. Peacock (2008), 'Mindful or mindless: do UK student drinking cultures and stereotypes undermine intercultural contact?', in Higher Education Academy (ed.), *University Life Uncovered: Making Sense of the Student Experience*, pp. 44–56. Available at: <https://www.heacademy.ac.uk/system/files/university-life-uncovered_0.pdf> (last accessed 10 December 2016).

Hechanova-Alampay, R., T. A. Beehr, N. D. Christiansen and R. K. van Horn (2002), 'Adjustment and strain among domestic and international student sojourners: a longitudinal study', *School Psychology International*, 23(4), 458–74.

Hibell, B., U. Guttormsson, S. Ahlström, O. Balakireva, T. Bjarnason, A. Kokkevi and L. Kraus (2009), *The 2007 ESPAD Report: Substance Use Among Students in 35 European Countries*, The Swedish Council for Information on Alcohol and Other Drugs, Stockholm, Sweden. Available at: <http://www.emcdda.europa.eu/attachements.cfm/att_77168_EN_ESPAD_summary_EN.pdf> (last accessed 18 December 2018).

Jacob, E. J., and J. W. Greggo (2001), 'Using counselor training and collaborative programming strategies in working with international students', *Journal of Multicultural Counseling and Development*, 29, 73–88.

Khawaja, N. G., and H. M. Stallman (2011), 'Understanding the coping strategies of international students: a qualitative approach', *Australian Journal of Guidance and Counselling*, 21(2), 203 24.

Kudo, K., and K. A. Simkin (2003), 'Intercultural friendship formation: the case of Japanese students at an Australian university', *Journal of Intercultural Studies*, 24(2), 91–114.

Lee, L.-Y., and B. M. Sukoco (2010), 'The effects of cultural intelligence on expatriate performance: the moderating effects of international experience', *The International Journal of Human Resource Management*, 21(7), 963–81.

Leong, C.-H. (2007), 'Predictive validity of the Multicultural Personality Questionnaire: a longitudinal study on the socio-psychological adaptation of Asian undergraduates who took part in a study-abroad program', *International Journal of Intercultural Relations*, 31(5), 545–59.

Li, A., and M. B. Gasser (2005), 'Predicting Asian international students' sociocultural adjustment: a test of two mediation models', *International Journal of Intercultural Relations*, 29(5), 561–76.

Maundeni, T. (2001), 'The role of social networks in the adjustment of African students to British society: students' perceptions', *Race, Ethnicity and Education*, 4(3), 253–76.

Montgomery, C. (2010), *Understanding the International Student Experience*, Basingstoke: Palgrave Macmillan.

Montgomery, C., and L. McDowell (2009), 'Social networks and the international student experience: a community of practice?', *Journal of Studies in International Education*, 13(4), 455–66.

OECD (2012), *Education at a Glance 2012: OECD Indicators*. Available at: <https://www.oecd-ilibrary.org/education/education-at-a-glance-2012_eag-2012-en> (last accessed 10 December 2018).

Peacock, N., and N. Harrison (2009), '"It's so much easier to go with what's easy": mindfulness and the discourse between home and international students in the United Kingdom', *Journal of Studies in International Education*, 13(4), 487–508.

Plant, M., and M. Plant (2006), *Binge Britain: Alcohol and the National Response*, Oxford: Oxford University Press.

Rosenthal, D. A., V. J. Russell and G. J. Thomson (2006), *A Growing Experience: The Health and Well-being of International Students at the University of Melbourne*. Available at: <https://services.unimelb.edu.au/__data/assets/pdf_file/0011/358436/GrowingExperience.pdf> (last accessed 13 December 2018).

Schartner, A. (2015), '"You cannot talk with all of the strangers in a pub": a longitudinal case study of international postgraduate students' social ties at a British university', *Higher Education*, 69(2), 225–41.

Schutz, A., and M. Richards (2003), 'International students' experience of graduate study in Canada', *Journal of the International Society for Teacher Education*, 7(1), 10–26.

Smart, R. G., and A. C. Ogborne (2000), 'Drug use and drinking among students in 36 countries', *Addictive Behaviours*, 25(3), 455–60.

Smith, R. A., and N. G. Khawaja (2011), 'A review of the acculturation experiences of international students', *International Journal of Intercultural Relations*, 35(6), 699–71.

Sovic, S. (2009), 'Hi-bye friends and the herd instinct: international and home students in the creative arts', *Higher Education*, 58(6), 747–61.

Swami, V. (2009), 'Predictors of sociocultural adjustment among sojourning Malaysian students in Britain', *International Journal of Psychology*, 44(4), 266–73.

Tajfel, H., and J. Dawson (1965), *Disappointed Guests*, London: Oxford University Press.

Thomson, G., D. Rosenthal and J. Russell (2006), *Cultural Stress Among International Students at an Australian University*, Paper presented at the Australian International Education Conference, Canberra, October. Available at: <http://aiec.idp.com/uploads/pdf/Thomson%20%28Paper%29%20Fri%201050%20MR5.pdf> (last accessed 18 December 2018).

UKCOSA (UK Council for Overseas Student Affairs) (2014), *International Students in UK Universities and Colleges: Broadening our Horizons. Report of the UKCOSA Survey*. Available at: <http://www.ukcosa.org.uk/files/pdf/BOHreport.pdf> (last accessed 10 December 2018).

UNITE (2006), *The International Student Experience Report*, Bristol: UNITE. Available at: <http://www.unite-group.co.uk/sites/default/files/2017-03/international-student-experience-report-2006.pdf> (last accessed 18 December 2018).

van der Zee, K. I., and J. P. van Oudenhoven (2000), 'The Multicultural Personality Questionnaire: a multidimensional instrument of multicultural effectiveness', *European Journal of Personality*, 14(4), 291–309.

van Oudenhoven, J. P., S. Mol and K. I. van der Zee (2003), 'Study of the adjustment of Western expatriates in Taiwan ROC with the Multicultural Personality Questionnaire', *Asian Journal of Social Psychology*, 6(2), 159–70.

van Oudenhoven, J. P., and K. I. van der Zee (2002), 'Predicting multicultural effectiveness of international students: the Multicultural Personality Questionnaire', *International Journal of Intercultural Relations*, 26(6), 679–94.

Vivancos, R., I. Abubaker and P. R. Hunter (2009), 'Sexual behaviour, drugs and alcohol use of international students at a British university: a cross-sectional survey', *International Journal of STD & AIDS*, 20(9), 619–22.

Volet, S. E., and G. Ang (1998), 'Culturally mixed groups on international campuses: an opportunity for intercultural learning', *Higher Education Research & Development*, 17(1), 5–23.

Volet, S. E., and A. Tan-Quigley (1999), 'Interactions of South-east Asian students and administrative staff at university in Australia: the significance of reciprocal understanding', *Journal of Higher Education Policy and Management*, 21(3), 95–115.

Ward, C. (2004), 'Psychological theories of culture contact and their implications for intercultural training and interventions', in D. Landis, J. M. Bennett and M. J. Bennett (eds), *Handbook of Intercultural Training*, Thousand Oaks, CA: Sage, pp. 185–216.

Ward, C., S. Bochner and A. Furnham (2001), *The Psychology of Culture Shock*, 2nd edn, Hove: Routledge.

Ward, C., C. Leong and M. Low (2004), 'Personality and sojourner adjustment: an exploration of the Big Five and the cultural fit proposition', *Journal of Cross-Cultural Psychology*, 35, 137–51.

Ward, C., Y. Okura, A. Kennedy and T. Kojima (1998), 'The U-curve on trial: a longitudinal study of psychological and sociocultural adjustment during cross-cultural transition', *International Journal of Intercultural Relations*, 22(3), 277–91.

Ward, C., and A. Rana-Deuba (2000), 'Home and host culture influences on sojourner adjustment', *International Journal of Intercultural Relations*, 24, 291–306.

Wright, C., and A. Schartner (2013), '"I can't … I won't?" International students at the threshold of social interaction', *Journal of Research in International Education*, 12(2), 113–28.

Yang, R. P.-J., K. A. Noels and K. D. Saumure (2006), 'Multiple routes to cross-cultural adaptation for international students: mapping the paths between self-construals, English language confidence, and adjustment', *International Journal of Intercultural Relations*, 30(4), 487–506.

Yeh, C. J., and M. Inose (2003), 'International students' reported English fluency, social support satisfaction, and social connectedness as predictors of acculturative stress', *Counselling Psychology Quarterly*, 16(1), 15–28.

Young, T. J., P. G. Sercombe, I. Sachdev, R. Naeb and A. Schartner (2013), 'Success factors for international postgraduate students' adjustment: exploring the roles of intercultural competence, language proficiency, social contact and social support', *European Journal of Higher Education*, 3, 151–71.

Yuan, W. (2011), 'Academic and cultural experiences of Chinese students at an American university: a qualitative study', *Intercultural Communication Studies*, 20(1), 141–57.

# 7
# ASSOCIATIONS BETWEEN ADJUSTMENT DOMAINS

In this chapter, we present both quantitative and qualitative data related to the interrelationships between ISs' academic, psychological and sociocultural adjustment and adaptation, and discuss conceptual overlaps between the three domains. Below, we first present data related to the relationship between sociocultural and psychological adjustment and adaptation (7.1), followed by data on the association between academic and psychological adjustment and adaptation (7.2) and, finally, on that between sociocultural and academic adjustment and adaptation (7.3). Below, we refer to and integrate previously published research, and we extend our previous contributions with a specific focus on the interactions between the different domains that were our focus in Chapters 4 to 6 above. By presenting the quantitative and qualitative data together, we hope to portray any 'measurable' associations between the domains whilst also reporting on any perceived interactions as experienced by the students *in situ*. We end with a brief conclusion and implications for research and practice (7.4).

Before we present our empirical data, we feel it is important to reiterate how the three domains are commonly conceptualised in the literature (see also Chapter 2 of this book). Academic adjustment/adaptation[1] may include factors such as academic lifestyle, academic motivation and academic achievement (Anderson et al. 2016). A common indicator of the latter are grade point averages (GPAs; Andrade 2006). Sociocultural adjustment/adaptation is conceptualised as the acquisition of knowledge and social skills that individuals need to 'fit in' with and effectively negotiate their new cultural environment (Masgoret and Ward 2006). Psychological adjustment/adaptation commonly refers to psychological wellbeing or satisfaction with life (Searle and Ward 1990).

Research on ISs' academic, psychological and sociocultural adjustment and adaptation is burgeoning (see Chapter 2), but a review of this literature reveals that most studies appear to treat them as three separate domains of enquiry (Schartner and Young 2016). They also tend to be portrayed as distinct units in most prevailing conceptual models. Although various authors have pointed to the conceptual interrelatedness of the three domains, especially between psychological and sociocultural adjustment (see, especially, work by Colleen Ward and colleagues, Chapter 2), empirical research exploring the spillover effects between the three domains is relatively sparse. Consequently, we still know very little about whether, how and to what extent they interact with one another. Further explorations to ascertain their interrelationships are needed if we are to get a fully rounded perspective (Zhou et al. 2008). On a more practical level, many university support systems tend to be divided, broadly, into those three domains, with academic support, psychological/wellbeing support and social support provided separately at many host universities (Wintre et al. 2009). Any overlaps between these three areas therefore not only are important for the conceptual advancement of the field but are also relevant to those working with and supporting ISs.

In sum, our survey of the literature suggests that there appears to be, firstly, very little research measuring interactions between academic, psychological and socio-cultural adaptation using quantitative measures, and secondly, a lack of longitudinal studies that 'track' the relationships of the three adjustment domains over time using qualitative methods of enquiry (cf. Wang and Xiao 2014). To address these gaps in the literature, we report below on our own data, starting with the relationship between sociocultural and psychological adjustment/adaptation.

## 7.1 SOCIOCULTURAL AND PSYCHOLOGICAL ADJUSTMENT AND ADAPTATION

Firstly, we were interested in the association between sociocultural and psychological adaptation. These two domains are largely treated as conceptually distinct in the literature but have been found to be interrelated, with social difficulties probably having an impact on the individual's psychological wellbeing (Searle and Ward 1990). Indeed, unfamiliar customs and social norms encountered in the new cultural milieu are often the primary source of psychological stressors for cross-cultural sojourners (see Chapter 5), and studies have shown that sojourners who are better adapted to their host environment tend to report higher wellbeing (Berry et al. 2006). It is thought that psychological difficulties can be minimised if the individual manages to acquire the appropriate skills to 'fit in' with the host environment (Wu and Mak 2012).

There are some recent studies that have attempted to measure the relationship between psychological and sociocultural adaptation, such as Wu and Mak (2012), who found a significant interrelationship between sociocultural maladaptation and psychological distress in a sample of mainland Chinese students in Hong Kong. Similarly, in their study of ISs and staff at a British university, Demes and Geeraert (2014) found sociocultural adaptation and psychological adaptation to be positively interrelated: that is, respondents who reported high sociocultural adaptation also tended to report high levels of psychological adaptation ($r = 0.55$). They also found that greater sociocultural adaptation was significantly related to a range of wellbeing indicators, including lower stress and anxiety levels and higher self-esteem and satisfaction with life. Similarly, perceived difficulty in daily life was found to be a significant predictor of self-reported psychological stress in Spencer-Oatey and Xiong's (2006) study of Chinese English language students at a British university. Greater sociocultural adaptation was also found to have a positive impact on the psychological wellbeing of ISs sojourning in Australia (Leung 2001).

The literature further suggests that students who report greater levels of anxiety also tend to report greater sociocultural adjustment difficulties (Wang and Xiao

2014). In a USA-based student sample, Mahmood and Burke (2018) found a significant negative, albeit weak, relationship between levels of acculturative stress and sociocultural adaptation. Finally, in their study of Cape Verdean ISs in Portugal, Neto and Wilks (2017) found that subjective wellbeing correlated positively with sociocultural competence. The latter emerged as a significant predictor of subjective wellbeing.

Some of the earliest research on the relationship between psychological and sociocultural adaptation in different groups of cross-cultural sojourners (students, volunteers, business people, domestic workers and diplomats) was conducted by Colleen Ward and colleagues in the early to mid-1990s. This body of work has consistently produced significant correlations between the two domains ranging from 0.23 to 0.72 (Ward et al. 1998). However, the strength of this relationship has been found to be affected by a range of variables, including time and 'cultural distance'. In their study of Japanese students sojourning in New Zealand, Ward and colleagues (1998) found sociocultural and psychological adaptation to be significantly related ($r = 0.36$) after twelve months in the new environment, but no significant relationship was found for the early sojourn stages. Their research also suggests that the association might be stronger for sojourners who make a 'small' cross-cultural transition: for example, Malaysian students in neighbouring and culturally similar Singapore (Ward and Kennedy 1993). Finally, Ward and colleagues have found that sociocultural adjustment and psychological adjustment appear to follow somewhat different trajectories over time (Ward et al. 1998; Ward et al. 2001). In line with social skills and culture-learning approaches, sociocultural adjustment is thought to follow a learning curve with a steep beginning that gradually levels off over time. Psychological adjustment, on the other hand, is thought to follow a less stable temporal pattern and has been found to fluctuate over time (Ward and Kennedy 1996).

Literature on expatriate adjustment also suggests a relatedness between psychological adaptation and aspects of sociocultural adaptation. In a study of 'Western' expatriate business managers in mainland China, Selmer (1999) found statistically significant correlations between subjective wellbeing on the one hand, and general adjustment ($r = 0.22$), interaction adjustment ($r = 0.25$) and work adjustment ($r = 0.33$) on the other.

Based on our review of previous literature, we presumed a positive relationship between the adaptation domains in our IS sample:

> *H1a: There is a positive association between the sociocultural adaptation and the psychological adaptation of ISs on a one-year postgraduate programme.*
> *H1b: Sociocultural adaptation predicts the psychological wellbeing of international postgraduate students on a one-year postgraduate programme.*
> *H1c: Sociocultural adaptation predicts the satisfaction with life of international postgraduate students on a one-year postgraduate programme.*

Analysis revealed that all three hypotheses were upheld in our data. First, a Pearson's correlation showed that the sociocultural adaptation measure correlated significantly with indicators of psychological adaptation, psychological wellbeing ($r$ = .35, p < .01) and satisfaction with life ($r$ = .43, p < .01), indicating that students who feel well adjusted to the new social and cultural milieu also tend to feel happier and more satisfied with life, and vice versa. There appears, then, to be a positive association between the level of sociocultural adaptation and the degree of psychological adaptation of ISs.

Next, a simple linear regression analysis showed that sociocultural adaptation alone explained 12 per cent of the variance of psychological wellbeing, $F(1, 141) = 19.65$, $p < .001$, and was a significant predictor, $\beta = .35$, t(141) = 4.43, $p < .001$. Another simple linear regression analysis showed that sociocultural adaptation alone explained 19 per cent of the variance in satisfaction with life, $F(1, 141) = 32.43$, $p < .001$, and was a significant predictor, $\beta = .43$, $t(141) = 5.70$, $p < .001$. It appears that if students manage to achieve high levels of sociocultural adaptation in the host environment, they are also likely to feel happier and well in themselves, and more satisfied with life in general.

In the qualitative dataset we also found indications for possible interactions between students' sense of wellbeing and aspects of sociocultural adjustment. The 'cold' and 'rainy' weather in the host city appeared to put a strain on psychological wellbeing throughout the one-year sojourn. Coping with cold weather was a pre-arrival concern for many, especially those from warmer climates:

> The snow, I've never lived in the snow [...] I've never had to walk in it [...] that's probably the only thing that I'm nervous about, being cold. (US student, female, Time 1)

The cold weather during the winter months remained a dominant topic of conversation and some students pointed to the implications of the 'depressing' British weather.

One aspect that appeared to impact negatively on students' satisfaction with life in the host environment was a reported lack of contact with British people (cf. Schartner 2015). Students reported finding it difficult to instigate and maintain meaningful contact with local people, most especially younger people and 'home' students, often to their great perceived detriment. 'I don't have any British friends' was a common statement across the interview sample.

> I don't have British friends and I'm really keenly searching for people (...) where can I find them? (...) in a pub, but you cannot talk with all of the strangers in a pub. (Turkish student, female, Time 2)
>
> I always feel depressed since I cannot communicate better with local people in Newcastle. It makes me feel very upset. (Chinese student, female, Time 1)

One reason for the dearth of host national contact appeared to be differences in how students socialised, with several interviewees reporting feeling scared to approach young people in the host city.

> I am afraid to talk with them. They made their hair in colourful so I don't think they are friendly to talk with. (Chinese student, female, Time 1)

The vibrant nightlife in the host city and related consumption of alcohol appeared to affect students, with some reporting feeling anxious when walking home at night. Negotiation of everyday communication episodes was a cause of concern for a number of interviewees, most especially in the early sojourn stages, with some students feeling they lacked appropriate knowledge to interpret social cues in the host environment. The local accent also appeared to add to this feeling.

> I have sometimes difficulty in understanding other accents, including British accent. That's the basic concern for me. This is the most different. Sometimes I don't know how to react or how to behave in certain situations so I hope I will learn. (Turkish student, male, Time 1)
>
> They have difficult accent, sometimes I just cannot understand, maybe it's the [local variety] accent not all British. (Latvian student, female, Time 1)

English language ability for everyday life, or lack thereof, was a significant source of worry for many students.

> I don't know how to conquer barriers about language [...] it's hard for me to communicate with other people. (Chinese student, female, Time 1)
>
> [...] I'm not very confident about my English. (Chinese student, female, Time 1)

Our results largely corroborate those of previous studies and add further evidence for a close empirical relationship between sociocultural and psychological aspects of IS adaptation.

## 7.2 ACADEMIC AND PSYCHOLOGICAL ADJUSTMENT AND ADAPTATION

Studies of both 'home' and 'international' students across different HE contexts seem overwhelmingly to suggest a strong link between student wellbeing and academic performance. For example, in a study of undergraduate students in Canada, higher levels of psychological wellbeing were linked with better academic outcomes (Chow 2010). Similarly, a longitudinal study of Swedish students found that psychological difficulties, such as anxiety, depression and tiredness, negatively affected academic achievement (Vaez and Laflamme 2008). Subjective wellbeing was also linked to academic achievement in a sample of Lebanese university students (Ayyash-Abdo and Sanchez-Ruiz 2012). Buddington (2002) found that lower stress levels led to higher academic achievement among Jamaican immigrant college students in the USA, and Kotze and Kleynhans (2013) reported that better psychological wellbeing was positively related to the academic performance of first-year undergraduate students at a South African university.

The few quantitative studies that aimed to measure the relationship between academic and psychological adaptation among student sojourners suggest a close link between the two. In a sample of ISs at four Malaysian universities, Othman and colleagues (2014) found that affective adjustment (that is, the ability to regulate emotions or feelings) was a significant predictor of academic performance. Bulgan and Çiftçi's (2017) study of married ISs sojourning in the USA found that academic self-efficacy was a significant predictor of both psychological wellbeing and satisfaction with life. Academic self-efficacy had previously also been linked to psychological adaptation in a study of international postgraduate students by Poyrazli and colleagues (2002). Higher levels of acculturative stress were related to lower levels of academic adaptation among a sample of ISs sojourning in Turkey (Cura and Isik 2016). Spencer-Oatey and Xiong (2006) found significant correlations between self-reported psychological stress and academic achievement (students who reported greater levels of stress tended to obtain lower end-of-degree GPAs) among a sample of Chinese students in the UK, and Neto and Wilks (2017) found that academic life satisfaction was a significant predictor for subjective wellbeing in a sample of Cape Verdean students in Portugal.

In light of the above literature we presumed a positive relationship between academic and psychological adaptation in our data:

*H2a: There is a positive association between the academic adaptation and the psychological adaptation of ISs on a one-year postgraduate programme.*
*H2b: Academic achievement predicts the psychological wellbeing of ISs on a one-year postgraduate programme.*
*H2c: Academic achievement predicts the satisfaction with life of ISs on a one-year postgraduate programme.*

Analysis showed that H2a could be only partially verified and H2b was not upheld. Firstly, all three indicators of academic achievement correlated positively with satisfaction with life – the taught GPA ($r$ = .33, p < .01), the research GPA ($r$ = .30, p < .01) and the overall degree GPA ($r$ = .34, p < .01). This suggests that students who performed well academically also tended to feel more satisfied with their lives, and vice versa. No significant associations were found between academic achievement and psychological wellbeing.

Next, a simple linear regression analysis showed that the overall degree GPA was a significant predictor of satisfaction with life, $\beta = .34$, $t(138) = 4.30$, $p < .001$, and explained 12 per cent of the variance, $F(1, 138) = 18.51$, $p < .001$. This suggests that students who achieve a good academic outcome at the end of their degree programme are also likely to feel more satisfied with life. H2c was therefore sustained in our data. Overall, our results suggest that academic adaptation appears to be closely related to satisfaction with life but not with psychological wellbeing.

We were able to discern some evidence for a link between academic adjustment and student wellbeing in the interview data. Adjustment to the new academic environment and the *modus operandi* at the host university were key concerns for the students in the early sojourn stages, with some students expressing a fear of failure early on:

> I am worried about not being able to complete the programme because otherwise when you come back to Turkey, like you have to pay for the money, that's the problem. So I am a little bit under stress that I should complete it successfully. (Turkish student, male, Time 1)

The academic demands of the degree programme, especially practices such as self-directed learning, were a source of great concern for some interviewees, who felt that they were inadequately prepared for the essay-based nature of their course. The prospect of regular assessed essays caused students to feel 'worried' and 'nervous':

> I'm worried that I might not have this good level of academic writing. (Latvian student, female, Time 1)

Beyond the first few weeks, it became evident that students' psychological wellbeing was associated, to some extent, with the nature and intensity of coursework. Several students reported a strain put on their wellbeing by busy assessment periods:

> [...] most of the things were written assignment in the first semester, so you had to do a lot and it was your first semester. It made me depressive. (Turkish student, female, Time 2)
>
> I also had the pressure of writing all the assignments [...] it really wasn't that good I guess. (Latvian student, female, Time 2)
>
> I'm a bit stressed with the exams and the assignments because they are all concentrated in this month mainly, so yeah it's a very intense period of my life. (Romanian student, female, Time 3)

While our quantitative data showed significant links between academic adaptation and satisfaction with life, the interview data provided some evidence that aspects of academic adjustment can also have an impact on students' own sense of psychological wellbeing.

## 7.3 SOCIOCULTURAL AND ACADEMIC ADJUSTMENT AND ADAPTATION

Zhou and Todman (2009: 481), in their study of Chinese postgraduate students in the UK, concluded that student sojourners' academic adaptation could 'not be considered in isolation from general life and social aspects of their adaptation'. However, empirical studies on the link between sociocultural and academic adaptation are sparse. There are some indications of the importance of social connectedness for academic adaptation. For example, greater perceived social support has been linked to academic adaptation in a sample of Jordanian 'home' students (Malkoush 2000) and in a sample of ISs sojourning in Turkey (Cura and Isik 2016). In one of the few studies explicitly measuring the relationship between the two domains, Leung (2001) found that greater sociocultural adaptation had a positive impact on the academic outcomes of student sojourners in Australia.

A link between sociocultural adaptation and aspects of academic adaptation has been reported in literature from the high-school context, where social adaptation has been found to have an impact on schoolchildren's GPAs, academic self-esteem and absenteeism (deRosier and Lloyd 2011). The literature on expatriate adjustment has pointed to spillover effects between general adjustment and work adjustment,[2] and between interaction adjustment and work adjustment (see a review by Bhaskar-Shrinivas et al. 2005). For example, Takeuchi and colleagues (2002), in their investigation of USA-based Japanese business expatriates, found significant spillover effects between general adjustment and work adjustment. In their study of expatriate academics in China and Taiwan, Selmer and colleagues (2015) found a positive relationship between general adjustment and interaction adjustment on the one hand, and job adjustment on the other hand. They also reported a significant and strong correlation between general and interaction adjustment ($r$ = 0.69). However, contrary to previous studies, in their investigation of public sector expatriates, Selmer and Fenner (2009) found no significant association between general adjustment and interaction adjustment on the one hand, and work adjustment on the other.

Nonetheless, based on prior studies, we assumed a positive relationship between sociocultural and academic adaptation in our IS sample:

*H3a: There is a positive association between the sociocultural adaptation and academic adaptation of ISs on a one-year postgraduate programme.*

*H3b: Sociocultural adaptation predicts the academic achievement of ISs on a one-year postgraduate programme.*

Both hypotheses were upheld in our data. Firstly, correlation analyses yielded moderately strong positive associations between sociocultural adaptation and all three indicators of academic adaptation – the research GPA ($r$ = .35, p < .01), the taught GPA ($r$ = .28, p < .01) and the overall degree GPA ($r$ = .33, $p$ < .01). This suggests that students who managed to cope well with the practical and behavioural aspects of living in a new social and cultural milieu were also likely to achieve a good academic outcome, and vice versa.

Next, simple linear regression analyses yielded significant relationships between sociocultural adaptation and all three academic achievement measures. Firstly, sociocultural adaptation was a significant predictor for the taught GPA ($\beta$ = .28, $t$(140) = 3.41, $p$ < .01), explaining 8 per cent of the variance in the data, $F$(1, 140) = 11.64, $p$ = .001. Secondly, sociocultural adaptation was a significant predictor of the research GPA ($\beta$ = .35, $t$(138) = 4.41, p < .01), explaining 12 per cent of the variance, $F$(1, 138) = 19.49, $p$ < .001. Thirdly, sociocultural adaptation was a significant predictor of the overall degree GPA ($\beta$ = .33, $t$(138) = 4.12, $p$ < .01, explaining 11 per cent of the variance in the data, $F$(1, 138) = 16.94, $p$ < .001. These results suggest that students who manage to achieve a good 'fit' with the host environment are also likely to achieve good academic outcomes on both the teaching-focused and the more student-led aspects of the degree programme.

The data also provided some indications for an association between sociocultural adjustment and academic adjustment. For example, a number of interviewees commented on the impact of coursework on social activities and felt they had missed opportunities to get to know the host environment:

> Actually I thought that we didn't spend enough time to know much thing about acculturate because we had to do the assignments. I couldn't go to the other cities or I couldn't explore the other parts of the city. (Turkish student, male, Time 2)

As academic workload and pressure increased, the time students spent socialising appeared to have subsequently decreased. A number of interviewees explained how, as academic workload intensified, they had less contact time with their friends. Thus, course demands and busy assignment periods sometimes became an impediment to social contact.

> I had very limited contact with other students, with other people. And I also had the pressure of writing all the assignments (Latvian student, female, Time 2)
> I have lots of jobs to do and I will not be socialising until mid of June, so I'm not very active socially. (Lithuanian student, male, Time 3)
> [...] a lot of times I was too busy to meet with friends [...] (Finnish student, female, Time 3)

## 7.4 CONCLUSION

Amongst the small body of published quantitative research, there are strong indications for close empirical relationships between the three adaptation domains (see our literature review above). Our findings were largely in line with those of these previous studies. The quantifiable 'outcome'-focused data provided evidence for significant associations between the adaptation domains. It appears that IS sojourners who achieve high levels of adaptation in one area are also likely to achieve high levels of adaptation in another. The interview data, very broadly, supported the quantitative findings. Although the interviewees were not asked explicitly about any interactions between the adjustment domains, it became evident from their accounts that challenges experienced in one area could have an impact on another. This was especially true for the relationship between academic and psychological adjustment, which stood out as possibly having the strongest spillover effect.

Some tentative conclusions can be drawn from the findings above. Firstly, they provide further evidence that sociocultural and psychological adaptation are closely linked (Ward et al. 2001). This is hardly surprising. It seems likely that students who manage to settle into the unfamiliar host environment socially and culturally will feel happier and more satisfied with their lives. Likewise, it seems plausible that students who feel happy and well in themselves and with their lives will also embrace the new social and cultural milieu more fully. Secondly, the association found between sociocultural and academic adaptation provides further evidence that sociocultural adaptation should not be considered in isolation from academic performance (Zhou and Todman 2009). Our findings suggest that students who cope well with the practical and behavioural aspects demanded of them in the host environment are also likely to be successful academically. This seems plausible, as academic functioning and adjustment to university life could well be seen as aspects of sociocultural adjustment. Sociocultural adaptation is traditionally viewed as an outcome variable and is therefore seldom used as an independent variable in studies of IS adaptation. However, it seems plausible that students who acquire the knowledge and skills necessary to 'fit into' the sociocultural environment in the host country (Ward et al. 2001) will also be successful academically. Finally, the results suggest an association between academic adaptation and aspects of psychological adaptation. It seems instinctively obvious that more 'successful' students will feel happier and more satisfied with their lives. Surprisingly, we did not find significant associations between academic achievement and psychological wellbeing in our survey data. However, our results do suggest that students who perform well academically are more likely to feel satisfied with their lives, and students' own accounts suggest that aspects of academic adjustment may well impinge on subjective wellbeing.

On a final note, it is important to acknowledge that we measured our adaptation indices only at sojourn end-point (that is, nine months into the sojourn) and we recognise that the extent of the relationship between the three domains may be influenced by time. Future research could very usefully include mid-sojourn adaptation measures to account for this.

## NOTES

1. In this chapter, we use 'adaptation' when referring to measurable outcomes, and 'adjustment' when referring to processes and trajectories tracked over time. As there is much variation in terminology, when reporting on individual studies we will adopt the term(s) used by the respective author(s).
2. Work adjustment can be seen as the equivalent of academic adjustment for expatriate business sojourners.

## REFERENCES

Anderson, J. R., Y. Guan and Y. Koc (2016), 'The academic adjustment scale: measuring the adjustment of permanent resident or sojourner students', *International Journal of Intercultural Relations*, 54, 68–76.

Andrade, M. S. (2006), 'International students in English-speaking universities: adjustment factors', *Journal of Research in International Education*, 5(2), 131–54.

Ayyash-Abdo, H., and M.-J. Sanchez-Ruiz (2012), 'Subjective wellbeing and its relationship with academic achievement and multilinguality among Lebanese university students', *International Journal of Psychology*, 47(3), 192–202.

Berry, J. W., J. Phinney, D. Sam and P. Vedder (eds) (2006), *Immigrant Youth in Cultural Transition: Acculturation, Identity and Adaptation Across National Context*, Mahwah, NJ: Lawrence Erlbaum.

Bhaskar-Shrinivas, P., D. A. Harrison, M. A. Shaffer and D. M. Luk (2005), 'Input-based and time-based models of international adjustment: meta-analytic evidence and theoretical extensions', *Academy of Management Journal*, 48(2), 257–81.

Buddington, S. A. (2002), 'Acculturation, psychological adjustment (stress, depression, self-esteem) and the academic achievement of Jamaican immigrant college students', *International Social Work*, 45(4), 447–64.

Bulgan, G., and A. Çiftçi (2017), 'Psychological adaptation, marital satisfaction, and academic self-efficacy of international students', *Journal of International Students*, 7(3), 687–702.

Chow, H. P. H. (2010), 'Predicting academic success and psychological wellness in a sample of Canadian undergraduate students', *Electronic Journal of Research in Educational Psychology*, 8(2), 473–96.

Cura, U., and A. N. Isik (2016), 'Impact of acculturative stress and social support on academic adjustment of international students', *Egitim ve Bilim – Education and Science*, 41(184), 333–47.

Demes, K. A., and N. Geeraert (2014), 'Measures matter: scales for adaptation, cultural distance, and acculturation orientation revisited', *Journal of Cross-Cultural Psychology*, 45(1), 91–109.

deRosier, M. E., and S. W. Lloyd (2011), 'The impact of children's social adjustment on academic outcomes', *Read Writ Q*, 27(1), 25–47.

Kotze, M., and R. Kleynhans (2013), 'Psychological well-being and resilience as predictors of first-year students' academic performance', *Journal of Psychology in Africa*, 23(1), 51–9.

Leung, C. (2001), 'The psychological adaptation of overseas and migrant students in Australia', *International Journal of Psychology*, 36, 251–9.

Mahmood, H., and M. G. Burke (2018), 'Analysis of acculturative stress and sociocultural adaptation among international students at a non-metropolitan university', *Journal of International Students*, 8(1), 284–30.

Malkoush, R. (2000), 'Social support and scholastic adjustment among students of the University of Jordan', *Dirasta Journal*, 27(1), 161–72.

Masgoret, A.-M., and W. Ward (2006), 'Culture learning approach to acculturation', in D. L. Sam and J. W. Berry (eds), *The Cambridge Handbook of Acculturation Psychology*, Cambridge: Cambridge University Press, pp. 58–77.

Neto, F., and D. C. Wilks (2017), 'Predictors of psychological adaptation of Cape Verdean students in Portugal', *Journal of College Student Development*, 58(7), 1087–100.

Othman, A. K., Y. M. Yusoff, M. I. Hamzah and M. Z. Abdullah (2014), 'The influence of psychological adjustment on academic performance of international students: the moderating role of social support', *Australian Journal of Basic and Applied Sciences*, 8(2), 272–83.

Poyrazli, S., R. McPherson, C. Arbona, S. Pisecco and A. Nora (2002), 'Relation between assertiveness, academic self-efficacy, and psychosocial adjustment among international graduate students', *Journal of College Student Development*, 43, 632–42.

Schartner, A. (2015), '"You cannot talk with all of the strangers in a pub": a longitudinal case study of international postgraduate students' social ties at a British university', *Higher Education*, 69(2), 225–41.

Schartner, A., and T. J. Young (2016), 'Towards an integrated conceptual model of international student adjustment and adaptation', *European Journal of Higher Education*, 6(4), 372–86.

Searle, W., and C. Ward (1990), 'The prediction of psychological and sociocultural adjustment during cross-cultural transitions', *International Journal of Intercultural Relations*, 14, 449–64.

Selmer, J. (1999), 'Culture shock in China? Adjustment pattern of Western expatriate business managers', *International Business Review*, 8, 515–34.

Selmer, J., and C. R. Fenner (2009), 'Spillover effects between work and non-work adjustment among public sector expatriates', *Personnel Review*, 38(4), 366–79.

Selmer, J., J. Lauring, J. Normann and A. Kubovcikova (2015), 'Context matters: acculturation and work-related outcomes of self-initiated expatriates employed by foreign vs. local organizations', *International Journal of Intercultural Relations*, 49, 251–64.

Spencer-Oatey, H., and Z. Xiong (2006), 'Chinese students' psychological and sociocultural adjustments to Britain: an empirical study', *Language, Culture and Curriculum*, 19(1), 38–53.

Takeuchi, R., S. Yun and J. E. A. Russell (2002), 'Antecedents and consequences of the perceived adjustment of Japanese expatriates in the USA', *International Journal of Human Resource Management*, 13(8), 1224–44.

Vaez, M., and L. Laflamme (2008), 'Experience stress, psychological symptoms, self-rated health and academic achievement: a longitudinal study of Swedish university students', *Social Behavior and Personality*, 36(2), 183–96.

Wang, Y., and F. Xiao (2014), 'East Asian international students and psychological well-being: a systematic review', *Journal of International Students*, 4, 301–13.

Ward, C., S. Bochner and A. Furnham (2001), *The Psychology of Culture Shock*, 2nd edn, Hove: Routledge.

Ward, C., and A. Kennedy (1993), 'Where's the "culture" in cross-cultural transition? Comparative studies of sojourner adjustment', *Journal of Cross-Cultural Psychology*, 24(2), 221–49.

Ward, C., and A. Kennedy (1996), 'Before and after cross-cultural transition: a study of New Zealand volunteers on field assignments', in H. Grad, A. Blanco and J. Georgas (eds), *Key Issues in Cross-cultural Psychology*, Lisse: Swets & Zeitlinger, pp. 138–54.

Ward, C., Y. Okura, A. Kennedy and T. Kojima (1998), 'The U-curve on trial: a longitudinal study of psychological and sociocultural adjustment during cross-cultural transition', *International Journal of Intercultural Relations*, 22(3), 277–91.

Wintre, M. G., S. K. E. Gates, W. M. Pancer, M. S. Pratt, J. Polivy, S. Birnie-Lefcovitch and G. Adams (2009), 'The student perception of university support and structure scale: development and validation', *Journal of Youth Studies*, 12(3), 289–306.

Wu, E. K. Y., and W. W. S. Mak (2012), 'Acculturation process and distress: mediating roles of sociocultural adaptation and acculturative stress', *The Counseling Psychologist*, 40(1), 66–92.

Zhou, Y., D. Jindal-Snape, K. Topping and J. Todman (2008), 'Theoretical models of culture shock and adaptation in international students in higher education', *Studies in Higher Education*, 33(1), 63–75.

Zhou, Y., and J. Todman (2009), 'Patterns of adaptation of Chinese postgraduate students in the United Kingdom', *Journal of Studies in International Education*, 13(4), 467–86.

# 8

# RETROSPECTIVES ON THE INTERNATIONAL STUDENT EXPERIENCE

In this chapter, we present and discuss data collected from alumni of the MA degree programmes, which provided the datasets referred to in Chapters 3 to 7, above. Here, we first discuss the aims for gathering retrospective accounts (8.1). We then detail our two-stage qualitative research design, the participants and our analysis (8.2). Next, we present findings from the two stages (8.3), and finally draw conclusions relevant to an exploration of IS adaptation and adjustment, and the nature of the students' intercultural transitions (8.4).

## 8.1 WHY 'RETROSPECTIVE' ACCOUNTS?

Our research, reported above, impressed strongly on us that the 'international student experience' goes beyond the time spent abroad – what students learn on their degree programmes (and the qualification they obtain) will later influence their professional choices and pathways (see also Maiworm and Teichler 1996; Engel 2010). The experiences they have in the new environment are also likely to have a strong, possibly profound, effect on them, more broadly, as people (Frändberg 2006; King and Ruiz-Gelices 2003; Paige et al. 2009). This study has attempted to integrate new knowledge about the longer-term effects of study abroad into our understanding of study abroad as intercultural transition, and to add a new temporal perspective to our attempts to understand the IS experience in all its complexity. Such retrospective accounts, where people have had time to reflect on their time as ISs and to relate that experience to their subsequent lives, seemed highly likely to offer valuable perspectives.

## 8.2 DESIGN, PARTICIPANTS AND ANALYSIS

Our specific research focus was on two interrelated questions. Firstly, how do alumni of 'international' degree programmes retrospectively describe and evaluate their experiences in terms of their (1) academic, (2) psychological and (3) sociocultural adjustment? Secondly, what effects did they feel attending such an international programme had had on their subsequent professional and occupational lives, and on them as people?

Two datasets were collected and analysed within a multi-method (qualitative Stage 1 and qualitative Stage 2) design. These were, firstly, written qualitative responses to a questionnaire, and secondly, in-depth spoken responses in interviews conducted with a subsample of these alumni to explore and develop themes arising further. Participants in Stage 1 were sixty-six alumni of heavily 'internationalised' taught postgraduate programmes, who had studied at a single British university between 1991 and 2013; these were the degrees also undertaken by the participants in the research reported in Chapters 4 to 7, above. Their nationality mix and gender profile broadly matched those of student participants in the research reported in the above chapters, so a majority were female and the sample was very 'international' in composition, although in this instance, as detailed below, we did also tap into the experiences of 'home' students, in this case British ones. All the alumni who participated in this investigation had successfully passed the degree programmes they were subsequently asked about. These represented all of the respondents to an emailed request for participants sent by the authors, who were subsequently able to participate. Texts from each participant varied in length from 300 to 1,000 words, and were typically around 750 words. The sixty-six texts gave us a corpus for analysis of nearly 50,000 words.

The subgroup for Stage 2 were eight participants from Stage 1, who had agreed to take part in follow-up work and who were available for interview during a specified time period. Of these, four were female and four male, with three Asian participants (from Japan, South Korea and the People's Republic of China) and five British participants. The interviewees graduated from the degree programmes between 1994 and 2012. The broad timespan allowed us to access the experiences of a larger number of former students than might otherwise have been the case. It also allowed for the possibility of different perspectives related to different retrospective timespans. Five were interviewed face to face and three by phone or Skype, as they were based outside of the UK at the time of the interviews. Interviews lasted between fifteen and twenty-five minutes, this timeframe largely being determined by the degree of detail the participants gave. The interviews were audio-recorded, transcribed and anonymised. Transcription gave us a corpus for analysis of around 15,000 words.

Stage 1 participants completed an online survey. This consisted of three questions inviting an open-ended written qualitative response:

- What are your main memories of doing the programme?
- How has the programme influenced your professional life?
- How has the programme influenced your personal life?

Responses were collated, and then analysed as below.

Stage 2 consisted of using the same questions in a semi-structured interview format. In Stage 2, each question subsequently led to different subquestions, depending on the original responses from the participants to the broad initial questions. These tended to be 'prompt' questions, designed to encourage more developed responses where an issue or recollection seemed to be particularly relevant to the participant – 'Can you tell me more about that?' Our aim in this stage was to add, as far as possible, nuance and detail to our findings from Stage 1, in close relation to participants' own perceptions of the salience of aspects of their experiences.

For the data from each stage of the enquiry, a thematic analysis (Braun and Clarke 2006) was conducted, based on the following stepped framework. Each step was

Table 8.1 Analytical categories and example comments in relation to sociocultural adjustment

| Analytical category | Example comments |
|---|---|
| Positive | 'I love being involved with students from other countries.'<br>'I worked well with all my friends in the group assignments we did.' |
| Negative | 'Communication was a big problem because they had issues with English.'<br>'Sometimes I felt I had to teach my course mates and that I didn't expect'. |
| Problematising | 'It is a little bit more challenging to do group assignments with more of those students.'<br>'We must look up the words all the time and then translate into Chinese.' |

conducted independently by two researchers, who then compared versions and resolved differences, where these occurred, to agree on a final version of each dataset.

- *First analytical step:* Based on Ward and colleagues' (2001) sojourner adjustment framework and our work reported in Chapters 4 to 7, above, we focused on three thematic areas: (1) academic adjustment, (2) psychological adjustment and (3) sociocultural adjustment. In addition, the focus on retrospective accounts warranted a fourth thematic area: (4) professional and personal outcomes of study abroad. Relevant comments from the texts were placed into the best-matching thematic area.
- *Second analytical step:* Students' responses from each thematic area were then divided into 'positive', 'negative' and 'problematising' categories. Table 8.1 gives examples of coding criteria, analytical categories and example comments that were judged to fit these categories for one of the thematic areas.

## 8.3 FINDINGS

Findings are presented here, firstly, with an overall summary of the Stage 1 written responses, then with quotes and examples from these texts, related to each thematic category, in order to illustrate general points and give further detail. In a similar way, we then present findings from Stage 2, the interviews, first as an overall general summary, and then with examples drawn from former students' spoken responses related to the relevant thematic category.

### 8.3.1 FINDINGS FROM STAGE 1 – WRITTEN ACCOUNTS

Analysis of responses to the Stage 1 questionnaires showed that, overall, a majority of former students' retrospective accounts were positive or highly positive. This was especially the case for those related to sociocultural aspects of the experience as recalled retrospectively, and to professional outcomes of study subsequent to being abroad to obtain the qualification. Relatively little comment was made on psychological aspects of the experience of being an 'international' student *per se*. There was, however, considerable comment on the (generally very positive) psychological outcomes of obtaining a degree, largely related to an increase in self-confidence and a sense of a more positive self-concept. Relative to sociocultural and psychological aspects, comments on academic aspects were most balanced between positive and negative/problematising comments. There was a slight majority of positive comments, most especially related to people (that is, classmates, staff). Some comments on intensity of workload and English language issues were also made.

It became very clear that what people remember most are the sociocultural aspects of study, reflected in the vast amount of comments on cohort composition, opportunities for cross-cultural interaction, interactions with staff, and social contacts and friendships in general. This area seemed to be the one that has the most profound and long-lasting impact. There was little direct indication in responses that students struggled in terms of sociocultural adjustment, although there were some negative/problematising comments on the 'international' study environment related to cohort and class composition.

**Academic adjustment – negative and problematising comments**

Comments on academic adjustment issues related mainly to academic workload and English language issues:

> It was a lot of work due to the fact that I had to improve my English a lot in order to follow the courses.
>
> Much more reading/writing assignments than expected, with which I had trouble from time to time.

Some students made suggestions for induction for ISs and stressed how useful they thought this would have been:

> I'm Chinese and Chinese studying and teaching style is very different. I'd be very grateful if I can get to know British studying and teaching style before I start the course. That way I wouldn't need to spend one semester learning 'how to study'!
>
> I think it can be improved through giving more induction to international students as it was very challenging to adapt to the system in the UK.
>
> I learned grammar and vocabulary before I came but not about writing in university, what you need to do to be good.

A range of negative/problematising comments related to the perceived lack of practical, 'real-life' examples and 'hands-on' experience on the kind of MA programmes these former students had followed:

> Less theory, more practical application. I can't say that enough.
>
> More real-life, hands-on experience. There was a lot of theory, but I didn't understand the theory until I practiced a lot of hands-on stuff here in the USA.

Students also wished for clearer links at the time of study between the degree and prospective careers/job market/alumni:

> The University could focus more on negotiating the transition of students from school to the work force. Content of study, in many cases, is not as important as connections!
> Let alumni to go back to [name of university] to talk about their own experiences.
> It would be great to have one or a couple of university trips throughout the year to some of the main international organizations (EU, European Central Bank, UNESCO, etc?) in Europe.

Many former students' comments reflected, either negatively or in a problematising way, on student cohort composition, mainly related to a perceived skewed student intake (that is, too many East Asian ISs) and 'native' versus 'non-native' speaker issues:

> I remember thinking that the native English speaker/non-native speaker was a difficult mix simply because of the cultural and educational differences between natives/non-natives ... there was often a reluctance to share/lack of confidence from those classmates, and often the 3 native speakers were left to give their ideas in class and lead the discussion.
> Form more mixed classes with more native speakers of English.
> Too many Chinese people in my class, I wanted to meet and work with others.

Interestingly, negative comments about large numbers of 'Chinese' students on the programmes came as often from Chinese students as from non-Chinese.

A lot of comment related to staff competencies and approachability, including teaching skills, availability and cultural awareness:

> Some qualified teachers who is familiar with eastern culture should be employed.
> I found that the tutors were not easily approachable.

Comments on the broad and generalised nature of the degree programmes were also common, with this seen as a positive or a negative attribute. Some former students commended what they saw as the range of module choice, and the degree of autonomy possible in 'building' their own programmes. Others actually wished for more choice, while others expressed concern about the over-generalised 'broad sweep' nature of the programmes:

> As the course is a taught MA with a combination of Cross-cultural Studies and Marketing, I found that we ended up touching lightly upon both topics instead of going deep into the two fields.
> It was good to get a range of ideas and views.

> I liked how much choosing you could do.
>
> The subjects are not wide enough for us to choose.

**Academic adjustment – positive comments**

Overall, there were more positive than negative/problematising comments on academic aspects of adjustment. A majority of comments related to people, most especially the 'international' make-up of the classes and opportunities for experiential learning and 'real-life', 'real-time' 'cross-cultural' communication:

> The good thing is, rather than lecturing the cultures, there are live examples – different people from different cultures. We can have practical experience by communicating with them.
>
> It was great to have such a variety of people all on the same course.
>
> The degree is good as a place for very different people to get together. To actually learn from each other our different cultures, and therefore living out the theories introduced to us.

There were a lot of positive comments on university staff, and how university staff had interacted with them as students seems to have been a very important part of how the experience was evaluated.

> All the lecturers were very skillful [sic] and dedicated, and nice persons.
>
> Staff all went extra mile.
>
> A supportive, friendly, but nevertheless professional environment.

Similarly, there were many positive comments on practical aspects of programmes, and (perhaps unsurprisingly) the structure and organisation of their programmes made a strong impression on, and was an important part of the evaluation of, the overall experience:

> It's practical. I still use the approaches and methods I learned from the lectures.
>
> It was well organised and clear how to do things.
>
> I thought the course had the right balance of theory and practice.

There were plenty of comments on the topic range that had been made available to students:

> Being able to choose the modules enabled the student to have a degree as if it was his own because it suites his needs.
>
> The flexibility and openness regarding the students' module selection.

There were some comments on very specific positive memories:

> Doing a case study in an elementary school.
>
> The video class was one of my favorite.

**Psychological adjustment – positive, negative and problematising comments**
Interestingly, and as noted above, analysis revealed very little comment on psychological aspects other than psychological outcomes of doing the degree – increased confidence and the perceived value of qualification:

> I have always had confidence in my intelligence and abilities, but I suppose having an MA kinda makes it official!
> I feel more comfortable due to an internationally recognized degree.
> I've felt more confident in what I was able to achieve overseas.

There were only two negative comments on psychological adjustment, but both are perhaps very revealing of the kind of psychological experiences that have an impact upon and stay with people who have been ISs:

> There were difficulties and frustrations, of course: sharing a flat with 4 other people; worrying about money … course deadlines; the cold …
> Suddenly losing the ability to learn anything at all, needing to take anti-depressants, missing my friends and living abroad.

Getting through such difficulties, in a new sociocultural environment where the 'normal rules' are different, is, of course, profoundly difficult. Where people are able to do so – and the vast amount are – this is, in itself, a great achievement.

**Sociocultural adjustment – positive, negative and problematising comments**
The comments made in relation to sociocultural adjustment were almost exclusively positive. Many comments related to cross-cultural interaction and its benefits as outcomes, which people experienced and still remember. This specifically related to aspects of intercultural awareness, effectiveness and competence:

> I also remember all the great people I met from all parts of the world, which provided me with interesting cross-cultural experiences.
> I became more open to different cultures. I wouldn't be so shy anymore when talking to someone abroad.
> After completing this MA, I became a more culturally aware person as well as more open and globally minded.
> Studies taught me not to jump to conclusions about nationality and culture.

There was also a lot of comment on the long-lasting nature of contacts formed during the degree:

> The contacts I made during my stay … were of great importance for many years.
> I made the most amazing friends […] they are connections for a lifetime.
> I am still connected via social media to many of my classmates.

There were many comments on informal, out-of-class discussions that people had had:

> The informal coffee talks about our various teaching contexts.
> Outside of class discussions with friends and colleagues.

There were also many remarks about the host environment, including the host city and experiencing the 'local culture':

> Wonderful student life.
> I was amazed by the beauty of the [region], and the vibrant social life in [the host city].
> I still remember that I had spent a wonderful time at a home stay with a family during Christmas time.
> The pubs and clubs were the places I went every weekend and I enjoyed the culture a lot too.

Across the whole dataset, there were only two negative accounts of sociocultural experiences, the second of which can perhaps only loosely be described as 'sociocultural':

> I found the cross culture thing difficult as learners, which was unexpected, I thought I would thrive in a cross-cultural situation.
> Getting burgled, unfortunately.

**Professional and personal outcomes – positive, negative and problematising comments**

Comments on the professional and interrelated personal outcomes of their programmes and their subsequent careers were almost exclusively positive. There were many comments on the acquisition of specific skills/knowledge and attributes that subsequently proved useful in career terms:

> After taking the course, I found it easier for me to write various kinds of texts logically in English.
> I think I am a better, more well-informed teacher now because of the reading that I did.
> It has given me more awareness and confidence in dealing with people from different background.

There were many comments on links between getting the degree and subsequent jobs and/or promotions secured:

> It has helped me get my current job and equipped me with some knowledge and skills required.
> I think my MA was important in the hiring process, and led to me getting hired.

> I am the money-maker and have been able to be a successful mom and provide for my family because of my degree.
> It led me to my lecturing post and then led me to a PhD.

There was also a lot of comment on the value of the qualification and the opportunities it provides in career terms in general:

> It gave me the qualification to apply for the teaching job in public and private schools.
> I guess my degree helps build up my professional credibility.
> My experience abroad and language proficiency won myself many chances in the job market.
> It has helped set me apart in the job market.

Related to this, there was a lot of comment on the link between the degree and finding or working out a career path:

> It has had a huge impact in that it set me on the course of my current career.
> The international element of the course influenced my choice of career and how it has progressed.
> It changed my professional and career goals completely.
> It provided me with the inspiration and motivation to pursue further studies (PhD) and become a researcher/lecturer.

There were very few problematising or overtly negative comments on professional outcomes of the degree, but a strong sense of disappointment emanates from these:

> My degree doesn't really influence my professional life.
> I would be in exactly the same place had I not done the CCC degree.

### 8.3.2 FINDINGS FROM STAGE 2: INTERVIEWS

Findings from Stage 2 tended, for the most part, to confirm, reinforce and add nuance and detail to those of Stage 1; the two datasets were found to be very complementary. Most comments in the interviews related to sociocultural aspects of the experience, as they had also done in the written questionnaire comments. Strong links emerged in the interview data between memories of issues of workload and general management of academic matters and the psychological wellbeing of people when they were students during the programmes. This had especially been the case in the early stages of the former students' programmes. An apparent tension emerged between a high number of positive or very positive comments on the 'international' and 'intercultural' aspects of academic adjustment and the general experience of the degree: where a former student's cohort or class composition was seen as skewed towards a particular nationality – with students' from the People's Republic of China being the most usual one specified – this had been experienced as a problem. There was a very high number of comments on the professional and career outcomes of doing the degree, almost entirely positive in nature. Also emerging strongly was a sense of major – in many cases, life-changing – personal outcomes, spanning the sociocultural and psychological. A summary of representative example quotes illustrating these findings is presented below. It is noteworthy that a majority of participants in this part of the investigation were British alumni of the kind of 'internationalised' postgraduate programmes described in Chapters 3 to 7 above.

**Academic adjustment – positive, negative and problematising comments**

In respect of academic adjustment, overall, a balanced mix of positive, negative and problematising comments were made by the interviewees. Several positive comments were made on the 'international' learning experience and learning outcomes:

> It was probably the best academic year I'd had.
> Enjoying it, just like enjoying picking an essay topic for the assignment and like digging into that.
> I learned from the textbook, from the lecture, so I used that for my work later on.
> If I participate in some communicating and some you know discussion part in class … that is really good for me I think.

There were several problematising/negative comments on workload. The initial stages were experienced by several interviewees as particularly intense:

> At first like two months or three months I was so stressed out because when I read articles and books it takes so much time.
> Kind of nightmare for me because it is very different story in comparing Japanese language learning situation and also Japanese university system because I was really surprised of some gaps between Japanese style and the English style.
> I didn't know what the expectations were, so there was this huge element of doubt at the start and maybe that was just my own insecurity at the time but like just wondering whether the work I produced was good enough. Having no frame of reference whatsoever …
> For me because my English wasn't really good … so personally I think a little bit heavy for me.

A large number of problematising comments were made on student cohort composition (that is, on the balance of 'home' versus 'international' students). A related and strongly emergent area was associated with perceived differences between being a native- or first-language speaker of English on a programme where English is the medium of instruction, and being a non-native second or other language speaker. These comments were made almost exclusively by the British participants in this stage of the investigation.

> In my class I think it's around 60, like only have two or three English students … I would like to meet more local students to observe how they study.
>
> There was a 100-ish people in the class and of that 90 per cent plus were non-home students which was great, I mean good for collaboration and getting new viewpoints and things like that, but also I think that caused challenges for the department.
>
> I think sometimes the home students were put in a position of being experts by experience even though they didn't really want to be an expert by experience.
>
> In some ways it was quite a difficult year because … there were only three native speakers of English on the course … we were older than perhaps the rest of the cohort and we had teaching experience … my memories of it were finding it quite frustrating.
>
> They [non-English first language ISs] did the classic thing of deferring to our experience, necessarily or unnecessarily really and it meant that in classes we consciously tried to stay quiet to let them speak and if we spoke it had the aura of authority … I remember it being quite a strange experience.

**Psychological adjustment – positive, negative and problematising comments**

Interviewees tended to report positive, negative and problematised experiences, with a sense of getting on top of the expectations and their psychological consequences as they became more experienced as postgraduate students. The majority of comments related to links between academic workload and psychological wellbeing:

> At first I think I to be honest I was really depressed because I had to do so many things like because this is my first experience to read so many books … But last half of my master course I think I got acclimatised to this situation.
>
> For two months I was really overwhelmed, stressed out. And then every time I went to the modules, they always introduced what the essay will be, so they always 'Oh, you have to write 4,000 words of essays', the number itself is really overwhelmed and I didn't have any you know experience that writes in second language that much long.
>
> There was some heavy workload times and then family illness kind of occurring, essays and family illness co-occurring … and adding to the stress of each other.
>
> I think the summer was probably when I felt the most stressed out because I wasn't really talking to people about my project anymore or their projects or how we were getting on as much as we had been.

There was one specific account of loneliness, although loneliness and how to cope with and alleviate isolation was a recurrent theme across the sample.

> Sometimes maybe I feel a little bit lonely because XXX is a small city compared to cities in China.

**Sociocultural adjustment – positive, negative and problematising comments**

A great many of the comments made by the interviewees related to sociocultural adjustment. The vast majority of these were positive and tended to confirm the life-changing and life-affirming nature of the experience in sociocultural terms. Comments mostly related to the community spirit of the student cohort and opportunities for positive cross-cultural interaction:

> It was very sociable, there was a big community-feel to it. It wasn't particularly cliquey, everyone spoke to everyone.
> I have some connection between the people having different background, completely different background, different ethnicity, different races yeah and then it is really good for me to talk to them about so many topics.
> I just remember it being very nice and there were just lovely, lovely students on the course from all over the place and we met a lot.
> We always invite each other in our flat and then cook together, we always try to make some really home-made, some traditional food and then we share talks at the same time.
> I think it was just really nice to have a sort of really heterogeneous group to study with basically and all the people that you meet from different countries.

**Professional and person outcomes**

A great many comments were made in these areas and they were overwhelmingly positive; in career and personal development terms, all the interviewees reported some degree of growth, success and positivity. Some comments related to career change in the direction of academic and further study:

> I decided to go to PhD and I think this is because this master course.
> Changed my career direction, yeah, completely. I was getting a postgraduate qualification to try and make myself more employable instead I discovered actually what I really wanted to do was academia.

International and intercultural awareness, effectiveness and competence (variously framed) as a professional outcome was a strongly recurrent theme:

> After graduate I work in Beijing, always in an international company. So I think I can communicate with my colleagues better and the way they doing business.
> They are a lot of chance that you have to like communicate with the people from different cultures, so I think it would be very helpful and useful.
> I suppose it gave me interpretations of being somebody living in a very different society and linguistically, culturally different community.

Many interviewees saw doing the degree as the foundation of their subsequent career:

> I mean it was the grounding for what I do now really and I couldn't be doing what I do now if I hadn't done that course.

> I suppose it served its purpose in that it gave me a good, solid foundation that I managed to keep up on since.
> I became an academic so the content was, had an impact on me and I'm still using it either directly or indirectly to inform my teaching and my research.

Finally, and in purely human terms, most importantly, was an emergent theme relating to personal change and growth (variously framed) as a strongly-felt outcome of study:

> I think I was too spoiled in China … I always have to rely on my parents … since I went to the UK I become more independent person … I'm much more confident than before.
> I like to think it made me a bit more of an accepting and open person.
> Now become more positive person, compared to the past. So it was such a wonderful year and very inspirational, very insightful. I grow up mentally, so I really satisfied.

## 8.4 CONCLUSIONS

We found the process of obtaining 'retrospective' data, and the findings from that data, to be an extremely valuable exercise. At a personal level, as people who had been involved in studying and/or teaching on some of the programmes that the alumni had undertaken, we were delighted to read and hear the largely positive responses to the questions we had been asking.

This did not, we are confident, interfere with an appropriately distant and objective perspective on the data themselves but should nevertheless be acknowledged. These data gave us very valuable extending and confirmatory ideas to feed into the model we were developing, which attempted to capture aspects of the full temporal range of the experience. The fact that the study periods of the alumni who gave us their retrospective accounts spanned an eighteen-year period (between 1994 and 2012, as noted above) enabled us to access the experiences of people whose impressions ranged from the fairly recent to the more distant. A danger with retrospective accounts, we acknowledge, is the possible fallibility of people's memories; we found, however, that people's recollections of events and impressions were, in general, strong and sustained.

Overall, these data gave us a complex, if largely positive, picture in terms of describing and evaluating the transition to being an 'international student' or, in the case of our British participants in Stage 2, being a 'home' student on an overwhelmingly 'international' degree programme. This seemed true, even for those whose experience of a heavily 'internationalised' degree was anything up to eighteen years before participation in this research; we were impressed at how strong experiences remained for people, even at a long time distance. Answers to our research questions indicated that, in reflecting on their experience, alumni had strong, positive and still resonant feelings about most aspects of the experience. Our first question asked how international alumni retrospectively describe and evaluate their experiences in terms of their (1) academic, (2) psychological and (3) sociocultural adjustment. We found here that sociocultural aspects of the experience were particularly intense – how they as 'strangers in a strange land' had found or made a social place for themselves and a *modus vivendi* within the host academic institution and the wider host society through friendships and strong social support networks largely formed *in situ*. Responses in related aspects of psychological adjustment indicated that the process was tough and demanding, but ultimately manageable for most. In terms of academic adjustment, there was a *lot* of adjustment to make but again, most people, on reflection, managed it and seem to have developed perspective and resilience, to a certain extent, because of it. Some tensions emerged from the data in relation to actual 'doing the intercultural' under the high pressure of a one-year MA degree; working collaboratively with people from different backgrounds was a challenge and an abiding memory. This seemed to be particularly the case when working closely with cultural others where there were also perceived issues of asymmetrical abilities with the language of instruction. Nevertheless, the data did, on the whole, tell us something positive and affirming. It showed how people were faced with the transitionary challenges of simultaneous academic, psychological and sociocultural adjustment, plus adjustment to a new level of study. It told us how, in most cases, most of the time, they managed and, in their own terms, succeeded. This became increasingly the case as they developed experience of and in the new environment.

Our second research question asked what effects doing an 'international' programme had on alumni's subsequent professional and occupational lives, and, more broadly, on them as people. Again, answers were complex but largely positive. An overwhelming impression from the datasets as a whole is that this was an important life event for people: it was one that has been highly significant for most, and in some cases, profoundly so. It has subsequently played a role in how they have seen themselves as people and how they have lived their lives. It has also been a strong – and, for some, a profound – influence on how they have forged a place for themselves in their chosen professional spheres after graduation and beyond.

## REFERENCES

Braun, V., and V. Clarke (2006), 'Using thematic analysis in psychology', *Qualitative Research in Psychology*, 3(2), 77–101.

Engel, C. (2010), 'The impact of Erasmus mobility on the professional career: empirical results of international studies on temporary student and teaching staff mobility', *Belgeo, Revue belge de géographie*, 4, 351–63.

Frändberg, L. (2006), 'International mobility biographies: a means to capture the institutionalisation of long-distance travel?', *Current Issues in Tourism*, 9(4–5), 320–34.

King, R., and E. Ruiz-Gelices (2003), 'International student migration and the European "year abroad": effects on European identity and subsequent migration behaviour', *International Journal of Population Geography*, 9(3), 229–52.

Maiworm, F., and U. Teichler (1996), 'Study abroad and early career: experiences of former ERASMUS students', *Higher Education Policy Series 35*, ERASMUS monograph no. 21.

Paige, R. M., G. W. Fry, E. M. Stallman, J. Josić and J. E. Jon (2009), 'Study abroad for global engagement: the long-term impact of mobility experiences', *Intercultural Education*, 20(sup1), S29-S44.

Ward, C., S. Bochner and A. Furnham (2001), *The Psychology of Culture Shock*, 2nd edn, Hove: Routledge.

# PART III

# 9

# CONCLUSIONS

In this chapter, we revisit the aims of this book and offer conclusions related to its empirical, methodological and theoretical contributions. We first revisit the research questions and briefly summarise key empirical findings (9.1). We then present a guiding conceptual model of IS adjustment and adaptation, detailing its underpinning theoretical foundations and empirical background (9.2). We conclude with an agenda for future research (9.3).

## 9.1 REVISITING THE RESEARCH QUESTIONS

We aimed to answer the following research questions:

1. How do commonly identified contributory factors (host language ability, knowledge about the host country, prior overseas experience, autonomy in the decision to study abroad, intercultural competence, social contact and social support) relate to different aspects of academic adaptation measured over the whole programme?
2. How do these contributory factors relate to psychological adaptation?
3. How do they relate to sociocultural adaptation?
4. What are the patterns and dynamics of student sojourners' academic, psychological and sociocultural adjustment over the course of the programme?
5. What are the interrelationships of academic, psychological and sociocultural adjustment and adaptation?

Questions 1 to 3 had a predictive aim: here, our interest was in the effects of a range of contributory factors on adjustment outcomes, specifically academic, psychological and sociocultural adaptation. Our findings suggest that, firstly, dispositional 'pre-sojourn' factors impinge on the level of adaptation achieved, and that, secondly, social connectedness, developed 'in sojourn', plays a crucial role in this process. We summarise below the key findings regarding each adaptation domain.

**Academic adaptation (see Chapter 4)**
Our findings suggest that an academically successful student sojourner is likely to be somebody who has prior overseas experience and good knowledge about the host

country. They are also likely to be able to speak the host language well and to have made the decision to study abroad independently from others. They are likely to be proactive individuals who exhibit high levels of flexibility, as well as empathy for cultural 'others'. During their time abroad, they most likely have strong international networks and experience high levels of socio-emotional support. All these variables emerged as significant predictors of academic success in our research.

**Psychological adaptation (see Chapter 5)**

Knowledge about the host country, proficiency in the host language and independence in the decision to study abroad were key predictors of a sense of satisfaction during the sojourn. Students reporting high levels of satisfaction with life were also likely to be proactive and emotionally stable individuals who exhibit high levels of cultural empathy. During the sojourn, they were likely to have developed and have been able to draw on strong networks with non-co-national ISs and to receive high levels of socio-emotional support. Students who reported high levels of psychological wellbeing at the end of their sojourn were likely to be emotionally stable individuals who had made the decision to study abroad independently of others.

**Sociocultural adaptation (see Chapter 6)**

Students who reported high levels of sociocultural adaptation were highly likely to be proficient in the host language, to have prior knowledge about the host country and to have made their decision to study abroad independently of others. They were also likely to have high levels of cultural empathy and to be proactive and emotionally stable. During their sojourn, they had strong networks with British and non-co-national ISs, and received high levels of socio-emotional support. In sum, then, the 'pre-sojourn' contributory factors that were predictive across the three adaptation domains were: knowledge about the host country, autonomy in the decision to study abroad, cultural empathy and social initiative. 'In-sojourn' factors predictive of all three domains included: contact with non-co-national ISs and socio-emotional support.

Research question 4 had a monitoring aim: here, our interest was in the dynamics of students' academic, psychological and sociocultural adjustment trajectories over time. Our findings suggest that, by and large, all three trajectories followed a more or less ascending curve, with the greatest difficulties experienced in the early sojourn stages, followed by improvements as time progressed. Despite a similar overall trend, there were some distinct patterns:

- Academic adjustment appeared to followed a relatively steady upward curve (Chapter 4), pointing to a gradual acquisition of 'academic cultural competence' (Brown 2008) over time.
- Psychological adjustment remained more variable over time, with periodical drops in student wellbeing reflected in a more uneven curve (see Ward et al. 2001 and Chapter 5).
- Sociocultural adjustment generally followed an upward curve (Chapter 6), much in line with Ward and colleagues' (2001) original conceptualisation (Chapter 2).

However, some adjustment difficulties persisted over time, such as lack of contact with local people, which remained an issue for most students throughout their sojourn.

Research question 5 focused on the interrelationships between academic, psychological and sociocultural adjustment and adaptation. Our findings strongly indicate that there are close relationships between the three domains, as revealed by both our quantitative and our qualitative data. Our survey data showed that when students were successful academically, they were also more likely to feel satisfied with life in the host environment and to achieve high levels of sociocultural adaptation, and vice versa. The qualitative data largely supported this and further showed that students felt happy and well in themselves when they were able to perform well academically and function effectively in everyday life. A particularly strong spillover effect was noteworthy between academic and psychological adjustment. Our findings serve to confirm what prior literature has alluded to – that academic, psychological and sociocultural adjustment are not three separate domains but are instead strongly interwoven and highly interdependent processes. They are thus portrayed as such in our conceptual model, discussed below and detailed in Figure 9.1 later.

## 9.2 A CONCEPTUAL MODEL OF INTERNATIONAL STUDENT ADJUSTMENT AND ADAPTATION

In this section, we begin by introducing the model that conceptualises and integrates the experience of ISs' intercultural transitions to study abroad. We then explain why a model of this kind and scope is timely (9.2.1). We then reiterate its theoretical foundations (9.2.2) and the empirical data that led to its development (9.2.3). The next section presents a research agenda arising from our research (9.3), and suggests and explores how the model might be applied and developed in future studies.

### 9.2.1 THE MODEL

Our model is presented in Figure 9.1. It is informed by our empirical work, reported in Chapters 4 to 7, above, as well as the broader research literature detailed in Chapter 2, above, and 9.2.3 below. An earlier version of the model, whose development was then a work in progress, was also presented in Schartner and Young (2016). The model fulfils three aims, on an empirical, a methodological and a practical level:

1. To provide an organising framework for the synthesis of a burgeoning body of research on IS adjustment and adaptation (empirical)
2. To provide a template that researchers can use to design future empirical studies (methodological)
3. To provide a heuristic for practitioners working in the internationalising university, and for 'home' and 'international' students (practical).

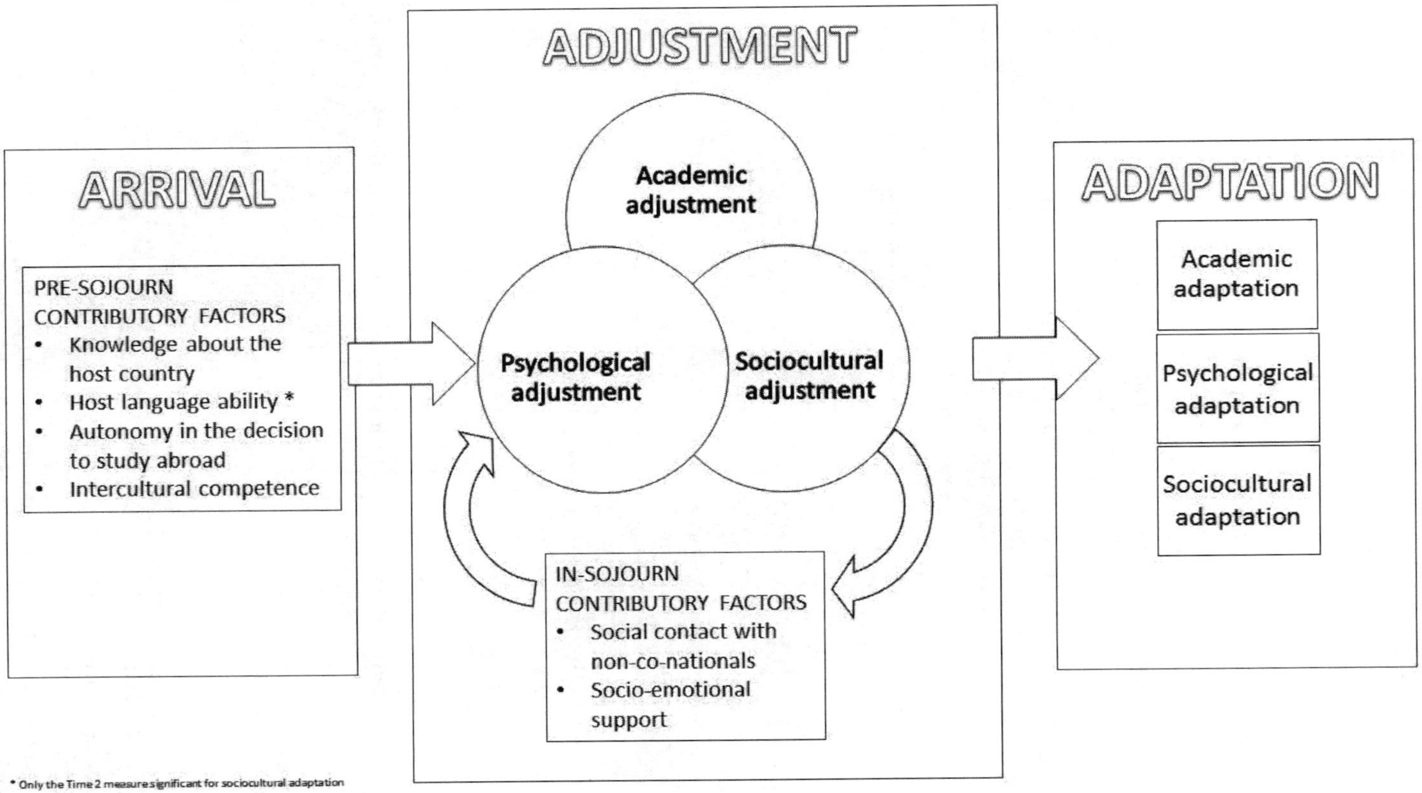


*Figure 9.1* *An integrated model of international student adjustment and adaptation*

Our model is a response to the paucity of conceptual work on the 'international student experience'. Conceptual models in the acculturation literature are, by and large, more specific to the experiences of longer-term sojourners or permanent immigrants (see Chapter 2, above, and a review by Smith and Khawaja 2011). We argue that a 'one size fits all' model cannot fully accommodate the unique circumstances of internationally mobile students, which are inherently different from those of other sojourner groups, such as business people or refugees. The model adopts a micro-level focus, with the individual student sojourner and their intra- and interpersonal experiences at the centre of enquiry (Kim 2001). In order to capture the full temporal range of the 'international student experience', it encompasses both 'pre-sojourn' factors (local language proficiency, knowledge about the host country, motivation for study abroad, prior overseas experience, and intercultural competence) and 'in-sojourn' factors (social contact and social support) (Berry 2006). As we have seen, it also provides a useful heuristic to explore the 'after-effects' of an academic sojourn on people's lives (Chapter 8).

The model distinguishes between psychological and sociocultural adjustment/adaptation (cf. Ward et al. 2001), where the former is understood as affective responses to the new environment, including psychological wellbeing and satisfaction with life, and the latter is viewed as behavioural responses related to 'fitting in' with the host environment. It also captures adjustment/adaptation beyond the psychosocial and includes an academic domain that, despite its absence from other conceptual models, is of particularly high salience to student sojourners. This includes adjustment to the specific demands of academic study, including styles of teaching and learning at the host university (Ryan 2005; Young et al. 2013; Schartner and Young 2016). The three domains (portrayed as overlapping circles) are presented in the model as intertwined processes (see Figure 9.1), in response to empirical research that found significant associations between them (see Chapter 7 and Jindal-Snape and Ingram 2013).

Our model offers a unique and significant contribution in several ways. Firstly, it encompasses a holistic perspective, integrating a broad range of contributory and outcome factors from across academic, psychological and sociocultural adjustment, which are usually pursued as distinct and separate domains of enquiry (Zhou and Todman 2009). Secondly, in response to some terminological ambiguity in the intercultural sojourner literature (see Chapter 1, above, and Matsumoto and Hwang 2013), it makes a clear conceptual distinction between 'adjustment' and 'adaptation', with the former reflecting a process (that is, the experience of change), and the latter reflecting outcomes of this process that are of high salience to the person going through the transition. From this methodological perspective, 'adjustment' can best be monitored over time using qualitative methods of enquiry, whilst 'adaptation' can best be measured using a range of outcome indices, such as academic grades (Chapters 2 and 3, above). A mixed-methods longitudinal perspective of this kind is unusual in the literature on IS adjustment and adaptation: it enables us to combine a broad, generalisable perspective with a fine-grained perspective that recognises the individuality of adjustment and adaptation. We argue that studies with this design are needed if we are to operationalise successfully the 'ecumenical' epistemological position we detail in Chapter 1, and so address the full range of factors that are influences on, and outcomes of, the 'international student experience' (see also Zhang and Goodson 2011).

The model comes at a critical point in time: a shift towards more inclusive, sustainable and ethically focused approaches to internationalisation agendas is now evident across much of the HE landscape (cf. Robson et al. 2018 and Chapters 1 and 2). As a result, attention is being increasingly paid to the quality of the 'student experience' for both internationally mobile students and non-mobile 'home' students. A conceptual model that attempts to capture what this experience might look like can therefore provide a useful and timely frame of reference for those working in the internationalised university, and a useful reflective tool for the students themselves. Although the model is predominantly informed by research conducted among taught postgraduate students in the UK HE context, we discuss below (Chapter 10) how it can be used as a heuristic to gauge the totality of the international student experience anywhere. As we will argue, we believe that it is also, in most particulars, applicable to other groups of internationally mobile students, in other national contexts. Moreover, it can serve as a reference point for other researchers and for practitioners striving to achieve 'internationalisation at home' in a climate where ISs' perspectives and experiences are an often underused resource at their host universities. It will also show how an interest in ISs' experiences can help hosts – both institutions and individuals – benefit from the range of possibilities for growth and change offered by real engagement with an IS population. Such possibilities encompass the academic and the more generally sociocultural and intercultural domains, and so offer a real way forward in helping universities worldwide in their attempts to become truly 'global', connected and inclusive.

### 9.2.2 THEORETICAL BASIS FOR THE MODEL

Figure 9.2 illustrates the theory underpinning our model. As detailed in Chapter 2, two dominant, broad theoretical approaches to the study of adjustment have become well established in the literature exploring intercultural sojourning and sojourners: firstly, stress and coping approaches, and secondly, culture-learning and social skills approaches. Drawing on research from the fields of international education and social psychology, both approach intercultural sojourners as agentive, potentially proactive individuals who can respond to change rather than being passive victims of 'culture shock' (Zhou et al. 2008). Stress and coping approaches emphasise affective elements and highlight the significance of life changes in the sojourner's transition. Advocates of stress and coping approaches argue that cognitive appraisal and coping strategies are required to tolerate acculturative stress (e.g. Berry 1997). If adequate coping strategies are employed on the part of the sojourner, the acculturative stress experienced may be low, or at least manageable; if the coping strategies or resources are not sufficient, however, the acculturative stress experienced may be high and can result, in severe cases, in anxiety or depression (Smith and Khawaja 2011).

Culture-learning and social skills approaches, in contrast, highlight specifically behavioural elements of the sojourner experience. Proponents of this approach assume that sojourners usually arrive in the host environment with a deficit of appropriate social and cultural skills (e.g. Furnham and Bochner 1982, 1986). Given this lack, learning about the salient characteristics of the new environment becomes essential. Adjustment is conceptualised here as a growth-facilitating experience, where initial difficulties are followed by steady improvement as the sojourner acquires the culture-specific skills required to function effectively and successfully in the new environment (Ward et al. 2001). Although the notion of acquiring 'culture-specific' skills may take an overly narrow view of both 'acquisition' and 'culture' (see Chapter 1), both approaches nevertheless provide a useful starting point and basis for the study of ISs' adjustment and adaptation.

Clearly, an IS sojourn is a major life event (Chapter 1; Berry 2006), which can trigger affective (A), behavioural (B) and cognitive (C) processes in the individual (see Chapter 2). 'Becoming' an IS usually involves major changes, at least temporarily, in familiar social support systems and exposes students to an unfamiliar academic and sociocultural environment, within which they are expected to operate with some degree of expertise. In order to experience a 'successful' sojourn, some kind of adjustment is therefore needed. To reflect this, and in line with Ward and colleagues (2001), psychological adjustment is viewed in our model through a stress and coping lens, where coping strategies are employed to deal with acculturative stress. The degree of success in employing these coping strategies will ultimately influence the degree and quality of psychological adaptation achieved. Academic adjustment and sociocultural adjustment, on the other hand, are viewed through a culture-learning and social skills lens: the acquisition of culture-specific knowledge and social skills will ultimately determine students' academic achievement

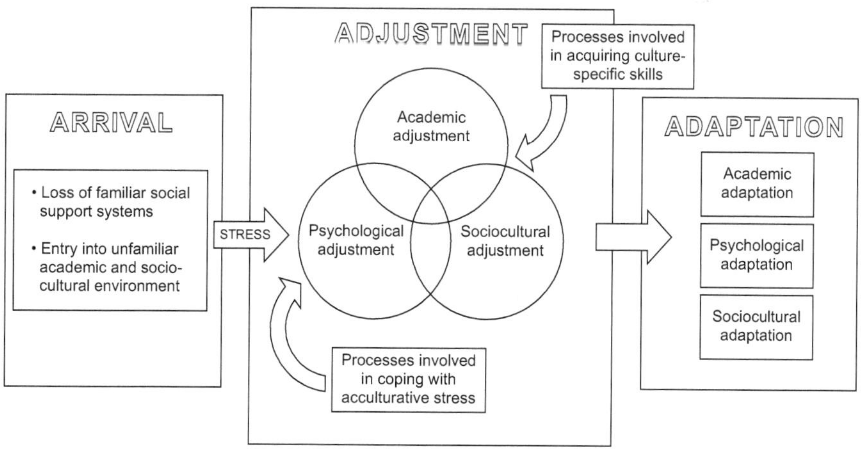


*Figure 9.2 The broader theoretical background underpinning the model (Source: Schartner and Young 2016)*

and degree of sociocultural adaptation. All three adjustment processes involve, we feel, complex cognitive processes that can ultimately lead to value changes in the individual.

### 9.2.3 EMPIRICAL BASIS FOR THE MODEL

Two empirical studies conducted by the authors form the specific empirical basis for this model, as detailed below. The first (Young et al. 2013), an exploratory mixed-methods study, was triggered by a research interest in factors associated with the successful adjustment of ISs to life and study overseas. A total of 108 ISs undertaking one-year postgraduate taught MA programmes in the UK took part in this initial study. Of these, 102 completed a self-report survey in December of the year of study with quantitative responses to items on a number of adjustment subscales (see Table 9.1, below), and an open response section with qualitative responses that asked participants for 'any other comments about yourself and your adjustment to life in the UK'. Six students also took part in three waves of semi-structured interviews.

Quantitative findings from this first, preliminary, study indicated significant associations between, on the one hand, students' academic achievement, satisfaction with life in the new environment and psychological wellbeing (as outcome factors and aspects of measures of the nature and degree of 'success'), and, on the other hand, aspects of their intercultural competence, contact with non-co-nationals, including hosts, and their language proficiency (as contributory factors). The qualitative data showed various dimensions of broadly successful or unsuccessful adjustment, both within and beyond the university. These tended to reinforce the findings from the quantitative survey data – emphasising the importance of language skills, aspects of intercultural competence, social contacts, especially with non-co-nationals, and social and institutional support systems and networks. Interviewees all reported a sense of generally increasingly successful adjustment to the new academic and sociocultural environment over time, although, as a small and self-selected subsample, it was difficult to generalise this pattern of adjustment beyond that group, who were surmised to be more self-confident and linguistically able than was the norm in the sample as a whole.

These findings informed a more extensive follow-on study of 226 ISs undertaking one-year postgraduate taught MA degrees in the UK (Schartner 2014). In response to the prevalence of cross-sectional research (Zhang and Goodson 2011), this study included a stronger longitudinal element and tracked students over an entire programme of study running from October to June. Instruments used to collect data included self-report surveys at 'entry' and 'exit' points (N = 224), and three waves of semi-structured interviews (N = 20). The findings of this study are detailed in Chapters 4 to 7 of this book. For the purpose of illustrating the empirical underpinning of our model, a brief summary of findings from both studies is presented in Table 9.1.

Table 9.1 Significant associations between contributory factors and adaptation measures in Young et al. (2013) and Schartner (2014), reported in Schartner and Young (2016)[1]

| Study 1 | | Study 2 | |
|---|---|---|---|
| *Contributory factors* | *Outcome* | *Contributory factors* | *Outcome* |
| Host language proficiency ($r = .37$)*<br>Cultural empathy ($\beta = .58$)<br>Open-mindedness ($\beta = -.50$)<br>Contact with non-co-national international students ($\beta = .32$) | Academic achievement | Host language proficiency ($\beta = .30$)<br>Knowledge about the host country ($\beta = .25$)<br>Autonomy in the decision to study abroad ($\beta = .38$)<br>Cultural empathy ($\beta = .43$)<br>Open-mindedness ($\beta = -.34$)<br>Social initiative ($\beta = .25$)<br>Flexibility ($\beta = .20$)<br>Contact with non-co-national international students ($\beta = .44$)<br>Socio-emotional support ($\beta = .33$) | Academic achievement |
| Host language proficiency ($r = .26$)*<br>Emotional stability ($\beta = .71$)<br>Open-mindedness ($\beta = .25$)<br>Contact with host nationals<br>Social support ($r = .20$) | Psychological wellbeing | Autonomy in the decision to study abroad ($\beta = .26$)<br>Emotional stability ($\beta = .40$) | Psychological wellbeing |
| Emotional stability ($\beta = .52$)<br>Contact with host nationals ($\beta = .25$) | Satisfaction with life | Host language proficiency ($\beta = .21$)<br>Knowledge about the host country ($\beta = .20$)<br>Autonomy in the decision to study abroad ($\beta = .37$)<br>Cultural empathy ($\beta = .37$)<br>Social initiative ($\beta = .26$)<br>Emotional stability ($\beta = .21$)<br>Contact with non-co-national international students ($\beta = .34$) | Satisfaction with life |

Table 9.1 Continued

| Study 1 | | Study 2 | |
|---|---|---|---|
| *Contributory factors* | *Outcome* | *Contributory factors* | *Outcome* |
| | | Contact with home students ($\beta$ = .14)**<br>Socio-emotional support ($\beta$ = .31) | |
| | | Host language proficiency ($\beta$ = .40)***<br>Knowledge about the host country ($\beta$ = .34)<br>Autonomy in the decision to study abroad ($\beta$ = .45)<br>Cultural empathy ($\beta$ = .19)<br>Social initiative ($\beta$ = .35)<br>Emotional stability ($\beta$ = .22)<br>Contact with home students ($\beta$ = .15)**<br>Contact with non-co-national international students ($\beta$ = .33)<br>Socio-emotional support ($\beta$ = .36) | Sociocultural adaptation |

Note: *Only correlation analysis was conducted for this factor; **significant at the 90 per cent level; ***only the Time 2 measure was significant for sociocultural adaptation.

## 9.3 AGENDA FOR FUTURE RESEARCH

In this book, we have integrated theory and empirical data on IS adjustment and adaptation, and put forward a conceptual model based on this data. We intend the model to be used as, firstly, a discussion document for students, both 'home' and 'international', and for those working in the 'internationalised' university, and secondly, a methodological toolkit for researchers wishing to study IS adjustment and adaptation (see Chapter 10). The model opens up a number of possible future research directions. First and foremost, we argue that the model should be further tested with a multitude of student samples across locations and degree programmes, in particularly in 'non-Western' HE contexts, where research on IS adjustment and adaptation is still in its infancy (for a recent example of the latter see Srisakda 2018). It might also be usefully tested on international staff – preliminary work indicates that it might be useful in this regard, with very slight adaptations (Young and Snodin 2018). Secondly, comparative research across levels of study (that is, undergraduate, postgraduate taught and postgraduate research) and disciplines beyond the humanities and social sciences will be important to ascertain the applicability of the model across different student sojourner groups. Thirdly, macro-level factors specific to the host country or university, such as internationalisation agendas and national discourses on immigration, could also be usefully explored. From a methodological perspective, measures of adaptation could be taken at different points across the sojourn to track changes and variations of adjustment outcomes over time. Finally, the model provides scope for a more detailed exploration of the 'post-sojourn' or 're-entry' stage. Future research could very usefully explore whether the same set of contributory factors, shown to have an impact on adjustment to the host environment, might also impinge on readjustment to the 'home' context.

We hope that this model can provide a useful heuristic to explore and explain what the 'international student experience' is like, and how it might be understood as an academic, sociocultural and psychological phenomenon of adjustment and adaptation. We also hope that it can make a positive contribution to enhancing this experience, to the benefit of individual ISs, whether current or prospective, university staff, and other students who interact with them, and the institutions and wider societies that host them (Schartner and Young 2016). More broadly, we feel that this book complements others in the series by employing a broader conception of 'social interaction', one that, rather than looking at the detail of talk, focuses on the experiences of a unique social group – student sojourners in HE – and how they interact with hosts, host institutions, academic expectations and standards, and with each other.

## NOTE

1. A significance level of $p < .05$ was set in both studies as is common in the social sciences (Capraro, 2007). All associations were significant at the 95 per cent level unless indicated otherwise.

## REFERENCES


Berry, J. W. (1997), 'Immigration, acculturation, and adaptation', *Applied Psychology*, 46(1), 5–34.

Berry, J. W. (2006), 'Stress perspectives on acculturation', in D. L. Sam and J. W. Berry (eds), *The Cambridge Handbook of Acculturation Psychology*, Cambridge: Cambridge University Press, pp. 43–57.

Brown, L. (2008), *The Adjustment Journey of International Postgraduate Students at a University in England*, Unpublished doctoral thesis, Bournemouth University, UK.

Furnham, A., and S. Bochner (1982), 'Social difficulty in a foreign culture: an empirical analysis of culture shock', in S. Bochner (ed.), *Cultures in Contact: Studies in Cross-cultural Interaction*, Oxford: Pergamon, pp. 161–98.

Furnham, A., and S. Bochner (1986), *Culture Shock: Psychological Reactions to Unfamiliar Environments*, London: Methuen.

Jindal-Snape, D., and R. Ingram (2013), 'Understanding and supporting triple transitions of international doctoral students: ELT and SuReCom Models', *Journal of Perspectives in Applied Academic Practice*, 1(1), 17–24.

Kim, Y. Y. (2001), *Becoming Intercultural: An Integrative Theory of Communication and Cross-cultural Adaptation*, Thousand Oaks, CA: Sage.

Matsumoto, D., and H. C. Hwang (2013), 'Assessing cross-cultural competence: a review of available tests', *Journal of Cross-Cultural Psychology*, 44(6), 849–73.

Robson, S., J. Almeida and A. Schartner (2017), 'Internationalization at home: time for review and development?', *European Journal of Higher Education*, 8(1), 19–35.

Ryan, J. (2005), 'Improving teaching and learning practices for international students: implications for curriculum, pedagogy and assessment', in J. Carroll and J. Ryan (eds), *Teaching International Students: Improving Learning for All*, Abingdon: Routledge, pp. 92–101.

Schartner, A. (2014), *Cross-cultural Transition in Higher Education: The Academic, Psychological and Sociocultural Adjustment and Adaptation of International Postgraduate Students at a British University*, Unpublished doctoral thesis, Newcastle University, UK.

Schartner, A., and T. J. Young (2016), 'Towards an integrated conceptual model of international student adjustment and adaptation', *European Journal of Higher Education*, 6(4), 372–86.

Smith, R. A., and N. G. Khawaja (2011), 'A review of the acculturation experiences of international students', *International Journal of Intercultural Relations*, 35(6), 699–71.

Srisakda, N. (2018), *A Study of International Vietnamese Undergraduate Students' Psychological, Sociocultural and Academic Adaptation and Adjustment at a Thai Higher Education Institution*, Unpublished doctoral thesis, Newcastle University, UK.

Ward, C., S. Bochner and A. Furnham (2001), *The Psychology of Culture Shock*, 2nd edn, Hove: Routledge.

Young, T. J., P. G. Sercombe, I. Sachdev, R. Naeb and A. Schartner (2013), 'Success factors for international postgraduate students' adjustment: exploring the roles of intercultural competence, language proficiency, social contact and social support', *European Journal of Higher Education*, 3, 151–71.

Young, T. J., and N. S. Snodin (2018), 'The "international student and staff experience" in higher education: a multiregional narrative enquiry from Thailand', *Global Conference on Education and Research*, University of Nevada, Las Vegas.

Zhang, J., and P. Goodson (2011), 'Predictors of international students' psychosocial adjustment to life in the United States: a systematic review', *International Journal of Intercultural Relations*, 35(2), 139–62.

Zhou, Y., D. Jindal-Snape, K. Topping and J. Todman (2008), 'Theoretical models of culture shock and adaptation in international students in higher education', *Studies in Higher Education*, 33(1), 63–75.

Zhou, Y., and J. Todman (2009), 'Patterns of adaptation of Chinese postgraduate students in the United Kingdom', *Journal of Studies in International Education*, 13(4), 467–86.

# 10

# IMPLICATIONS

Implications of the work presented in this book constitute its final chapter. We present these in terms of interest groups affected by the phenomenon of 'internationalisation', specifically HEIs (10.1), researchers (10.2) and policy makers (10.3). We briefly detail some implications of our findings for aspirant students (10.4), and give the final word to a former IS reflecting on his experience of study abroad and its effects on him as a person, along with some of the implications it has had for his subsequent life.

## 10.1 HEIs

We briefly stated in Chapter 1 that we very much see adjustment as a two-way reciprocal process involving both students and their host institutions. We therefore detail below examples of the kinds of adjustive institutional responses that might serve to advance a more values-based and ethically focused internationalisation agenda of the kind we advocate. Our findings, reported in Chapters 4 to 8, and the model of IS transitions we presented in Chapter 9 all serve to suggest that students' preparedness for study abroad and their degree of social connectedness in the host environment greatly influence the extent to which they experience a happy and successful sojourn. This has important implications for the training and support offered to ISs by the universities that host them.

Although student sojourners are generally seen as an active and highly motivated sojourner group (Russell et al. 2010) and have been portrayed in the literature as strategic agents of their own adjustment process (Montgomery 2010), host university support is needed and can aid the students in their adjustment and enhance their learning experience (Trice and Yoo 2007). Ramsay and colleagues (2007) point out that university support generally is strategically focused on the early sojourn period. While, as we have seen, this is a time of particular stress and nervousness for most, a combination of early pre-departure orientation and ongoing long-term support seems most desirable. We detail below what this support might most usefully look like.

### 10.1.1 INTERCULTURAL TRAINING

The importance of intercultural competence (IC) for student sojourners' adjustment has implications for the orientation and training offered to ISs, and the provision of intercultural training either pre-arrival or as part of the sojourn. Intercultural training is widely used in the preparation of expatriate business personnel (Bennett et al. 2000), but thus far remains a neglected feature in the pre-departure training of student sojourners, if this is offered at all. Pre-arrival preparation tends to be confined to preparation for language tests such as IELTS or TOEFL to fulfil the host universities' language entrance requirements (Gu et al. 2010; Young et al. 2013). In an earlier report (Young and Schartner 2014), we found that the study of intercultural communication was associated with academic success. Additionally, as the findings we present above in Chapters 4 to 7 have shown, host language ability, while very important, is not the sole determinant of students' cross-cultural adaptation. Given the inextricable relationship between language and culture (Young and Sachdev 2011), training aimed at developing IC could very usefully be incorporated into pre-sojourn language preparation (Byram and Feng 2004) or, alternatively, host universities could offer experiential reflective in-sessional intercultural training. This could be provided as part of induction programmes or could be incorporated into other existing support structures provided to incoming students. The 'multicultural campus' (Valverde and Castenell 1998) would certainly provide a fruitful setting for applied intercultural training techniques such as critical instances, case studies and role playing (Fowler and Blohm 2004).

It must be noted, though, that the 'trainability' of some IC dimensions may be limited and that there is no clear consensus in the literature as to which competencies can be acquired or improved through training (Leiba-O'Sullivan 1999). It might be that dimensions such as social initiative and cultural empathy are more trainable than, for example, emotional stability, which is widely seen as a more fixed and impermeable personality trait (Ones and Viswesvaran 1997). In the future, the MPQ could therefore very usefully be deployed as a diagnostic tool to help to establish the specific training needs of ISs (van der Zee and van Oudenhoven 2000).

It should also be stated that the type of intercultural training offered needs some thought. Very little research, as we note above (Chapter 1), has tested the efficacy of the myriad intercultural training courses and programmes on offer. Our own research in the area (Young and Schartner 2014) indicated that programmes that encouraged an explicitly critical perspective on key concepts such as culture, communication and social and cultural identity, and on the influence of human communication on culture, and culture's influence on human communication, are more likely to be effective. However, in spite of considerable criticism over a sustained period (Chapter 1, above), much intercultural sensitivity and effectiveness training education is still dependent for its main conceptual frames of reference on *a priori* cultural categorisation, which tends to equate nationality and culture. Our research provided evidence that working with alternative approaches that explicitly resist or at least interrogate such reductive categorisations may be associated with successful academic adaptation, perhaps because they inculcate an interrogative approach to concepts that the students and staff in 'internationalising' universities are actually experiencing on a day-to-day basis, promoting a positive interaction between experiential, immersive learning and training informed by a critically focused academic model.

As part of intercultural training, host institutions in the UK and elsewhere should also consider the benefits of community placement schemes for their ISs. Placements with local organisations such as charities, social care facilities or neighbourhood associations could facilitate the development of IC through experiential learning, and would additionally facilitate meaningful engagement with the host society, which was so desired by the students in this study and others (Chapter 2). The centrality of experience in the development of IC is also emphasised by Deardorff (2006), who points to the importance of involvement in a process of exposure through which student sojourners not only learn factual information about the new environment and improve their language, but also become more flexible, open-minded and empathetic to other cultures in general. Host universities could offer accredited or supernumerary community-based learning as part of their degree programmes or at least encourage community placements as an extra-curricular activity. This would also help to enhance relationships between the university and the local community by 'internationalising' the local community while at the same time 'localising' the international community (Green and Finn 2010).

We also suggest that IC development opportunities should not be aimed solely at ISs. Host students, administrative and support staff, and academic staff could and would all benefit from the provision of such opportunities. In contexts where HE 'internationalisation' is seen in the more rounded, values-driven terms we detail in Chapter 1, then the development of intercultural understanding, respect and dialogue is, indeed, perhaps a prerequisite in moving away from more solely recruitment-driven approaches. Such training needs to be provided for 'hosts', as well as IS sojourners, if a truly international environment is to be established and maintained.

### 10.1.2 HOST LANGUAGE REQUIREMENTS AND LANGUAGE SUPPORT

English language ability played a crucial role in students' adjustment and emerged as a significant predictor of all three adaptation domains. This confirms the findings of most recent research in the area (see Chapter 2) and clearly has important implications for HEIs in terms of the language requirements they set for entry and the language support they offer, both pre- and in-sessional.

In terms of language requirements, the authors have observed tendencies across HE programmes that they have been involved with internationally to set the lowest possible language entry requirements in many cases, often below those recommended by the testing agencies themselves. This seems to be especially the case in relation to postgraduate taught and even postgraduate research programmes in the humanities and social sciences, where the linguistic demands needed to fulfil the programmes successfully might themselves be expected to be particularly strenuous. Pressure to set low language entry requirements for programmes relative to competitors' requirements applies if programmes have difficulties recruiting, or where pressures from institutions on academic selectors to recruit high numbers of ISs for financial reasons are particularly high. Students, to a certain extent, can tend to collude in this process, understandably seeking out the best programmes in the best institutions that their level of funding and qualifications – including language qualifications – can 'buy' them entry to. An important implication of our findings is that this process of downward pressure on language requirements is likely to be negatively consequential: this is true both for the students, who may find themselves signed up for programmes that they will have difficulty participating in, and for the host institutions themselves. Essentially, low levels of ability in the host language, or in a 'world' language like English if it is the medium of instruction, are likely to correlate with higher numbers of students who will struggle, with all the consequences this implies in terms of academic and pastoral support needed. These students are more likely to be unhappy, with consequences in terms of their own wellbeing and in how they feel about their own 'international student experience'. Damage to institutional reputations is likely to be the very least negative consequence that universities who set low language entry requirements will suffer. We encourage institutions to set appropriate language entry requirements – and to resist the urge to 'sell themselves cheap' in this regard – for moral as much as practical reasons.

Overall, our findings indicate that in-sessional language support should be further strengthened but this should be less standardised than preparation for (for example) the IELTS or TOEFL tests. A sufficiently high score on a standardised pre-programme language test does not necessarily equate to confidence in actually using the language once students have entered the host environment (Takahashi 2009). Thus, student sojourners would certainly benefit from more applied communicative pre-sojourn language training, including exposure to local varieties of English and informal language (Lewthwaite 1996). Most especially, host institutions should consider the linguistic merits of home stays with local families as part of their ongoing language support.

It is also doubtful whether passing a TOEFL or IELTS test will necessarily guarantee that students will perform well academically (Melnick et al. 2011). Our interview findings have shown that although students fulfilled the English language requirements of their host university, language ability and its impact on academic performance were still a key concern for the students as they progressed through their programmes of study. This shows that it is the 'specialised nature of academic discourse' (Schmitt 2005: 65), rather than general English language ability, that causes problems for ISs in actually engaging actively and successfully with their programmes of study. Although most English language support centres at many universities aim to provide contextual study skills that endeavour to acclimatise students, to some extent, to the culture of a host university, it is not, generally speaking, part of their core function, which remains rooted in general approaches to 'academic' versions of the local language, and it is doubtful whether these courses are specific enough to prepare students adequately for the demands of their chosen programme of study. Course-specific terminology and academic language might differ quite considerably across disciplines and departments (Scudamore 2013). Thus, academic language support is probably most usefully provided at course level and, in light of international student recruitment, should be offered at the host department as part of an 'after-sales service' (Addison and Cownie 1992). Other language support services often either involve additional costs for the students or are very generic and thus of limited use to students during their actual degree programmes.

### 10.1.3 KNOWLEDGE (IN-ACTION) TRAINING

Pre-sojourn knowledge about the UK was predictive of all three adaptation domains and although the effect was moderate, this provides some indication for the importance of pre-departure orientation and preparation. Factual knowledge about the host country's history, politics, institutions and social conditions could very easily be integrated into orientation offered to ISs prior to departure from home in the form of a course-specific pre-arrival website and/or as part of induction programmes at the host university, and should most appropriately be specific to the immediate host environment (that is, the host university and host city). This type of knowledge can help prospective student sojourners to establish realistic expectations about the host environment (Leiba-O'Sullivan 1999) and can provide them with the factual information necessary to carry out daily tasks successfully. Moreover, programme-specific information is key for facilitating adjustment to new learning and teaching approaches at the host university. It is important for host universities to be explicit in their communication with ISs (Carroll 2005), pre-arrival and during induction, and expectation management (QAA 2015) is crucial. For example, concepts such as 'independent learning' and 'criticality' are highly ambiguous and can mean 'different things to different people' (Scudamore 2013). Thus, these concepts should be explored and unpacked for student sojourners, so that they know what is required of them on their degree programme – both during any induction periods and throughout the programme at key times: for example, as part of preparation for assignments.

However, it is important to note that merely providing students with factual information might be inefficient, as presenting 'facts' about the host environment could tend towards cultural oversimplification and stereotyping, and might not represent a sufficiently accurate picture of the host society (Louie 2005). There is also a danger that specific cultural expectations and behaviours could be imposed on student sojourners (Turner 2006). Thus, a less ethnocentric approach through more generic cultural training programmes, encouraging cultural empathy and open-mindedness among students prior to their arrival, could be more useful. Deardorff (2006) believes that it is through a widening of perspective that students engage in cultural learning, rather than through a mere assumption and transmission of 'facts' and behavioural conventions. However, that is not to say that certain factual, practical information about the immediate host surroundings (that is, where to eat, how to use the transport system) cannot be helpful to student sojourners, but it is important for content knowledge to be transformed into 'knowledge in action' (Etherington and Spurling 2007). In other words, factual knowledge alone might not be sufficient for successful adjustment: some researchers suggest that if one lacks experience in applying existing knowledge, considerable anxiety may result (e.g. Black and Mendenhall 1990). Host universities should therefore go beyond handbooks and leaflets, and offer knowledge in action training where incoming students can practise their newly acquired knowledge in structured and 'safe' environments. Examples may include guided shopping tours of local supermarkets or organised journeys on the public transport system.

### 10.1.4 THE MOTIVATIONAL VARIABLE

Our finding that degree of autonomy in the decision to study abroad was a significant contributory factor for all three adaptation domains points to the importance of motivational variables in student sojourners' adjustment. It seems plausible that students who fully endorse their decision to study abroad will be more proactive socially and will work more productively academically than those who feel they were pushed to study abroad by external factors (Chirkov et al. 2007). This contributes to our understanding of why some ISs adapt better to the host environment than others (Ryan and Twibell 2000), and can assist host institutions in providing tailored support services to those students who are studying abroad not of their own choosing but due to external factors such as parental pressure. Institutional interventions may be necessary to enhance the adaptation potential and experiences of these students. There are indications in prior research that ISs from East Asian countries might be particularly susceptible to external pressure in their decision to study abroad (Bodycott and Lai 2012); thus future research could explore differences in the degree of self-determined motivation between student sojourners from different countries.

### 10.1.5 SOCIAL CONNECTEDNESS

The importance of companionship and interpersonal connectedness in student sojourners' adjustment experience was an obvious and recurrent feature of our interview data. Moreover, degree of social contact was a major contributory factor for all three adaptation domains in our model. What stands out from our findings is the crucial role of contact with non-co-national ISs, which emerged as a significant predictor across the adaptation domains, and a persistent lack of host national contact. In light of these findings, links among student sojourners (that is, 'international ties') should be actively fostered by host institutions by encouraging peer interaction in the classroom through, for example, group activities in mixed-nationality teams. Outside the formal classroom setting, interaction among student sojourners could be encouraged by setting up more informal multicultural reading groups or, for oral assessment, practice sessions for group presentations. The dearth of host contact might be more difficult to tackle on degree programmes with an already low number of domestic students, as tends to be the case on UK taught postgraduate degrees (Chapter 1). None the less, there are some strategies that host universities could more actively pursue, including expanding 'buddy schemes' from the campus to the wider local community, and encouraging 'home' students to interact more proactively with their international peers. The latter is especially important in light of discussion surrounding the 'internationalisation' of HE, where inter- or cross-cultural communication competence is increasingly seen as an objective for all students: this applies whether students are 'international' or not, and as we note in Chapter 9, has been framed as an aspect of 'internationalisation at home' (see also Sanderson 2008;

Stier 2006). This warrants research into the perceptions and attitudes of domestic students and the wider local community toward growing international student numbers and the internationalisation of HE (Brown 2009). Only if the perceptions of members of the host society are fully understood can host institutions offer an effective impetus for interactions between the hosts and the student sojourners.

### 10.1.6 SOCIAL SUPPORT

Closely related to social contact, socio-emotional support emerged as a significant predictor of all three adaptation domains and there were strong indications in the interview data of the importance, to students' own sense of adjustment, of the social support derived from interaction with peers who were also going through the sojourn. Challenges associated with study abroad, such as lack of language confidence and homesickness, were moderated in supportive mixed-nationality groups, mainly through a sense of a collective group solidarity based on shared experiences. It seems that close links with fellow ISs temporarily replaced the familiar support systems that students had left behind in their home countries, a finding also reported in other previous research on student sojourners (e.g. Montgomery and McDowell 2009; Moores and Popadiuk 2011).

None the less, emotional compatriot support, in the host country and via social media with family members, should also be recognised as important (Lewthwaite 1996). There were indications in our interview data that co-national contact in the UK fulfilled a particularly important support function in the initial sojourn stage, in terms of mitigating loneliness and homesickness by sharing a common language and 'cultural' characteristics. Moreover, it seems that links to home and family can function as an important source of emotional support to student sojourners (Rosenthal et al. 2006), and the interview findings suggest that students generally had strong connections with 'home' throughout the sojourn. Future research could very usefully explore the impact of online communication technology (e.g. Skype, WhatsApp, Facebook) on student sojourners' adjustment, and the role of virtual 'e-ties' (Coleman and Chafer 2011). Bearing in mind the importance of socio-emotional support for student sojourners' adjustment, there is also a need to make counselling services more sympathetic to ISs' adjustment issues and provide intercultural training for wellbeing advisers and counsellors (Arthur 2004). In the academic domain, access to responsive and culturally aware tutors is equally desirable (Young et al. 2013). Thus, and as we have noted above, suitable intercultural training should be offered to academic and administrative staff with the aim of providing practical strategies for working with diverse student populations.

## 10.2 RESEARCH IMPLICATIONS

We note above an agenda for future research based on the Conceptual Model of International Student Adjustment and Adaptation (Chapter 9, Figure 9.1). It may be sufficient therefore to add here that we can commend this as a new and, we hope, useful conceptual model of the IS experience, which can gauge the adjustment and adaptation trajectories of this unique and important sojourner group in all their richness and complexity. Its integration of recent empirical research exploring the academic, psychological and sociocultural aspects of, and influences on, the experience of study abroad offers a heuristic that may well be applicable in any international HE context. As such, we very much hope that it will inspire other researchers to use it as a key conceptual tool in their own investigations.

In terms of further implications for researchers interested in 'internationalisation' and how it is experienced, we can also commend to others our 'ecumenical' epistemological position in relation to culture and cultural identity, and their relationships to behaviours and experiences, which we outlined in Chapter 1, and whose operationalisation we detailed in Chapter 3. This combines both quantitative and qualitative research methodologies into a single 'toolkit'. Bringing the two together has allowed us, and would allow others, to augment the strengths of each of these methods, while also mitigating at least some of the weaknesses, and could, we argue, be readily employed by research outside the 'Western' context of the study detailed in this book. In this respect, see also, for example, Young and Snodin (2018) for applications of this methodological toolkit by relatively inexperienced researchers in Thailand.

Specifically, our quantified data on the academic, psychological and sociocultural adaptation of ISs, and the inter-relationships between these different domains, are generalisable beyond the specific UK and postgraduate taught context of the research we have presented, and beyond the particular groups of students who were our participants. We also gathered and analysed qualitative interview data that were highly individual and person- and context-specific, with which to deepen our understandings of what particular people are going through, more or less while they are going through it, in terms of how they are perceiving and responding to the changed, transitional, circumstances in which they are finding themselves. We have converged each dataset together with the other, enabling a multilevel analysis of the complex experiential phenomena we are exploring. This convergence and corroboration, we contend, and as we note in Chapter 1, can only serve to improve the validity of our research outcomes. It can also help, we hope, to realise the 'ecumenical' position in the study of intercultural transitions, which we feel is the most fruitful, outward-facing and sustainable epistemology for researchers in any location who are interested in the phenomena in all their richness and complexity.

## 10.3 POLICY IMPLICATIONS

> If you believe you are a citizen of the world, you are a citizen of nowhere. You don't understand what citizenship means. (May 2016)

We refer in Chapter 1 to a call to arms, and we cannot end a book of this nature without addressing the sociopolitical context in which 'internationalisation' and the 'international student experience' occur. Former UK Prime Minister Teresa May's framing of citizenship as localised, nationalist social identity was part of a wider attack on an 'internationalised liberal establishment', who, as May put it, 'behave as though they have more in common with international elites than with the people down the road'. It chimes closely with what Goodhart (2017) sees as an increasingly apparent schism between 'Anywhere People' – with a mobile, 'achieved' identity and economic success – and 'Somewhere People' – with a marginalised, roots-based identity who feel they have been the losers from globalisation.

Such distinctions, as we note in Chapter 1, may have helped fuel the 2016 referendum vote in the UK to leave the European Union, the election of Donald Trump as President of the USA in 2017, the apparent decline of the political centre-left in the global North, and the rise of 'populism' across Europe, Western Asia and the Americas. They are distinctions that, of course, push strongly against the ethos that informs values-driven 'internationalisation', and a critical, interpretivist stance in intercultural studies that approaches cultural identities as emergent, dynamic, dialogically constructed, multiple and, perhaps necessarily, cosmopolitan. If the international experience in HE is about, in some way, helping people to become better 'global citizens', as we strongly contend it should be, then it has to be in the business of helping foster the aspects of people that can see the value of identification beyond any single location or community, who can be a citizen of a city, a region, a country and the entire globe. From such a position, issues of global justice, climate change, the prevention of international conflict, and the promotion of intercultural dialogue and understanding are much more approachable, and the world may be made a safer and happier place for humanity.

Our research, reported above, shows how life-changing, and life-affirming being an internationally mobile student can be. It has shown the value of such an experience to individuals and, by strong implication, to the institutions and countries that host them – and, it is hoped, to the countries to which they usually return. A result of this, we argue, is that the true worth and value of international HE need to be sustained as an aspiration for an increasing number of people and, at policy level, promoted rather than treated – as it currently is in the UK, at least – as a problem to be approached with the same level of hostility as is directed towards any other aspect of migration. If the purpose of international HE is purely financial and elite-building, then it perhaps deserves to be treated with suspicion at policy level, where policy makers have a genuine interest in social justice and equality of opportunity. If it serves a higher purpose of fostering global citizenship in its best and most inclusive manifestations, it deserves as much support as socioeconomic circumstances permit, given its value to individuals and to wider societies. Globalisation without striving towards some idea of global citizenship is merely neoliberal socioeconomic steamrollering. HE can play a central role in fostering ideas of global connectedness and global citizenship if it can remain truly international and intercultural in its outlook and ethos.

We argue, therefore, that the implications for national and supranational policy are that it should be essentially supportive of HE internationalisation and, at its heart, of positive and affirmative 'international student experiences'. Where resources permit, in the global South, state aid should, of course, be directed towards developing local–national HE, but also towards facilitating international study for as many people as want and need it, with a view to supporting and sustaining development and broadening perspectives. More widely, at the very least, countries receiving large numbers of ISs – the majority of them rich – should be welcoming and appreciative of their presence: ideally, they should offer financial and other help to aspirant educational sojourners, both incoming and outgoing. Supranational organisations like the European Union and the Association of South East Asian Nations should be commended for their promotion of higher educational exchange and should continue to see this as a core part of their purpose and mission. Policy makers and international HE providers need to see themselves as partners in the process of making globalisation work for everyone.

## 10.4 IMPLICATIONS FOR ASPIRANT STUDENTS

To close, we offer the following humble suggestions. Firstly, we would encourage anyone who can and who wants to learn and travel to become an 'international student'. If you decide to do this, make sure this decision is really yours – talk to others, particularly to those that love you, but decide, ultimately, for yourself. Do your prior research and choose the programme and the place that seems best for you – but make the best you can of what you find when you get there. Prepare as much as you can before you go – work on your language and intercultural skills especially, as these are key. While you are studying, expect ups and downs but persevere and work hard – learning is not always easy but it is always worth it. Make and help your friends. Keep in touch with home but try to be part of where you are – take every opportunity to be part of the university, and of the wider, community. Strive always to learn and to contribute to the wider world. Enjoy it all; it will stay with you for a long time, maybe always.

As promised, we offer the very final word on an 'international student experience' and intercultural transition to an 'international student', a participant in our research whom we are calling Robin, just before he went home at the end of his programme:

> I'm ready to go home, but I feel like it's been a life changing experience, the whole time I've been here. I've definitely grown as a person, I've learned a lot, developed a lot of skills that I probably wouldn't have been able to develop if I didn't come, and I've made a lot of friends and good lifetime contacts. It's really interesting about people you study abroad with because [...] when you live in another culture together, that's like a lifetime bond.

## REFERENCES

Addison, W., and F. Cownie (1992), 'Overseas law students: language support and responsible recruitment', *Journal of Law & Society*, 9(4), 467–82.

Arthur, N. (2004), *Counseling International Students: Clients from Around the World*, New York: Kluwer Academic.

Bennet, R., A. Aston and T. Colquhoun (2000), 'Cross-cultural training: a critical step in ensuring the success of international assignments', *Human Resource Management*, 39(2–3), 239–50.

Black, J. S., and M. E. Mendenhall (1990), 'Cross-cultural training effectiveness: a review and theoretical framework', *Academy of Management Review*, 15, 113–36.

Bodycott, P., and A. Lai (2012), 'The influence and implications of Chinese culture in the decision to undertake cross-border higher education', *Journal of Studies in International Education*, 16(3), 252–70.

Brown, L. (2009), 'The transformative power of the international sojourn: an ethnographic study of the international student experience', *Annals of Tourism Research*, 36(3), 502–21.

Byram, M., and A. Feng (2004), 'Culture and language learning: teaching, research and scholarship', *Language Teaching*, 37, 149–68.

Carroll, J. (2005), 'Strategies for becoming more explicit', in J. Carroll and J. Ryan (eds), *Teaching International Students: Improving Learning for All*, London: Routledge, pp. 26–35.

Chirkov, V. I., M. Vansteenkiste, R. Tao and M. Lynch (2007), 'The role of motivation to study abroad in the adaptation of international students: a self-determination theory approach', *International Journal of Intercultural Relations*, 31(2), 199–222.

Coleman, J. A., and T. Chafer (2011), 'The experience and long-term impact of study abroad by Europeans in an African context', in F. Dervin (ed.), *Analysing the Consequences of Academic Mobility and Migration*, Newcastle: Cambridge Scholars, pp. 67–96.

Deardorff, D. (2006), 'Identification and assessment of intercultural competence as a student outcome of internationalisation', in M. Byram and A. Feng (eds), *Living and Studying Abroad: Research and Practice*, Clevedon: Multilingual Matters, pp. 232–56.

Etherington, S., and N. Spurling (2007), *Knowledge in Action: International Students and Their Interaction with Cultural Knowledge*. Available at: <www.ece.salford.ac.uk/proceedings/papers> (last accessed 12 December 2013).

Fowler, S., and J. Blohm (2004), 'An analysis of methods for intercultural training', in D. Landis, J. Bennett and M. Bennett (eds), *Handbook of Intercultural Training*, 3rd edn, Thousand Oaks, CA: Sage, pp. 37–85.

Goodhart, D. (2017), *The Road to Somewhere: The Populist Revolt and the Future of Politics*, London: Hurst.

Green, P., and D. Finn (2010), *Defining the Global Village: Community-based Learning and its Implications for International Students and the HE Sector*. Available at: <http://www.hw.ac.uk/AEteam/Themes/D-Finn_HW_Confce_Dec2010_pptV2.pdf> (last accessed 3 May 2013).

Gu, Q., M. Schweisfurth and C. Day (2010), 'Learning and growing in a "foreign" context: intercultural experiences of international students', *Compare*, 40(1), 7–23.

Leiba-O'Sullivan, S. (1999), 'The distinction between stable and dynamic cross-cultural competencies: implications for expatriate trainability', *Journal of International Business Studies*, 30(4), 709–25.

Lewthwaite, M. (1996), 'A study of international students' perspectives on cross-cultural adaptation', *International Journal for the Advancement of Counselling*, 19(2), 167–85.

Louie, K. (2005), 'Gathering cultural knowledge: useful or handle with care?', in J. Carroll and J. Ryan (eds), *Teaching International Students: Improving Learning for All*, London: Routledge, pp. 17–25.

May, T. (2016), 'Prime Minister's Address to the Conservative Party Annual Conference. International Convention Centre, Birmingham, UK', October. Available at: <https://www.intelligencesquared.com/events/if-you-believe-you-are-a-citizen-of-the-world-you-are-a-citizen-of-nowhere/> (last accessed January 2019).

Melnick, G. A., G. Kaur and G. Yu (2011), 'Social integration and academic outcomes: the case of an international public policy and management program', *Journal of Public Affairs Education*, 17(4), 569–84.

Montgomery, C. (2010), *Understanding the International Student Experience*, Basingstoke: Palgrave Macmillan.

Montgomery, C., and L. McDowell (2009), 'Social networks and the international student experience: a community of practice?', *Journal of Studies in International Education*, 13(4), 455–66.

Moores, L., and N. Popadiuk (2011), 'Positive aspects of international student transitions: a qualitative inquiry', *Journal of College Student Development*, 52(3), 291–306.

Ones, D. S., and C. Viswesvaran (1997), 'Personality determinants in the prediction of aspects of expatriate job success', in D. M. Saunders and Z. Aycan (eds), *New Approaches to Employee Management: Vol. 4. Expatriate Management: Theory and Research*, Stamford, CT: JAI Press, pp. 63–92.

QQA (Quality Assurance Agency) (2015), *Supporting and Enhancing the Experience of International Students in the UK: A Guide for UK Higher Education Providers.* Available at: <http://www.qaa.ac.uk/Publications/InformationAndGuidance/Pages/International-students-studying- in-the-UK.aspx> (last accessed 26 February 2019).

Ramsay, S., E. Jones and M. Barker (2007), 'Relationship between adjustment and support types: young and mature-aged local and international first year university students', *Higher Education*, 54(2), 247–65.

Rosenthal, D. A., V. J. Russell and G. J. Thomson (2006), *A Growing Experience: The Health and Well-being of International Students at the University of Melbourne*. Available at: <https://services.unimelb.edu.au/__data/assets/pdf_file/0011/358436/GrowingExperience.pdf> (last accessed 26 February 2019).

Russell, J., D. Rosenthal and G. Thomson (2010), 'The international student experience: three styles of adaptation', *Higher Education*, 60(2), 235–49.

Ryan, M. E., and R. S. Twibell (2000), 'Concerns, values, stress, coping, health and educational outcomes of college students who studied abroad', *International Journal of Intercultural Relations*, 24, 409–35.

Sanderson, G. (2008), 'A foundation for the internationalization of the academic self in higher education', *Journal of Studies in International Education*, 12(3), 276–307.

Schmitt, D. (2005), 'Writing in the international classroom', in J. Carroll and J. Ryan (eds), *Teaching International Students: Improving Learning for All*, Routledge: London, pp. 63–75.

Scudamore, R. (2013), *Engaging Home and International Students: A Guide for New Lecturers.* Available at: <http://www.heacademy.ac.uk/resources/detail/RachelScudamoreFeb2013> (last accessed 26 February 2019).

Stier, J. (2006), 'Internationalisation, intercultural communication and intercultural competence', *Journal of Intercultural Communication*, 11, 1–11.

Takahashi, A. (2009), 'Self-perception of English ability: is it related to proficiency and/or class performance?', *Niigata Studies in Foreign Languages and Cultures*, 14, 39–48.

Trice, A. G., and J. E. Yoo (2007), 'International graduate students' perceptions of their academic experience', *Journal of Research in International Education*, 6(1), 41–66.

Turner, Y. (2006), 'Chinese students in a UK business school: hearing the student voice in reflective teaching and learning practice', *Higher Education Quarterly*, 60(1), 27–51.

Valverde, L., and L. Castenell (1998), *The Multicultural Campus: Strategies for Transforming Higher Education*, Walnut Creek, CA: AltaMira.

van der Zee, K. I., and J. P. van Oudenhoven (2000), 'The Multicultural Personality Questionnaire: a multidimensional instrument of multicultural effectiveness', *European Journal of Personality*, 14(4), 291–309.

Young, T. J., and I. Sachdev (2011), 'Intercultural communicative competence: exploring English language teachers' beliefs and practices', *Language Awareness*, 20:2, 81–98.

Young T. J. and A. Schartner (2014), 'The effects of cross-cultural communication education on international students' adjustment and adaptation', *Journal of Multilingual and Multicultural Development*, 35(6), 547–62.

Young, T. J., P. G. Sercombe, I. Sachdev, R. Naeb and A. Schartner (2013), 'Success factors for international postgraduate students' adjustment: exploring the roles of intercultural competence, language proficiency, social contact and social support', *European Journal of Higher Education*, 3, 151–71.

Young, T. J., and N. S. Snodin (2018), 'The "international student and staff experience" in higher education: a multiregional narrative enquiry from Thailand', *Global Conference on Education and Research*, University of Nevada, Las Vegas.

# INDEX


ABC model of culture shock, 24–5
academic achievement, 26, 56, 63–5, 70–1
academic staff, 65, 66, 182
accommodation, 125
acculturation, 171
acculturative stress, 24–5, 30, 36, 40, 65, 95, 104–5, 135, 142, 145, 172–3
adaptation, 14–15
  academic, 56, 63–5, 71–9, 145–9, 167, 181
  psychological, 56–7, 83–5, 106–12, 141–6, 148–9, 168, 173
  sociocultural, 57, 115–16, 127–36, 141–3, 146–9, 168–9, 174
adjustment, 14–15
  academic, 26–7, 63–80, 145–9, 155–7, 171–2, 165, 168
  interaction, 25–6, 142, 147
  psychological, 15, 25, 27, 55–6, 83–114, 85–106, 141–6, 162
  sociocultural, 15, 25, 28, 57, 116–27, 141–4, 146–8, 158–9, 163
  work, 25–6, 142, 147
affective component of transition, 24–5, 27, 171–3
alumni, 3, 52, 60, 152–66
Anglophone countries, 5, 6
anxiety, 23, 86, 89, 95, 102, 141
autonomy in the decision to study abroad *see* motivation for study abroad

behavioural component of transition, 24–5
Big Five dimensions, 33
Brexit, 4, 7
business sojourners, 25

China, 4, 5, 53–4, 69, 117, 123
cognitive component of transition, 24, 25
communication
  skills, 24, 71
  non-verbal, 24
community of practice, 39, 76
conceptual models, 169–7
contributory factors, 29, 55–6
country of origin, 4, 15–16, 23, 39, 117
cross-cultural communication *see* intercultural communication
cultural distance, 24, 28, 29, 142
cultural empathy, 33, 74, 75, 108, 129, 134, 175
cultural identity, 10, 12, 181, 187
cultural training *see* intercultural training
culture, 10, 11, 13
culture learning, 24, 173
culture shock, 23, 27, 102, 172

depression, 29, 30, 102
discrimination, 29–30, 88
domestic students, 16, 38, 66, 185–6

early sojourn stages, 66–8, 79, 80, 100, 102, 103, 116–19
ecumenical approach, 10, 13, 14, 52
educational exchange *see* international student mobility
emotional stability, 33, 74, 108, 129, 175
England *see* United Kingdom
English language ability, 30, 55, 72, 90, 91, 106–7, 119, 128, 131–3, 144, 182–4
English language proficiency *see* English language ability
Englishisation of universities, 6, 7
essentialism, 12
European Union (EU), 4–5, 7
expatriates *see* business sojourners
expectations, 24, 70–1, 73, 119, 184
experiential learning, 157, 182

family support, 92–3, 95, 97, 103
flexibility, 33, 74, 175
foreign students *see* international student
friendship networks, 36–7, 38–9, 76, 97, 100, 104, 123–4, 155, 165

globalisation, 4, 11, 188–9
global citizenship, 11, 188
grade point average (GPA), 26

higher education
  institutions, 3–6, 8–9, 11, 15, 180, 182
  market, 5, 6
  internationalisation, 7–9
homesickness, 91–2, 97, 99, 103
home students, 16
host language proficiency *see* English language ability
host relationships *see* friendship networks

IELTS (International English Language Testing System), 55
immigration, 7, 16, 29, 94, 177
in-sojourn factors, 29, 77, 168
intercultural
  training, 85, 180–2, 186
  transition, 10, 11, 22
  communication, 11
  competence, 11, 32–5, 54, 55, 74–5, 108, 129, 134–5
intergroup relations, 11, 24
international graduates *see* alumni
international postgraduate students, 9, 10, 16, 25
international student, 15, 16, 189
  enrolment, 4, 7, 51
  experience, 9, 16
  mobility, 3–7
  recruitment, 4, 5, 6
internationalisation, 7–9, 11
  ethical, 172, 180
interpretivism, 11, 12, 13
interview, 52, 58

knowledge about the host country, 30–1, 55, 72, 107, 128, 133, 184–5

language
  proficiency *see* English language ability
  support, 182–4
local people, 116, 119–20, 124–6; *see also* friendship networks
loneliness, 87, 92
longitudinal data, 51–2, 60

master's level, 6, 25
method (-ology), 13, 14, 51
mixed methods, 1, 2, 13, 14, 52–3, 60, 171, 174
mobility *see* international student mobility
motivation for study abroad, 31–2, 55, 73, 107–8, 129, 133, 185
multicultural effectiveness, 32–5
Multicultural Personality Questionnaire (MPQ), 33–5, 74–5

open mindedness, 33, 74, 75, 175
overseas experience, 31, 54, 133
overseas students *see* international student

Pearson's correlation, 57
personality, 24, 27, 29; *see also* Multicultural Personality Questionnaire (MPQ)
policy makers, 180, 187–9
positivism, 11–13
postgraduate degree, 6, 25, 64
pre-departure orientation, 180, 184–5; *see also* knowledge about the host country
preparedness for change, 30, 180; *see also* knowledge about the host country
pre-sojourn factors, 29, 79
proficiency in English *see* English language ability
psychological wellbeing, 26, 54, 83–5

qualitative method, 13–14, 52, 58–0
quantitative method, 13–14, 52–7
questionnaire, 52–5, 60, 154

ranking of universities, 5, 9, 10
re-entry, 23, 177
regression analysis, 57
Relative Autonomy Index, 55
research design, 51–3
retrospectives, 52–3, 60, 152–65

satisfaction with life, 26, 54, 83–5
  scale, 57
self-determination theory, 32; *see also* motivation for study abroad
social contact, 36–9, 56, 67, 76–7, 108–9, 129–30, 185–6
  co-national, 37–8
  host national, 37, 38–9, 123, 143
  international, 37, 39
social identification theories, 24
social initiative, 33, 74, 129, 134, 175
social network, 36, 37, 121; *see also* friendship networks
social psychology, 12
social skills, 24
social support, 39, 56, 77, 109–10, 130, 135–6, 186
social ties *see* social contact
Sociocultural Adaptation Scale, 57
sojourn, 22
sojourner, 15
Statistical Package for the Social Sciences (SPSS), 57
stress and coping model, 24, 27, 80, 104, 134, 136, 172, 173
student sojourners *see* international student

study abroad, 3–7; *see also* international student mobility
survey data, 52–7; *see also* questionnaire

thematic analysis, 58–9, 153–4
TOEFL (Test of English as a Foreign Language), 55
transition, 9
t-test, 57
  independent samples, 57
  paired samples, 57

U-curve model of adjustment, 22–3, 79–80, 100, 102–3
United Kingdom, 6, 7

W-curve model of adjustment, 23